Foundations of Affective Social Learning

Written by experts in comparative, developmental, social, cognitive and cultural psychology, this book introduces the novel concept of affective social learning to help explain why what matters to us, matters to us. In the same way that social learning describes how we observe other people's behaviour to learn how to *use* a particular object, affective social learning describes how we observe other people's emotions to learn how to *value* a particular object, person or event. As such, affective social learning conceptualizes the transmission of value from a given culture to a given person and reveals why the things that are so important to us can be of no consequence at all to others.

DANIEL DUKES holds research positions at the University of Fribourg and the Swiss Centre for Affective Sciences, University of Geneva, Switzerland. He also currently holds a Swiss National Science Fund visiting research post at the University of Oxford, UK.

FABRICE CLÉMENT is full professor and co-founder of the Cognitive Science Centre at the University of Neuchâtel, Switzerland.

STUDIES IN EMOTION AND SOCIAL INTERACTION
Second Series

Series Editors

Brian Parkinson
University of Oxford

Maya Tamir
The Hebrew University of Jerusalem

(Continued after Index)

Foundations of Affective Social Learning

Conceptualizing the Social Transmission of Value

Edited by

Daniel Dukes
University of Fribourg, Switzerland
Fabrice Clément
University of Neuchâtel, Switzerland

CAMBRIDGE
UNIVERSITY PRESS

CAMBRIDGE
UNIVERSITY PRESS

University Printing House, Cambridge CB2 8BS, United Kingdom

One Liberty Plaza, 20th Floor, New York, NY 10006, USA

477 Williamstown Road, Port Melbourne, VIC 3207, Australia

314–321, 3rd Floor, Plot 3, Splendor Forum, Jasola District Centre,
New Delhi – 110025, India

79 Anson Road, #06-04/06, Singapore 079906

Cambridge University Press is part of the University of Cambridge.

It furthers the University's mission by disseminating knowledge in the pursuit of
education, learning, and research at the highest international levels of excellence.

www.cambridge.org
Information on this title: www.cambridge.org/9781108473194
DOI: 10.1017/9781108661362

© Cambridge University Press 2019

First published 2019

Printed in the United Kingdom by TJ International Ltd Padstow Cornwall

A catalogue record for this publication is available from the British Library.

Library of Congress Cataloging-in-Publication Data
Names: Dukes, Daniel, editor. | Clément, Fabrice, editor.
Title: Foundations of affective social learning : conceptualizing the social
transmission of value / edited by Daniel Dukes, Fabrice Clément.
Description: Cambridge, United Kingdom; New York, NY: Cambridge University
Press, 2019. | Series: Studies in emotion and social interaction | Includes index.
Identifiers: LCCN 2019019728 | ISBN 9781108473194 (hardback) |
ISBN 9781108461054 (paperback)
Subjects: LCSH: Social learning. | Social values. | Affect (Psychology)
Classification: LCC HM686.F68 2019 | DDC 302/.12–dc23
LC record available at https://lccn.loc.gov/2019019728

ISBN 978-1-108-47319-4 Hardback

Fabrice would like to thank Laurence and Daniel would like to thank Romaine for their enduring patience, love and support, and we would both like to thank our respective children for teaching us so much about what is important to them through their emotional expressions. *Papa!*

This book is dedicated to all of them.

Contents

Figures

Contributors

Fabrice Clément is a social and cognitive scientist intrigued by the social and psychological mechanisms underlining human beliefs. After training in anthropology, philosophy and cognitive science, he developed a strong interest in developmental psychology. Now a full professor at the University of Neuchâtel, he is still working on bringing sociology and psychology closer.

Jozefien De Leersnyder is Assistant Professor in Cultural Psychology at the University of Amsterdam and a research associate at the Center for Social and Cultural Psychology at KU Leuven, where she graduated in 2014. Her research focuses on the interplay between culture, emotion and well-being, especially in changing sociocultural worlds.

Daniel Dukes received his doctorate from the University of Neuchâtel, Switzerland in 2017, having spent one year at UC Berkeley. He has since pursued postdoctoral studies at the Universities of Amsterdam and Oxford (thanks to SNSF funding) and at the Universities of Geneva and Fribourg. His research focuses on socio-emotional processes in clinical and non-clinical populations.

Agneta Fischer is currently Professor in Emotions and Affective Processes at the University of Amsterdam and chair of the Psychology Department. Her research interest is emotions in social contexts and she has published on facial expressions, emotional mimicry, culture and gender differences, embodiment and the social functions of emotions.

György Gergely is a professor of social cognitive development and founder of the Cognitive Development Center at Central European University, Budapest. His work represents significant milestones for the field of developmental psychology including the formulation of theoretical concepts such as the teleological stance, rational imitation and natural pedagogy.

Thibaud Gruber is a scientific collaborator at the Swiss Centre for Affective Sciences at the University of Geneva and a postdoctoral fellow at the University of Oxford. He is interested in the evolution of culture and communication in all great apes including humans.

Paul L. Harris is a developmental psychologist with interests in the development of cognition, emotion and imagination. He was Professor of Developmental Psychology at Oxford University before moving in 2001 to Harvard University where he is the Victor S. Thomas Professor of Education. His latest book is *Trusting What You're Told: How Children Learn From Others* (2012).

Ildikó Király is Professor of Cognitive Psychology at Eötvös Loránd University, Budapest. She has made wide-ranging contributions to cognitive developmental science, her recent work as the leader of the MTA-ELTE Social Mind Research unit focuses on the study of the developmental origins of human sociality.

Antony Manstead is Emeritus Professor of Psychology at Cardiff University. His DPhil in Social Psychology was awarded by the University of Sussex. Before moving to Cardiff in 2004 he held academic positions at the universities of Sussex, Manchester, Amsterdam and Cambridge. He has research interests in emotion, attitudes and social identity.

Christian Mumenthaler is a postdoctoral researcher at the University of Geneva. He earned his PhD from this same university in 2015 for his research on the impact of social information on emotion recognition. Since 2016, he has focused on big data analytics to investigate psychological and social processes on a large scale.

Brian Parkinson is Professor of Social Psychology at the University of Oxford, UK. His books include *Ideas and Realities of Emotion* (1995) and *Emotion in Social Relations* (with Fischer and Manstead, 2005). He is currently co-editor of the Cambridge University Press book series Studies in Emotion and Social Interaction.

Magdalena Rychlowska is a research fellow at Queen's University Belfast. She earned her PhD in 2014 from the University of Clermont-Ferrand. Her research focuses on production, perception and social functions of facial expressions, in particular smiles and laughter.

David Sander is Professor of Psychology at the University of Geneva. He mainly investigates the brain and cognitive mechanisms involved in emotion. He directs both the Laboratory for the study of Emotion

Elicitation and Expression and the Swiss Centre for Affective Sciences, where various approaches and methods are used to study emotions as well as their determinants and effects.

Caroline Schuppli is a postdoctoral researcher at the University of Zürich. Her research focuses on the role of the interplay of social and environmental factors during cognitive evolution by comparing humans to great apes and by using broader comparative approaches across species. Since 2010 she has studied wild orang-utans in Indonesia.

Christine Sievers is a researcher and teaching assistant at the University of Basel, working on the cognitive underpinnings of animal communication and the evolution of language. She wrote her PhD, 'Ostensive Intentional Communication in Non-Human Animals', at the University of Basel and the University of Neuchâtel.

Job van der Schalk is a lecturer (assistant professor) at Cardiff University's School of Psychology. His research investigates how displays of emotions influence relationships between people, behaviour towards others and interactions between individuals.

Carel van Schaik recently retired as Professor of Biological Anthropology at the University of Zurich. He uses primate behavioural ecology and cognition to reconstruct the evolution of human nature.

Preface

A number of people have contributed a great deal to the making of this book and this preface is our chance to thank them all.

We begin in 2017 and at a two-day workshop on affective social learning (ASL) organized with the wonderful help of Magali Mari in Montezillon, Switzerland. Thanks then to all those people – Brian Parkinson, Agneta Fischer, Christian Mumenthaler, David Sander, Tony Manstead, György Gergely, Paul L. Harris, Jozefien De Leersnyder, Thibaud Gruber, Christine Sievers, Caroline Schuppli and Carel van Schaik, who attended the workshop and who eventually contributed to this volume. We would also like to thank the excellent students who attended the workshop who came with lots of questions and positive energy and who left, like us, we hope, informed and inspired. Thanks too, to the people who have kindly joined the project since – Ildiko Király, Magdalena Rychlowska and Job van der Shalk.

For those of you interested in the historical beginnings of ASL, one would do well to start with Joseph Campos. Joe was kind enough to host both of us in his lab in Berkeley, decades apart, and his research on socio-emotional processes continues to inspire us greatly. Indeed, it was actually at a conference organized by Joe and Eric Walle where the origins of ASL can be found (ISRE, UC Berkeley, 2013). In one symposium, chaired by David Sander, Eric explained why he thought social referencing and social appraisal were essentially the same thing. His position was the opposite of ours, as we felt there were important differences between the two phenomena. We wrote up our different viewpoints, which were subsequently published in two separate papers in *Emotion Review*. It was while formulating our argument that we were struck by how social appraisal could be split into both interpersonal situations and situations between an observer and an agent who was unaware of being watched – a situation that we have since termed *affective observation*. The idea of a hierarchy of socio-emotional terms quickly emerged and ASL was born. Thanks then to Eric for accepting the challenge in 2013 to join us in writing conflicting views on social referencing and social appraisal. It is often in opposition to one idea that another idea grows best.

We would also like to warmly express our gratitude to Betty Repacholi, Brian Parkinson, Laurence Kaufmann and Paul L. Harris who read and commented upon earlier drafts of our introduction and/or conclusion. Each of them offered very helpful comments and valuable advice.

We are very grateful to Janka Romero and Emily Watton at Cambridge University Press for patiently and kindly guiding us through this process and of course, the series editors, Maya Tamir and particularly Brian Parkinson, who not only suggested that ASL might make an interesting subject for a book, but who also kindly accepted our invitation to contribute a chapter himself. Thanks too to the anonymous reviewers for their comments.

Of course, we would like to thank, once again, the generous sponsors of the initial workshop – Swissuniversities on behalf of the Swiss Centre for Affective Sciences, the Swiss National Science Foundation and the University of Neuchâtel. Indeed, the Swiss National Science Foundation continues to generously support Danny's research.

Merci beaucoup à tous.

A difficult introduction to affective social learning

Fabrice Clément and Daniel Dukes

I.1 A difficult introduction

It is reasonable to expect any introduction to a book to consider the question(s) that motivated the volume, to reflect upon the relevance of putting minds together to think and write about the topic and to define the main concepts that inspire the book's title. By putting 'learning', 'social' and 'affective' together, we have not made our task particularly easy. Indeed, each of these terms refers to a concept that has given rise to multiple lines of research, essays and debates in the history of psychology. Given that the task of covering all of these points is not possible within these few pages, our introduction will only scratch the surface of the many issues that are implicated, in order to highlight what we consider to be the originality of our approach.

As an introductory remark, it is interesting to note that the different words in our title more readily tend to repel each other than peacefully coexist in the history of psychology. Indeed, most standard definitions of 'learning' refer to modifications that take place in an organism's response to a particular stimulus based on prior experience, leading to an enduring change mediated by its nervous system. This process is therefore described as an *individual* endeavour by which the subject acquires new information or modifies its subsequent behavioural patterns. As the pioneer Hermann Ebbinghaus put it, learning has to deal with how people retain information, and the scientist's focus should therefore be concentrated on these internal processes (Ebbinghaus, 1885/2013). This perspective also characterized the beginning of developmental psychology: Jean Piaget conceived of learning as an essentially individual quest for the child to make sense of their environment. In interacting with objects, babies acquire their first sensori-motor schemes that will then assimilate an increasing number of the aspects of their world, accommodating themselves when reality cannot be reduced to existing schemes

This chapter is co-authored and the authors share responsibility equally for its contents.

(Piaget, 1936). From this constructionist viewpoint, the master builder is the individual, and the best fitting metaphor for his activity is the solitary scientist, testing hypotheses by experimenting and building increasingly complex and abstract theories (Gopnik, Meltzoff, & Kuhn, 2001).

This somewhat solipsistic view of learning was already criticized during Piaget's lifetime. Vygotsky, notably, insisted on the role of social interactions to guide the development of children; knowledge is 'co-constructed' and language, through its internalization by individuals, plays a crucial role in learning and in cognitive development (Vygotsky, 1978). Interestingly, the focus on the individual has also been criticized by former members of the Piagetian school who insist on the import-ance of social interaction in the development of cognitive abilities (Perret-Clermont, 1980). For instance, children who did not previously possess certain cognitive abilities involved in Piaget's conservation of liquids task, acquire them after using and practising them in a social coordin-ation task (Doise, Mugny, & Perret-Clermont, 1975). But the researcher that really brought together the notions of *social* and *learning* is, of course, Albert Bandura. Bandura questions the commonly held idea that learning results from direct experience: according to Bandura, virtually all learning can occur on a vicarious basis, by observing people's behaviours and the subsequent repercussions (Bandura, 1977). In a series of famous studies, he showed that children who observed an adult acting aggressively (towards Bobo the doll, for instance) might then behave more aggres-sively than would otherwise be expected, apparently through the imita-tion of what could be seen as a social model (Bandura & Huston, 1961). Initiating a long debate that is still ongoing, he and his colleagues also demonstrated that aggression modelled on film can have a similar effect (Bandura, Ross, & Ross, 1963).

More or less at the same time, anecdotes of 'animal traditions' were circulating among field biologists, who observed that members of different groups sometimes exhibited patterns of behaviour that were totally absent in other groups – signs, perhaps, of cultures of behaviour. It seemed therefore inevitable to imagine that these 'cultural traditions' were transmitted from individual to individual by a form of observa-tional learning. Galef and Clark (1971) then showed experimentally that adult rats could play an active role in determining their young's behav-iour in order that the young avoid poisoned food. Learning could no more be seen as a purely individual endeavour, and the way was paved for accepting the idea of animal cultures (Boesch & Tomasello, 1998; van Schaik et al., 2003; but see also Galef, 1992).

Since then, it has come to be generally accepted that an important part of what we learn is socially transmitted. Given the importance of culturally informed practices for our species, it is hardly surprising that humans rely heavily on imitation to acquire the behaviours that are characteristic of their community (Meltzoff & Moore, 1977). It has even been hypothesized that children tend to be 'overimitators', that is, to copy even causally irrelevant elements in a sequence demonstrated by an actor (Lyons, Young, & Keil, 2007). However, the acknowledgement of the importance of social learning has until relatively recently been restricted to *behaviour*. At the beginning of the twenty-first century, this restriction was lifted to include *knowledge* through research conducted on testimony. As Paul L. Harris put it, children are not stubborn, auto-didacts but rather, they learn a lot thanks to others' statements (Harris, 2002), notably about facts that nobody can learn on their own, like history, science or religion (Harris & Koenig, 2006). Interestingly, it has been shown that this dependency on others is not absolute and that, on the contrary, children exhibit selective trust (Clément, 2010; Clément, Koenig, & Harris, 2004; Harris, 2012).

The goal of this book is to designate, beside behaviour and knowledge, another area where social learning is required to assure the transmission of any given culture: *values*. The objective this time is not so much to understand how efficient behaviour or reliable knowledge is transmitted, but to shed light on the mechanisms that enable children and indeed any newcomers to a social group, to make sense of what is worth attending to, interesting, *valuable*. It should explain, at least in part, why what matters to us, matters to us, either as an individual or as a collective. Sociologists have long shown how this kind of relevance is socially distributed: certain activities, objects or persons are considered as highly desirable – or even fascinating – for a given social group, while considered as boring and/or unworthy by other groups (Bourdieu, 1984). These preferences are not just reflected in superficial ways of speaking and acting; they are most often rooted in profound emotions that can motivate lifelong investments and deeply felt resentments. How are those social transmissions possible and how can they have such an influence on an individual's personality? This is what affective social learning (ASL) is about.

I.2   From value to social evaluation

It seems uncontroversial to say that most psychologists would consider values as being important for explaining human behaviour. Abstract concepts such as 'family values', 'cultural values' and 'political values' can all be used as explanations for why people think and act in a certain way, or even used as a shorthand explanation for others' behaviour or beliefs (as in 'He did that because he is an American liberal' or 'She thinks that because her parents were both environmentalists'). Not only do we imagine that people act as a result of their values but we like to think that our values are relatively stable and that, to some extent, they define who we are. For example, they can define our goals in life – we might want to work in the health industry because we value working to help others, or in the environmental sector because we value our planet. In short, our values can be defined as what matters to us, how we feel about something (Higgins, 2016). In a hypothetical world without any values, it is difficult to imagine how we could feel anything about anything – nothing would seem to matter more or less than anything else. With the possible exception of meeting our biological needs, this flattening of the evaluative landscape would result in a world without motivation, without pleasure and without displeasure. With this sobering illustration in mind, it is possible to consider values and how we feel about something as providing the impulse to acquire, acknowledge and act upon specific goals. In other words, our motivation to act seems to be intrinsically linked with the valence we attribute to the different aspects of our environment. This evaluation, or appraisal, is considered an essential property of emotions by many psychologists, enabling us to adapt to our environment by taking into account the potential hedonic consequences of daily events.

For a long time now, this process has been seen as essentially intra-individual. For instance, by the end of the 1960s, Paul Ekman described emotions as coherent responses, coordinated by 'affect programmes', which are triggered by events in the environment. Although partially inherited, these affect programmes can still incorporate information about how to adapt to certain recurring situations throughout the life-span (Ekman & Cordaro, 2011). When they have become learned, these programmes operate automatically and cannot be interrupted once in process, although they may last less than a second (Ekman, 2003). While the expression of the emotion can be adjusted depending on whether or not the expresser is in the company of others who may be sensitive to their response (Ekman, 1972), the expression comes automatically and naturally, even if only in barely perceptible micro expressions when someone tries to deliberately or unconsciously suppress their emotion (Ekman, 2003). Ekman's theory is therefore, for the most part, relatively uninformative concerning the social, interpersonal aspects of emotion.

This basic emotion theory was challenged by cognitive-appraisal theories of emotion, both in terms of its tight object–response relationship and eventually in terms of its rather asocial approach. Appraisal theory's first buds appeared in the 1960s (Arnold, 1960; Lazarus, 1966), but it took about two decades before it really began to flower when several different authors proposed different versions of the theory (Barrett & Campos, 1987; Frijda, 1986; Leventhal & Scherer, 1987; Oatley & Johnson-Laird, 1987; Roseman, 1984; Scherer, 1984a; Smith & Ellsworth, 1985). While some appraisal theorists focused on the relation between person and object (Campos, Mumme, Kermoian, & Campos, 1994; Lazarus, 1991) and others on the reactions that objects elicit (e.g. Scherer, 1984b), all appraisal theorists agree that it 'is not events per se that determine emotional responses, but evaluations and interpretations of events' (Roseman, 1991, p. 162). Of course, the word appraisal focuses attention on the evaluation of the object or its emotional meaning (Clore & Ortony, 2000), rather than the (intrinsic) value of the object itself. Whereas basic emotion theory suggests that there is a coherent response to give to the funny joke, for instance, the loosening of the object–reaction relationship inherent to appraisal theory can better explain, for example, how it is simultaneously possible for Samuel to find the joke funny but Ike to find it disgusting, or indeed, how it is possible for Francesca to have found a book interesting yesterday, but not anymore?

Again then, for appraisal theorists, it is not the stimulus or object itself that causes the reaction, but the evaluation of the stimulus. For example, perhaps it is more adapted to run than to fight, depending on how big the threatening person is in comparison to oneself or, perhaps the self-attribution of embarrassment can be mediated by the nature of an onlooker, who had done the same thing in the past and is therefore likely to be a less harsh judge. The emotion-eliciting question for appraisal theorists is whether the object is relevant to their goals or not, while for basic emotion theorists, the reaction to a particular object is more automatic (Frijda, 1986).[1]

As a more relational perspective then, appraisal theory is able to explain the differences that can exist between the evaluation processes made by different persons or by the same persons in different contexts. However, appraisal theory has been less successful in turning attention to social contexts and processes. Indeed, in a relatively recent review of appraisal theory written by some of its most notable proponents (Moors, Ellsworth, Scherer, & Frijda, 2013), the word 'social' was only used in terms of 'future research', the term 'relation' was only used concerning relations between the different mechanisms of appraisal and the word 'context' was only used once for describing 'events in their context' (Moors et al., 2013). While this does not mean that appraisal theories have nothing to teach us about the social context in which persons relate to objects, nor that its many adherents do not consider such issues, it does suggest that there is still more to do in terms of convincing some leading researchers of the importance of social context (Parkinson, 2011a).

This relative oversight comes in spite of the fact that, as early as 1981, Campos and Stenberg mentioned the possibility of 'social appraisal' in terms of taking into account how others react to events, comparing it to

---

[1] While it is important to stress that elements of appraisal become an important part of Ekman's theory (at least as early as 1985, see Ekman, Friesen, & Simons, 1985) and as such, this contrast might be somewhat overstated, it is nonetheless clear that appraisal theory insisted more on the evaluation of the object from its inception, rather than on the value of the object itself.

'intrinsic appraisal', which was an individual's appraisal of the objects in their environment (Campos & Stenberg, 1981), although it took another twenty years before the term was formalized. Antony Manstead and Agneta Fischer (2001) developed the concept in a bid to alert affective scientists to the fact that there was too much focus on the individual 'intrinsic appraisal' and not enough on the 'social' aspects of affect in appraisal theory (see also Parkinson 1995, 1996; Parkinson & Manstead, 1992). They stated that 'the behaviors, thoughts or feelings of one or more other persons are often appraised in addition to the appraisal of the event per se' (Manstead & Fischer, 2001, p. 222) and this concept has since then been a rich source of experimentation (e.g. Evers, Fischer, Rodriguez Mosquera, & Manstead, 2005; Mumenthaler & Sander, 2012, 2015; Parkinson & Simons, 2009; van der Schalk, Kuppens, Bruder, & Manstead, 2015). Indeed, Manstead, Fischer and colleagues have continued to incite researchers to focus more on the interpersonal aspects of emotions (Fischer & van Kleef, 2010; Hess & Fischer, 2016; Parkinson, Fischer, & Manstead, 2005; Parkinson & Manstead, 2015).

The debate about the nature of emotion has diversified then, from one where objects in the environment necessarily elicit quasi-automatic, universally recognisable reactions in individuals, to one where emotions involve the individual's context- and goal-dependent evaluations and where the evaluations of others' evaluations (or appraisals) may play an important role in the process. Klaus Scherer described one of the initial appraisal processes in terms of 'radar antennae scanning the environment' (Scherer, 1994) in the sense that an individual will locate and then evaluate objects on the basis of whether or not they can meet or obstruct the individual's goals. As such, other people can be identified as being, in the first instance, proxy relevance detectors and, more subtly, potential informers of value: we can learn from others what is worthy of further attention, and more specifically, how to qualify that attention – should I attend with fear, disgust, joy, etc. Thus, not only can we vicariously learn about efficient behaviours or reliable knowledge, we can also learn about values vicariously too.

Another important piece of the story comes from developmental psychology, and again has Joseph Campos at its origin: the visual cliff experiment and the phenomena of social referencing. Briefly, the social referencing paradigm used the visual cliff experiment (Gibson & Walk, 1960) to highlight how 12-month-olds would look to their mothers (i.e. reference them) when deciding to cross what apparently looked like it could be a dangerous drop to the infants (Klinnert, Campos, Sorce, Emde, & Svejda, 1983).[2] The results were spectacular: while a significant

[2] In fact, when the 'drop' was not too big, the infants crossed regardless of any signal from their parents, while when it appeared too great, the infants avoided it, irrespective of parent affective expression. This is important as some researchers insist that it is

majority of the infants crossed while their mothers looked at them with facial expressions of interest or joy, none of them crossed when the mothers looked at them with fear. Again, this finding has motivated many empirical studies that have added a great deal to our understanding of socio-emotional development (Boccia & Campos, 1989; Feinman & Lewis, 1983; Hirshberg & Svejda, 1990; Klinnert, 1984; Klinnert, Emde, Butterfield, & Campos, 1986; Sorce, Emde, Campos, & Klinnert, 1985; Walden & Baxter, 1989; Walden & Ogan, 1988; Zarbatany & Lamb, 1985). More recently, it has been shown that social referencing continues to be successfully used by adults (Parkinson, Phiri, & Simons, 2012). Clearly, there is a great deal of overlap between social referencing and social appraisal and, while some would have us believe that the two concepts are, in fact, indistinguishable (Walle, Reschke, & Knothe, 2017), we have argued that there are very good reasons to differentiate between the two (Clément & Dukes, 2013, 2017). As we see it, social referencing can be understood as a subtype of social appraisal.

In fact, it was while we were in the process of identifying the differences between social referencing and social appraisal that we struck upon the idea of a hierarchy of socio-emotional processes that could influence how people learn the value of the objects in their environment from others. This brings our introductory overview to the present day and to the title of this book. ASL describes how we can be influenced by the emotional expressions of others when acquiring knowledge about how to value the objects in our environment. Having outlined the historical motivation for this approach, we will now go into detail about its mechanisms.

I.3   The dimensions of ASL

We introduce the notion of ASL as an overarching concept to highlight research done within different fields while bringing important insights about the different ways people learn about what is valuable in their social environment. In a sense, these phenomena share the same function – the transmission of values – but differ in the cognitive and social mechanisms necessary for them each to function. Highlighting these differences is important to us for ontogenetic and phylogenetic reasons: while it seems that certain mechanisms are more complex than others, it is possible that they (a) are already present in very young children and (b) exist in other (non-human) species that to varying degrees appear to master specific competences that are transmitted from one generation to another.

To understand the differences between the phenomena we want to describe, let's start with some concrete illustrations. Marie, age 1,

---

particularly when there is an ambiguity to resolve that individuals look most readily to others for their 'advice'.

is playing alone in her room. She cannot help but hear her father and his friends watching television, enjoying a rugby match with loud and passionate enthusiasm. In such cases, nobody is addressing any direct message to an observer. Moreover, Marie does not really yet know what is so exciting about the event, or even what the object of excitement is. Marie is not intentionally trying to learn anything, nor is anybody trying to teach her anything. However, we suppose that she will learn to associate certain kind of objects with the very specific affective 'ambiance' that she feels during such emotional episodes. This is what we propose to label as *emotional contagion*. The second case requires an intentional search for information by the observer – the potential learner – and can be illustrated by the following 'stranger' situation: let's imagine that Marie is now waiting with her father for a medical appointment, browsing a picture book of some kind. Suddenly, an unknown person with a military uniform enters the waiting room and Marie does not know exactly how to feel about this interruption. She therefore turns her attention toward her father who, without paying attention to his child, addresses the newcomer with a warm greeting before starting a cordial conversation. Her father's reaction calms Marie who gets back to her book, with the probably enduring feeling that people dressed in uniform can be positively connoted. These kind of episodes are what we call *affective observation* (see Repacholi & Meltzoff, 2007, for a similar concept, *emotional eavesdropping*, discussed below). In the next illustration, the potential learner and the 'knower' have an intentional exchange on a given object in a spontaneous way. The classic example is the 'visual cliff experiment' designed by Joseph Campos and his colleagues, described above. In such cases, the child and the adult are engaged in an intersubjective relationship and their attention converges on the same object. However, the 'call' for information and the response do not require much cognitive elaboration: the learner is engaged in an action and his attention is already directed toward an object of interest. What he does not know is how to appraise the situation he is involved in, and whether he should stop or pursue his action. That is why he turns his attention to a significant other who, by means of an emotional expression, encourages or discourages the realization of the goal. This is what we called *social referencing* (for more on the specific criteria we use to describe something as *social referencing*, see Clément & Dukes, 2017). Finally, there are cases where the knower acts more as a 'teacher', influencing not only the kind of action to perform with a detailed demonstration, but also the kind of objects that are worth attending to. Marie's father can, for instance, systematically point to 'books of great worth', plead for the importance of literature, express his awe for great writers and systematically read several chapters of what he considers to be major works of art. Following Csibra and Gergely's (2009) denomination, we propose to call this kind of value transmission,

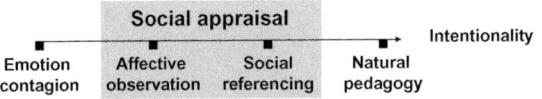

Affective social learning

Figure I.1 ASL along the dimension of intentionality, including the four major concepts and with social appraisal at its core.

where the affect is involved together with explicit explanations, *natural pedagogy.*

Figure I.1 shows how ASL was originally conceived (Clément & Dukes, 2017). As the name implies, the dimension of *intentionality* (in the sense of 'willingness' or 'purposiveness') relates to the increasing amount of purpose involved in the transmission of values. In other words, it is related to how much either the person wishing to communicate some information manifests her desire to communicate or how much the person wishing to receive the communication manifests this desire. In the case of emotional contagion (the rugby example, earlier), an emotion can be transmitted without it being intended at all. In the case of affective observation, the learner is aiming to get affective information. For social referencing and natural pedagogy, both social partners intend either to send or receive (to teach or to learn) affective information. In the specific case of natural pedagogy, this relationship is initiated by the teacher, but this may be implicitly or explicitly elicited by the child's desire to know something (Clément & Dukes, 2017).

It is important to note that this dimension is ordinal in the sense that we are not implying that 'social referencing' finds itself exactly half way between affective observation and natural pedagogy in terms of intentionality, but it is possible to say that there is less intentionality involved in affective observation than in natural pedagogy.

In Figure I.2, we propose to add a second dimension to specify the differences between the types of social learning: the amount of *social orientation* involved in the transmission of the information. By this we mean how much account is taken of the 'other' in these processes. In emotional contagion, for example, little or even no account is taken of the other as, in the strictest cases of emotion contagion, it is possible to imagine being affected by someone else's emotion without being aware that this was the case. In affective observation, the learner is clearly oriented to the knower, in social referencing, both are oriented briefly to each other (at least in a 'one-hit' exchange – an exchange of glances, for example), while in natural pedagogy, a much fuller exchange of views is given, as both people are oriented

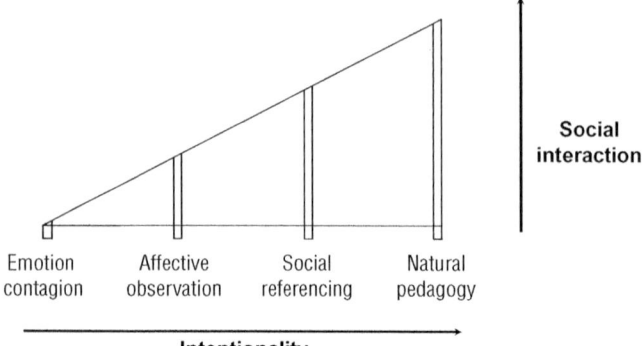

Figure I.2 ASL in two dimensions: intentionality and social orientation.

entirely towards each other. In the same way that levels of intentionality increase from emotional contagion to natural pedagogy, so too does the amount of social interaction, as will be explained in more detail for each component below.

In terms of the conceptual space, we consider that there is potentially more social orientation in social referencing than in affective observation (where only the learner is intentionally getting information via an other's affective reaction), but that there is potentially less in social referencing than in natural pedagogy (where each participant is coordinating his or her learning efforts for a more or less extended period of time). Again, these should only be seen in ordinal terms.

We argue then that ASL can be depicted by these two dimensions. Again, this will become clearer when each component is described in more detail.

Finally, we judge that our description is more complete and exact if we include a measure of trust that the observer may have with respect to the other, as shown in Figure I.3. This dimension is probably present in all social interactions when information is transmitted, irrespective of the type of information (beliefs, knowledge, affect, etc.), it particularly concerns the amount of trust a potential learner has in the source and can range from low or high for any of the components. The level of trust that the learner has in the 'knower' modulates how well the particular information is learned – when it is high, it means that the observer trusts the knower absolutely and we can expect the information to pass unchecked, while if it is low, the observer doesn't trust the knower at all and information would most likely not affect the learner. This may even be the case in emotional contagion when there is no 'intended' information at all (see Section I.4.1 below). It is even possible that in situations where the learner

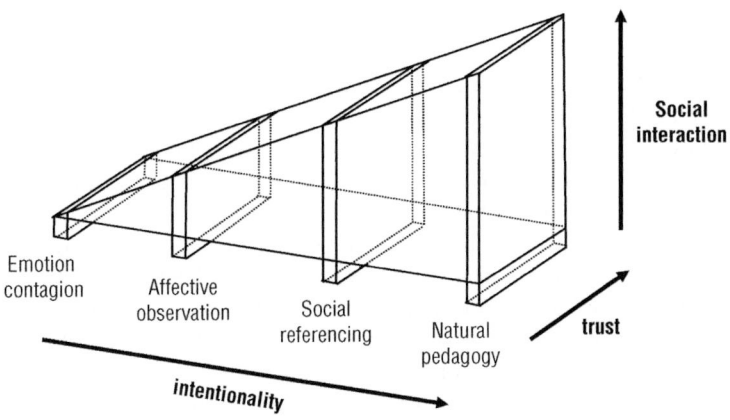

Affective social learning

Figure I.3 ASL structured along three dimensions: intentionality, trust and social orientation.

suspects that the knower is intentionally trying to cheat them, something entirely different to the intended message may be understood.

I.4 Four components of ASL

Now that we have a general picture of how ASL can be broken down into different mechanisms, we can detail the different components highlighted here and underline their relevance to understanding the acquisition of cultural values.

I.4.1 *Emotional contagion*

Emotional contagion is the process by which one person's emotion or mood can be directly influenced by someone else's. More formally, it has been described as 'the tendency to automatically mimic and synchronize expressions, vocalizations, postures, and movements with those of another person's and, consequently, to converge emotionally' (Hatfield, Cacioppo, & Rapson, 1994, pp. 153–154). We focus here on the minimal conditions necessary for emotional contagion to take place. For example, our hero, Marie, is playing with her toys on the kitchen floor while her father angrily does the cooking. (He is angry because he does not think that it is a man's role to do the cooking.) Initially unaware of her father's anger, Marie becomes angry too and starts making brusque movements with her toys. She has no understanding of what caused the anger, but her father's anger becomes transmitted nonetheless. Another example might involve a businesswoman walking into a boardroom of tense colleagues, making her feel tense too. It can be seen that the child's emotions and the businesswoman's affective state have been influenced by other people's emotions.

It may appear strange that we have included such phenomena in our account of ASL. As stated earlier, this is a relational account of how we can learn from others' relations to the objects in the environment but, in the examples provided here, the principal people in the story are not in perceptual contact with a particular object. In fact, as Parkinson (2011b) has pointed out, perhaps the key difference between emotional contagion and social appraisal processes is that there is no object in emotional contagion. However, these examples encourage us to include emotional contagion nonetheless. We argue here that there is an intermediate state between there being no object and there being an object: by feeling her father's enthusiasm and anger, the observer can associate, largely unconsciously, the emotion with the context. For instance, the association between kitchen and father(s) can start to be connotated negatively, favouring a rather traditional view of who is responsible for the household chores. Similarly, in the case of the businesswoman, the negative emotion that she felt in hierarchical contexts could encourage her to avoid such situations in the future, therefore impeding her career as a manager. In these examples, neither the child nor the businesswoman really knows what the 'object' or 'thing' is, but they have been made aware that there is a 'thing' and they have been influenced by others (the father, or the colleagues) about how to feel about those 'things'. They will probably then go on to imagine what the cause or the content of that thing might be. In more technical terms, we could describe these 'things' as placeholders for the object, wrapped in an affective envelope. In further encounters with this object, it is probable that this affective tone will still be associated with it as the placeholder will be 'filled' with more and more content. While it is true that this might be more cognitive than 'automatically mimicking or synchronizing expressions' (Hatfield, Cacioppo, & Rapson, 1994), it is not yet the same as reflecting on the object – the causes of the *ambiance*. Thus, while this 'awareness of the thing' does not meet the criteria for emotion contagion *stricto sensu*, it would certainly be closer to emotional contagion than affective observation.

We think that the dimension of trust can play an important role even for emotional contagion. Indeed, recent research on emotional mimicry suggests for instance that what had originally been thought of as an automatic process (Chartrand & Bargh, 1999) may actually be subject to certain constraints, including the relationship between the two actors (Bourgeois & Hess, 2008; Hess & Fischer, 2016). In fact, Hatfield and colleagues originally hypothesized that people whose self is construed as being more fundamentally interrelated to others in general would be more vulnerable to emotion contagion than people whose self is construed as distinct and unique (Hatfield et al., 1994). This suggests that someone who has a strong emotional link to a specific other may well be more vulnerable to emotional contagion from them than if they didn't know each other.

In terms of the dimensions mentioned earlier, and even if contagion works better when there is direct interaction, it seems that individuals can be influenced by others' emotions even when only minimal social interaction is involved. Second, neither the father nor the colleagues (in our earlier 'rugby' example) necessarily intended to communicate how they felt about the 'objects' to the person in question. As far as the level of trust is concerned, it is likely that contagion happens more quickly from a 'learner' to a 'knower' when the 'learner' trusts the 'knower'. For instance, it is more likely that a child becomes angry or anxious when confronted with her angry or anxious father than when witnessing a stranger's emotions. Similarly, the affective reaction of the business-woman is more likely to happen when she holds her colleagues in esteem, or at least respects them. The exact role played by trust in this moderation of emotional contagion is quite difficult to assess and experimentation is needed to settle the matter.

While emotion contagion is at the border of ASL, social appraisal is definitely at its heart. Elsewhere, we have made the case that social appraisal is a general term that covers occasions when the observer can learn from the other with or without the other knowing (Clément & Dukes, 2017; Dukes & Clément, 2017). This leads us to make a distinction between when the other communicates directly to the observer (as in social referencing) and when the other serves as a model without even being aware that they are being watched (affective observation).

I.4.2   *Affective observation*

Affective observation, as in our case of the 'stranger in a uniform', is rarely discussed by developmental psychologists, maybe because many psychological models insist – correctly in our Western world – on the crucial role of interpersonal relationships, notably between the child and her mother (Stern, 1985). One of the unintended consequences of this bias is the temptation to think of social learning uniquely in terms of interpersonal exchanges. However, when entering a group, individuals are prone to detect, simply by observing others' affective reactions, what is socially relevant and what is not. This kind of social learning by observation alone is particularly important in communities where schooling has not been prevalent (Paradise & Rogoff, 2009; Rogoff, 2003), but there is no reason to think that it does not play an essential role in every culture, and not only for children. We can imagine a dinner party, for example, where a curious guest, believing the host to be out of the kitchen, quickly tastes a spoonful of the sauce that is cooking in the pot. However, the host catches the guest stealing a taste of the sauce and looking disgusted. The host then pretends to re-enter the kitchen, perhaps with a warning cough, without letting the guest know that they have been seen, before adding some seasoning to their sauce to make it taste more agreeable.

In this perspective, Repacholi and Meltzoff (2007) demonstrated that children as young as 18 months old were able to regulate their behaviour as a function of how other people are expressing themselves, even when the other people are not expressing themselves directly to the children. In a process they call *emotional eavesdropping*, 18-month-old infants were able to detect a third-person's affective expression (anger) to evaluate whether the way the experimenter was acting on an object was appropriate or not. Concretely, children were less likely to imitate the demonstrators when their action was followed by an expression of anger towards them than when the third person expressed neutral affect. This specific example can be seen as a type of affective observation and this study tends to show how children can use third-party's affective reactions from a very early age. Our idea is that future research will show that children can use many other third-person affective reactions to figure out what their social environment is expecting people to do. It is therefore a powerful means to learn indirectly about the norms and values of any given cultural group.

When this affective observation is compared to emotional contagion, it is clear that the object is now much more central and is much more identifiable in each story. In terms of the dimensions that we are using to characterize ASL, given that one of the two people is aware of the other – it might be correct to describe this as minimal social interaction. As far as intentionality is concerned, it is clear that the observer is intentionally attending to the other, in order to gain some information perhaps, but that the other is not explicitly trying to communicate any information about value or affect to the observer. In cumulative terms then, there is greater intentionality than in emotional contagion. Clearly, trust must play a role here, too. It is presumably less likely that a child would copy and learn from someone they don't know than from someone they know and trust for example (Corriveau & Harris, 2009; Gruber, Deschenaux, Frick, & Clément, 2017), while the adult may dismiss their guest as someone whose judgement concerning food is flawed.

1.4.3   Social referencing

Social referencing is the second of the two social appraisal processes. While social referencing has been almost exclusively studied in terms of children and infants, one study was carried out on social referencing on adults when participants' behaviour was shown to be influenced by the facial expression of a friend (Parkinson et al., 2012). Outside of the lab, we would argue that social referencing is a very common occurrence in adulthood (Dukes & Clément, 2017). Indeed, whenever we seek and get verbal or non-verbal advice about how we should evaluate an object from someone could be described as social referencing (Clément & Dukes, 2017). For example, if you were looking at someone who is leaving a restaurant as you are considering trying it out, and they signal to you with a disgusted facial expression that you should not eat there, this would qualify as social referencing.

One important part of social referencing that needs to be determined perhaps is whether the information can be any subtler than preferences – a smile or a frown to suggest to 'go' or 'don't go', a look of disgust to suggest 'more salt' or 'less salt' or a nodding smile to suggest 'buy the book' rather than 'don't buy the book'. This conceptual fuzziness comes perhaps from the fact that most of the examples come from developmental psychology and even the one example that comes from an experiment with adults was non-verbal (Parkinson et al., 2012). Conceptually, it is possible that rather complex social learning can be enabled by social referencing. The classical cases involve an ongoing behaviour with a doubt about its relevance or danger that is then eliminated by the knower's affective expression. But presumably, the learner does not have to be herself engaged in a particular activity. Imagine a situation where Marie, walking with her father in the park, suddenly sees a girl doing something she has never seen before, for instance behaving aggressively towards a boy. Marie will then intentionally look at her father for an evaluation of the event and the shocked look that he shares with her will indicate that girls are not 'expected' to behave in such a way. Such indirect social learning can of course be involved in all sorts of activities or events. If they hear in the distance a brass-band concert, for instance, the depreciative pout and the accelerating pace of her father as he grabs her arm will be a clear signal to Marie that such music is not considered as 'socially relevant' for her.

In terms of the dimensions described earlier, clearly there is more social interaction and more intention on the part of the 'knower' to inform the 'learner' about the object in question than in affective observation. It is worth noting too, that, if we are to include instances where the information is more involved than simply suggesting 'go' or 'no-go' type information, there would be a greater amount of social interaction. This suggests again that, whether or not we regard this type of information sharing as social referencing or not, ASL should be considered as a continuum of behaviours, rather than a list.

1.4.4   Natural pedagogy

At the end of the spectrum we propose to place a phenomenon pinned down by Csibra and Gergely (2009): natural pedagogy. These are situations – like our 'love of literature' example – where teachers explicitly inform learners about the value of a given object, explaining why it deserves special attention and interest. For Csibra and Gergely, such triadic exchanges between two individuals about referent objects or classes of objects are essential for a species that, like ours, depends so much on culture (Gergely, Egyed, & Király, 2007). According to them, evolutionary pressures facilitated the emergence of cognitive abilities by learners as well as teachers. For instance, even babies are sensitive to higher pitches in voice ('motherese'), eye contact, eyebrow-raising, etc., which can be seen as 'natural' signals to attract their attention to ostensive communication. We reach the end of the spectrum in terms of intentionality and social interaction here because, not only do the teachers and learners explicitly intend to exchange information, but also the teachers make sure that their pupils are following their explanations, often using elaborate strategies (simplification, repetition, illustrations, exercises, metaphors, etc.) to assure an efficient transmission. Finally, trust is also essential at this level given the levels of attention and cognitive processing involved in these kinds of learning.

1.4.5   The end of the beginning

The following chapters each focus on different aspects of ASL. The chapters have been structured in such a way as to provide a phylogenetic and ontological basis for the concept before moving on to the mechanisms and applications thereof. While we feel that this chapter has provided a basic structure (with social appraisal at its core and emotional contagion and natural pedagogy as its end points) and even some meat on its relational bones, given that this is such a new concept, the details and the ramifications are somewhat up for debate. The reader therefore can expect some turbulence in terms of the definition as we have set it out, given that the researchers come from different disciplines (although all of them can be described as psychologists of one sort or another) and, as such, may like to tweak the definition in order that it makes most sense for their own discipline.

In Part I of this volume, comparative psychologists suggest different ways in which ASL could frame social learning research in non-human primates. In Chapter 1, Caroline Schuppli and Carel van Schaik describe research on wild orang-utans that suggests that the learner's interest and trust in the other may play an important part in the learning processes of immature orang-utans. Thibaud Gruber and Christine Sievers review the primate literature more generally in Chapter 2, concluding that, although it is unlikely that primates engage in natural pedagogy, there is a strong case for using the ASL framework as a basis for comparative research on the social transmission of value.

In Part II, the focus will turn to human developmental aspects of ASL. Paul L. Harris points out in Chapter 3 how important selectively learning from individuals who are representative of their own culture can be for a child's emotional development. In Chapter 4, György Gergely and Ildikó Király then discuss how emotion-based learning systems and the capacity for ostensive communication become integrated to serve ASL, even before acquiring language.

In Part III, the mechanics of ASL are considered more carefully. In Chapter 5, Brian Parkinson begins this section by insisting on the interpersonal nature of emotional experience, arguing that there may be cases of ASL that involve adjustments in interactants' orientations to what is happening, rather than changes to the perceived meaning of emotional objects. This is followed by Chapter 6, in which Christian Mumenthaler and David Sander focus on the socio-affective inferential mechanisms involved in emotion recognition and, in particular, the automaticity of social appraisal processing. The final chapter in this section (Chapter 7) is written by Agneta Fischer, who considers the mechanisms involved in learning from others' emotions generally before discussing the different types of learning that may be involved in ASL.

Finally, in Part IV, Antony Manstead, Magdalena Rychlowska and Job van der Schalk (Chapter 8) use the emotion of regret as an example to highlight how emotional expressions can provide lessons for observers, particularly when the regret is expressed by a member of a group to which we either belong or with which we are in competition and what the implications might be. In Chapter 9, Jozefien De Leersnyder gives an account of how ASL can be applied to culture and emotion research and how, she argues, culture, emotion and ASL scaffold one another.

We will close this book with a concluding chapter that takes into consideration the various viewpoints and research contributions made in these chapters, highlighting modifications that we will have to make in light of the criticisms made, as we lay the foundations for ASL and the conceptualization of the social transmission of value.

References

Arnold, M. B. (1960). *Emotion and personality* (2 vols.). New York, NY: Columbia University Press.

Bandura, A. (1977). *Social learning theory*. Oxford, UK: Prentice-Hall.

Bandura, A., & C. Huston, A. (1961). Identification as a process of incidental learning. *Journal of Abnormal and Social Psychology, 63*, 311–318.

Bandura, A., Ross, D., & Ross, S. A. (1963). Imitation of film-mediated aggressive models. *Journal of Abnormal and Social Psychology, 66*, 3–11.

Barrett, K. C., & Campos, J. J. (1987). Perspectives on emotional development II: A functionalist approach to emotions. In J. Osofsky (Ed.), *Handbook of infant development* (2nd ed., pp. 555–578). New York, NY: Wiley.

Boccia, M., & Campos, J. J. (1989). Maternal emotional signals, social referencing, and infants' reactions to strangers. *New Directions for Child and Adolescent Development, 44*, 25–49.

Boesch, C., & Tomasello, M. (1998). Chimpanzee and human cultures. *Current Anthropology, 39*, 591–614.

Bourdieu, P. (1984). *Distinction: A social critique of the judgement of taste*. Cambridge, MA: Harvard University Press.

Bourgeois, P., & Hess, U. (2008). The impact of social context on mimicry. *Biological Psychology, 77*(3), 343–352.

Campos, J. J., Mumme, D. L., Kermoian, R., & Campos, R. G. (1994). A functionalist perspective on the nature of emotion. *Monographs of the Society for Research in Child Development, 59*, 284–303.

Campos, J. J., & Stenberg, C. (1981). Perception, appraisal, and emotion: The onset of social referencing. In M. E. Lamb & L. R. Sherrod (Eds.), *Infant social cognition: Empirical and theoretical contributions* (pp. 217–314). Hillsdale, NJ: Erlbaum.

Chartrand, T. L., & Bargh, J. A. (1999). The chameleon effect: the perception–behavior link and social interaction. *Journal of Personality and Social Psychology, 76*, 893–910.

Clément, F. (2010). To trust or not to trust? Children's social epistemology. *Review of Philosophy and Psychology, 1*, 531–549.

Clément, F., & Dukes, D. (2013). The role of interest in the transmission of social values. *Frontiers in Psychology, 4*, 349.

   (2017). Social appraisal and social referencing: Two components of affective social learning. *Emotion Review, 9*(3), 253–261.

Clément, F., Koenig, M., & Harris, P. (2004). The ontogenesis of trust. *Mind & Language, 19*(4), 360–379.

Clore, G. L., & Ortony, A. (2000). Cognition in emotion: Never, sometimes, or always? In R. D. Lane & L. Nadel (Eds.), *The cognitive neuroscience of emotion* (pp. 24–61). New York, NY: Oxford University Press.

Corriveau, K. H., & Harris, P. L. (2009). Choosing your informant: Weighing familiarity and recent accuracy. *Developmental Science, 12*(3), 426–437.

Csibra, G., & Gergely, G. (2009). Natural pedagogy. *Trends in Cognitive Sciences, 13*(4), 148–153.

Doise, W., Mugny, G., & Perret-Clermont, A.-N. (1975). Social interaction and the development of cognitive operations. *European Journal of Social Psychology*, 5, 367–383.

Dukes, D., & Clément, F. (2017). Author reply: Clarifying the importance of ostensive communication in life-long, affective social learning. *Emotion Review, 9*(3), 267–269.

Ebbinghaus, H. (1885/2013). Memory: A contribution to experimental psychology. *Annals of Neurosciences, 20*(4), 155–156.

Ekman, P. (1972). Universals and cultural differences in facial expressions of emotions. In J. Cole (Ed.), *Nebraska symposium on motivation* (pp. 207–282). Lincoln, NE: University of Nebraska Press.

(2003). *Emotions revealed*. New York, NY: Times Books.

Ekman, P., & Cordaro, D. (2011). What is meant by calling emotions basic. *Emotion Review, 3*(4), 364–370.

Ekman, P., Friesen, W. V., & Simons, R. C. (1985). Is the startle reaction an emotion? *Journal of Personality and Social Psychology, 49*(5), 1416–1426.

Evers, C., Fischer, A. H., Rodriguez Mosquera, P. M., & Manstead, A. S. (2005). Anger and social appraisal: A 'spicy' sex difference? *Emotion, 5*(3), 258.

Feinman, S., & Lewis, M. (1983). Social referencing at ten months: A second order effect on infants' responses to strangers. *Child Development, 54*, 878–887.

Fischer, A. H., & van Kleef, G. A. (2010). Where have all the people gone? A plea for including social interaction in emotion research. *Emotion Review, 2*(3), 208–211.

Frijda, N. H. (1986). *The emotions*. Cambridge, UK: Cambridge University Press.

Galef, B. G. (1992). The question of animal culture. *Human Nature, 3*(2), 157–178.

Galef, B. G., & Clark, M. M. (1971). Social factors in the poison avoidance and feeding behavior of wild and domesticated rat pups. *Journal of Comparative and Physiological Psychology, 75*(3), 341–357.

Gergely, G., Egyed, K., & Király, I. (2007). On pedagogy. *Developmental Science, 10*(1), 139–146.

Gibson, E. J., & Walk, R. D. (1960). The 'visual cliff'. *Scientific American, 202*, 67–71.

Gopnik, A., Meltzoff, A., & Kuhl, P. (2001). *The scientist in the crib: What early learning tells us about the mind*. New York, NY: HarperCollins.

Gruber, T., Deschenaux, A., Frick, A., & Clément, F. (2017). Group membership influences more social identification than social learning or overimitation in children. *Child Development*. http://doi.org/10.1111/cdev.12931.

Harris, P. L. (2002). Checking our sources: The origins of trust in testimony. *Studies in History and Philosophy of Science, 33*, 315–333.

(2012). *Trusting what you're told: How children learn from others*. Cambridge, MA: Harvard University Press.

Harris, P., & Koenig, M. (2009). Choosing your informants: Weighing familiarity and recent accuracy. *Developmental Science, 12*(3), 426–437.

Hatfield, E., Cacioppo, J. T., & Rapson, R. L. (1994). *Emotional contagion*. New York, NY: Cambridge University Press.

Hess, U., & Fischer, A. (Eds.). (2016). *Emotional mimicry in social context.* Cambridge, UK: Cambridge University Press.

Higgins, E. T. (2016). What is value? Where does it come from? A psychological perspective. In T. Brosch & D. Sander (Eds.), *Handbook of value: The affective sciences of values and valuation* (pp. 43–62). Oxford, UK: Oxford University Press.

Hirshberg, L. M., & Svejda, M. (1990). When infants look to their parents I. Infants' social referencing of mothers compared to fathers. *Child Development, 61*(4), 1175–1186.

Klinnert, M. D. (1984). The regulation of infant behavior by maternal facial expression. *Infant Behavior and Development, 7*(4), 447–465.

Klinnert, M. D., Campos, J., Sorce, J. F., Emde, R. N., & Svejda, M. J. (1983). Social referencing: Emotional expressions as behavior regulators. *Emotion: Theory, Research and Experience, 2,* 57–86.

Klinnert, M., Emde, R., Butterfield, P., & Campos, J. (1986). Social referencing: The infant's use of emotional signals from a friendly adult with mother present. *Developmental Psychology, 22*(4), 427–432.

Lazarus, R. S. (1966). *Psychological stress and the coping process.* New York, NY: McGraw-Hill.

(1991). Progress on a cognitive-motivational-relational theory of emotion. *American Psychologist, 46*(8), 819.

Leventhal, H., & Scherer, K. (1987). The relationship of emotion to cognition: A functional approach to a semantic controversy. *Cognition & Emotion, 1*(1), 3–28.

Lyons, D. E., Young, A. G., & Keil, F. C. (2007). The hidden structure of over-imitation. *Proceedings of the National Academy of Sciences, 104*(50), 19751–19756.

Manstead, A. S. R., & Fischer, A. H. (2001). Social appraisal: The social world as object of and influence on appraisal processes. In K. R. Scherer, A. Schorr, & T. Johnstone (Eds.), *Series in affective science: Appraisal processes in emotion – theory, methods, research* (pp. 221–232). Oxford, UK: Oxford University Press.

Meltzoff, A., & Moore, M. (1977). Imitation of facial and manual gestures by human neonates. *Science, 198,* 75–78.

Moors, A., Ellsworth, P. C., Scherer, K. R., & Frijda, N. H. (2013). Appraisal theories of emotion: State of the art and future development. *Emotion Review, 5*(2), 119–124.

Mumenthaler, C., & Sander, D. (2012). Social appraisal influences recognition of emotions. *Journal of Personality and Social Psychology, 102*(6), 1118–1135.

(2015). Automatic integration of social information in emotion recognition. *Journal of Experimental Psychology: General, 144*(2), 392–399.

Oatley, K., & Johnson-Laird, P. N. (1987). Towards a cognitive theory of emotions. *Cognition and Emotion, 1,* 29–50.

Paradise, R., & Rogoff, B. (2009). Side by side: Learning by observing and pitching in. *Ethos, 37,* 102–113.

Parkinson, B. (1995). *Ideas and realities of emotion.* London, UK: Routledge.

(1996). Emotions are social. *British Journal of Psychology, 87,* 663–683.

(2011a). How social is the social psychology of emotion? *British Journal of Social Psychology, 50*(3), 405–413.

(2011b). Interpersonal emotion transfer: Contagion and social appraisal. *Social and Personality Psychology Compass, 5*(7), 428–439.

Parkinson, B., Fisher, A. H., & Manstead, A. S. R. (2005). *Emotion in social relations: Cultural, group, and inter-personal processes.* New York, NY: Psychology Press.

Parkinson, B., & Manstead, A. S. R. (1992). Appraisal as a cause of emotion. In M. S. Clark (Ed.), *Review of personality and social psychology, No. 13. Emotion* (pp. 122–149). Thousand Oaks, CA: Sage.

(2015). Current emotion research in social psychology: Thinking about emotions and other people. *Emotion Review, 7*(4), 371–380.

Parkinson, B., Phiri, N., & Simons, G. (2012). Bursting with anxiety: Adult social referencing in an interpersonal Balloon Analogue Risk Task (BART). *Emotion, 12*(4), 817–826.

Parkinson, B., & Simons, G. (2009). Affecting others: Social appraisal and emotion contagion in everyday decision making. *Personality and Social Psychology Bulletin, 35*(8), 1071–1084.

Perret-Clermont, A.-N. (1980). *Social interaction and cognitive development in children.* London, UK: Academic Press.

Piaget, J. (1936). *La naissance de l'intelligence chez l'enfant.* Neuchâtel and Paris: Delachaux et Niestlé.

Repacholi, B. M., & Meltzoff, A. N. (2007). Emotional eavesdropping: Infants selectively respond to indirect emotional signals. *Child Development, 78,* 503–521.

Rogoff, B. (2003). *The cultural nature of human development.* Oxford, UK: Oxford University Press.

Roseman, I. J. (1984). Cognitive determinants of emotion: A structural theory. In P. Shaver (Ed.), *Review of personality in social psychology* (Vol. 5, pp. 11–36). Beverly Hills, CA: Sage.

(1991). Appraisal determinants of discrete emotions. *Cognition & Emotion, 5*(3), 161–200.

Scherer, K. R. (1984a). Emotion as a multicomponent process: A model and some cross-cultural data. *Review of Personality & Social Psychology, 5,* 37–63.

(1984b). On the nature and function of emotion: A component process approach. In K. R. Scherer & P. Ekman (Eds.), *Approaches to emotion* (pp. 293–318). Hillsdale, NJ: Lawrence Erlbaum.

Scherer, K. (1994). An emotion's occurrence depends on the relevance of an event to the organism's goal/need hierarchy. In P. Ekman & R. Davidson (Eds.), *The nature of emotion: Fundamental questions* (pp. 227–231). New York, NY: Oxford University Press.

Smith, C. A., & Ellsworth, P. C. (1985). Patterns of cognitive appraisal in emotion. *Journal of Personality and Social Psychology, 48*(4), 813–838.

Sorce, J. F., Emde, R. N., Campos, J. J., & Klinnert, M. D. (1985). Maternal emotional signaling: Its effect on the visual cliff behavior of one-year-olds. *Developmental Psychology, 21,* 195–200.

Stern, D. (1985). *The interpersonal world of the infant.* New York, NY: Basic Books.

van der Schalk, J., Kuppens, T., Bruder, M., & Manstead, A. S. (2015). The social power of regret: The effect of social appraisal and anticipated emotions on fair and unfair allocations in resource dilemmas. *Journal of Experimental Psychology: General, 144*(1), 151.

van Schaik, C. P., Ancrenaz, M., Borgen, G., Galdidas, B., Knott, C. D., Singleton, I., ... Merrill, M. (2003). Orangutan cultures and the evolution of material culture. *Science, 299*, 102–105.

Vygotsky, L. S. (1978). *Mind in society: The development of higher cognitive processes.* Cambridge, MA: Harvard University Press.

Walden, T. A., & Baxter, A. (1989). The effect of context and age on social referencing. *Child Development, 60*(6), 1511–1518.

Walden, T. A., & Ogan, T. A. (1988). The development of social referencing. *Child Development, 59*, 1230–1240.

Walle, E. A., Reschke, P. J., & Knothe, J. M. (2017). Social referencing: Defining and delineating a basic process of emotion. *Emotion Review, 9*, 245–252.

Zarbatany, L., & Lamb, M. E. (1985). Social referencing as a function of information source: Mothers versus strangers. *Infant Behavior and Development, 8*(1), 25–33.

PART I

On the evolutionary foundations of affective social learning processes

Lessons from comparative psychology

CHAPTER 1

Social learning among wild orang-utans

Is it affective?

Caroline Schuppli and Carel van Schaik

Our goal in this chapter is to examine whether the rules through which young orang-utans acquire their skills and knowledge can be linked to affective social learning (ASL). Because the concept of ASL was developed with humans in mind, we will begin by identifying the ASL components that are relevant to social learning in non-human animals. We will then go on to describe the social learning processes we can observe in wild orang-utans before using this description to assess whether this framework must be amended for it to be applied to the social learning observed in great apes.

Dukes and Clément (Introduction, this volume) define ASL as a particular way of learning to assess the value of objects in our environment that is influenced by the emotional expressions of others manipulating or reacting to these objects. This definition implies that ASL is only a subset of all possible mechanisms involved in social learning. It is therefore possible for animals to engage in social learning without ever engaging in ASL, although it is equally possible that ASL is deployed extensively. It is therefore worth exploring this issue before undertaking a detailed comparison with social learning in immature orang-utans.

Dukes and Clément (Introduction, this volume) subdivide ASL into four categories: emotional contagion, affective observation, social referencing and natural pedagogy. These can be ordered by the centrality of the object (low in the first, high in the second, third and fourth), the degree of social interaction between role model and learner and the extent of active involvement of the role model (for both low in the first two, high in the third, highest in the last).

We thank Danny Dukes and Fabrice Clément for the invitation to participate in the meeting on affective social learning. We gratefully acknowledge the support for the orangutan fieldwork by SNF (grant 310030B_160363/1), the AH Schultz-Stiftung and the Leakey foundation (Primate research fund).

If we try to apply this human-oriented framework to non-human animals, we must first note that active participation by role models, in the form of informative signalling, such as pointing, or of facial expressions, such as disgust, are quite rare among animals (Burkart & van Schaik, 2010; van Schaik & Burkart, 2010) and full-blown natural pedagogy is unique to humans (Gergely & Csibra, 2013). However, we may expect some elements of social referencing and even pedagogy in cooperative breeders. Indeed, there is evidence for teaching from adults to infants in callitrichid primates (Humle & Snowdon, 2008; Martins & Burkart, 2013; Rapaport, 2011) and for cooperative signalling, i.e. active information donation, in them too, in the form of disgust reactions (Snowdon & Boe, 2003) or sentinel behaviour (Clutton-Brock, 2002), but further research is necessary (van Schaik & Burkart, 2010).

Given that the majority of non-human animals, including great apes (Matsuzawa et al., 2008; Tomasello, 2008; van Schaik, 2016), do not have active role-model involvement, this leaves emotional contagion and affective observation as the most likely candidates for ASL in non-human animals. In emotional contagion, the role model's emotional state affects the emotional state of the naïve observer, while the observer would not directly ascribe the emotional state of the role model to any object (see Clément & Dukes, Introduction, this volume). The naïve individual simply experiences the emotional state of the role model under a certain context and makes an association between the two. Importantly, the association between the emotional state of the role model and the context happens largely unconsciously. In affective observation, the naïve individual observes one or more role models interacting with some object and learns about the value or worth of the object's features or affordances from the role model's emotional responses. Notice that this is a form of social appraisal in the absence of any direct social interaction between role models and observers.

The first category, emotional contagion, is probably the same as the process through which maturing individuals learn the meaning of primate alarm calls, which has been called observational conditioning (Whiten, Horner, Litchfield, & Marshall-Pescini, 2004). The naïve immatures watch how experienced adults respond to particular vocalizations (usually with sudden, salient changes in behaviour) thereby learning how to respond to these alarm calls and how to recognize the stimuli that elicit these calls by association. This process has been described in detail for maturing vervet monkeys (Cheney & Seyfarth, 1990). However, while vocal learning may be the most common context of social learning in some species, it is a minor part in some others, such as great apes. In orang-utans, something similar may be found in maternal come-hither sounds (Hardus et al., 2009; Wich et al., 2012), where infants rush to their mother upon hearing this sound produced in the context of non-urgent danger, such as upon hearing a male long call – orang-utan mothers usually keep their infants away from flanged males, presumably because of the risk of infanticide.

The second category, affective observation, is ASL by observation alone: the learning individual is trying to find out about which objects are relevant in its environment and uses the role model's affective reactions to attribute values to different stimuli. The role model can be unaware of being observed or can be aware but doesn't care about it (see Clément & Dukes, Introduction, this volume).

In most cases of social learning in wild animals, the role model is presumably aware of being observed (because it happens at close range), but simply tolerates it, usually because it is a close relative or friend, and thus trusted by the naïve observer. What differentiates emotional contagion from affective observation is the importance of the object, which is less central and identifiable in emotional contagion. Another important element of affective observation is that the observer is intentionally attending to the role model, in order to gain information. However, even when the role model is aware of being observed, there is no active attempt on his or her part to communicate any information about value or affect to the observer.

For both emotional contagion and affective observation, the role model must be expressing a discrete emotion or at least some form of affective reaction to the object. However, in most cases of social learning in the wild, described below, the role model simply behaves normally, pursuing its daily activity, and it is the naïve observer who decides whether the role model's activity is salient enough to be worth attending to or not. How discrete does the emotional expression of the role model have to be to unleash the ASL cascade? In general, it is still a matter of debate to what extent emotions can be ascribed to non-human animals (Maestripieri, 2009). Defining the level of emotional engagement of the role model needed for ASL to work will thus not only determine how frequently ASL will be found among non-human animals but also how reliably its presence can be detected.

Defining emotions has proven to be extremely difficult (Cacioppo, Tassinary, & Berntson, 2007). Definitions range from emotions being quasi-automatic, universally recognizable reactions of individuals to objects in their environment, or of being the result of context- and goal-dependent evaluations by the individual, to being the result of the evaluations of others' evaluations (or appraisals) by the individual (see Clément & Dukes, Introduction, this volume). To what extent do the reactions wild great apes have to living their everyday lives, performing their everyday behaviours, qualify as being emotional?

Based on our many years of experience of observing wild primates, we would argue that for most of their average day, wild great apes do not display any discrete emotion at all. The exceptions to this may be rare or dangerous situations that likely trigger emotions like *excitement* or *fear*, or social interactions that plausibly may involve a broad spectrum of emotions in non-human primates just as in humans. However, is it necessary for someone to *display* an emotion (voluntarily or involuntarily) for an emotion to be detected? Would for example the satisfaction (and thus, presumably, a certain level of *happiness* or *joy*) a role model experiences while it is eating also qualify as an emotion and/or would it suffice to act as an emotional stimulus? What about the sheer act of focusing on an object while manipulating it? This must almost always be the result of some level of *interest* in the object (even in the most well-known and readily available food sources) and would thus arguably qualify as an emotion (Silvia, 2008). If these everyday scenarios are sufficient to elicit ASL, it may be that ASL is a central element in the skill acquisition process of all species when they learn socially from a trusted role model, but, if this is the case, then ASL itself becomes more difficult to differentiate from ordinary social learning.

Irrespective of the necessary level of emotional engagement required, ASL is a tool with which a naïve individual learns which objects are valuable in its environment. ASL describes learning from others about what is worth attending to, and how to qualify that attention, as in deciding on whether to attend and if to attend, then with which emotion (*fear, disgust, joy*). Through ASL from trusted role models, individuals can learn about efficient behaviours or reliable knowledge. These outcomes of ASL correspond nicely to the patterns we see during skill and knowledge acquisition in immature wild orang-utans, and that are most likely also representative of most natural learning in other great apes.

Below, we will describe social learning in immature orang-utans that we have studied extensively over the last ten years (Jaeggi et al., 2010; Schuppli, Forss et al., 2016; Schuppli, Meulman et al., 2016a). Since we argue that detecting the emotional states of role models is nearly impossible for wild great apes, we will focus on the emotional responses of the learners to the role models' behaviour. We will first give a description of how orang-utans socially learn in the wild, and then argue for a highly specific emotional arousal response of the immatures in the social-learning context. In the discussion, we will try to evaluate whether we should call this kind of social learning emotional, and if so, under which ASL category it would fall.

1.1   Social skill learning in orang-utans

We evaluated the amount of social interest individual orang-utans show in their conspecifics as a measure of (affective) social learning by scoring rates of peering behaviour (attentive close-range watching

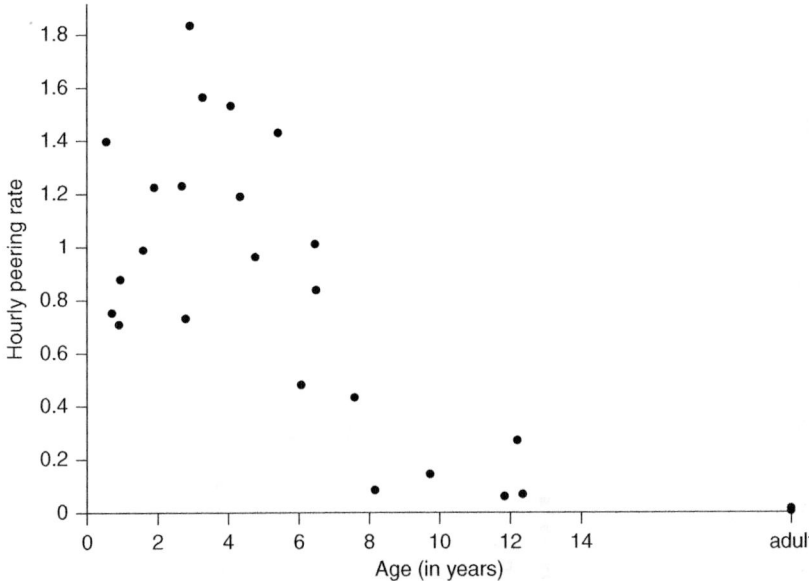

Figure 1.1 Hourly peering rates over age.
Note: Peering rates of immature Sumatran orang-utans at Suaq versus age. The "adult" points are based on data collected on five adult females.

of the activities of a conspecific, from a close enough distance to see the details of the activity, sustained over at least five seconds) in different contexts (feeding, nest building, social and others). Here we summarize and update various recently published studies (Jaeggi et al., 2010; Schuppli et al., 2017; Schuppli, Forss et al., 2016; Schuppli, Meulman et al., 2016).

Peering rates peak at around the age of 4 years and then decrease steadily throughout the rest of immaturity. By the onset of adulthood (around the age of 16), the social interest reaches values near zero, suggesting that adults show very low levels of social interest (Figure 1.1).

We found that peering events are followed by the *peerers* selectively practising the observed behaviour, thus providing strong evidence that peering is indeed part of social learning in immature orang-utans. For example, when we looked at the peering events that infants aimed at their mothers' behaviour, we found that when the infants were in the mother's feeding patch, the number of exploration events with the food item performed per unit of time increased significantly after each peering event (Figure 1.2). These peering-practice cycles suggest that even though orang-utan learning is socially induced, this learning includes a large amount of independent practice.

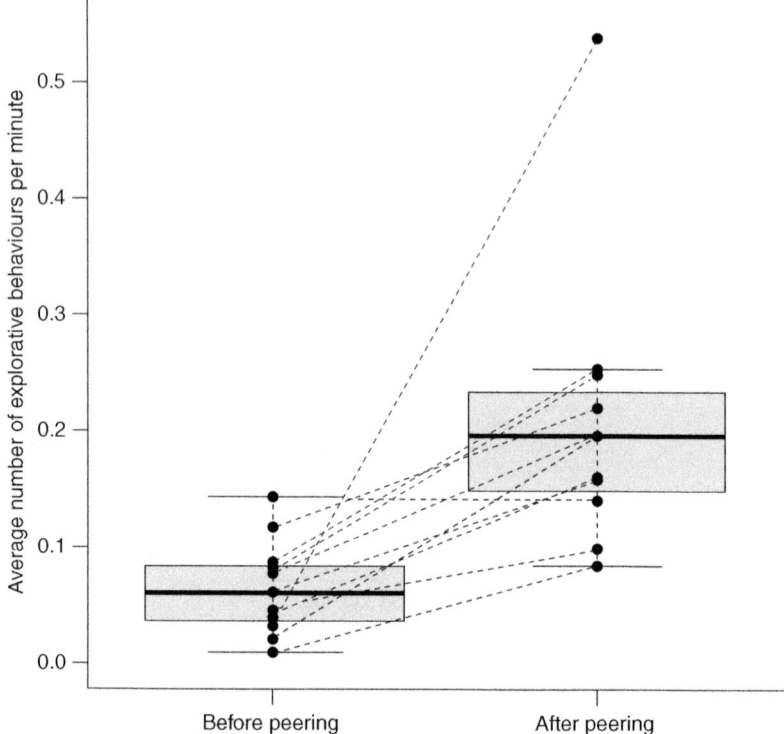

Figure 1.2 The peering-practice cycle: peering is followed by a steep increase in exploratory behaviour.

Note: Average number of exploration events per minute with the same food item before and after peering events at the mother, when the dependent immature is within the same feeding patch at Suaq. Data points represent exploration rates of the different infants before and after the peering event, averaged over all their recorded food peering events (GLMM: $N = 22$, $Estimate_{Timing} = 0.14$, $Std.Error_{Timing} = 0.04$, $P_{Timing} < 0.001$; $Estimate_{Age} = 0.01$, $Std.Error_{Age} = 0.01$, $P_{Age} = 0.256$).

In terms of role-model choice, one would expect that at a certain age the immature will have acquired all the skills and knowledge of its mother, and also, that with increasing age, role models other than the mother would become more interesting to pick up additional, novel skills. Indeed, our results indicate that, whereas young infants peer exclusively at their mothers, the proportion of peering that is directed at individuals other than the mother increases significantly with age (Figure 1.3).

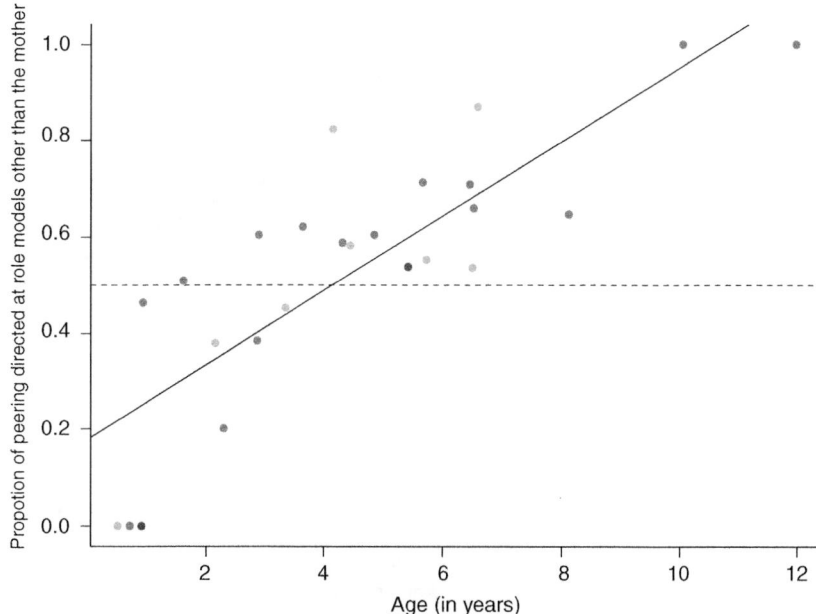

Figure 1.3 Peering preferences: mother versus other role models.

Note: The proportion of peering directed at role models other than the mother versus age. Peering proportions are corrected for the amount of time spent within two metres of each class of role model and thus depict true interest (i.e. are not biased by the availability of the role models). Black = data collected at Suaq, grey = data collected at Tuanan (Linear Mixed Effects Model: lmer(Peering at others ~ Age + Site + (1 | Focal)): $p_{Age} < 0.001$, Estimate$_{Age}$ = 0.08, Std.Error$_{Age}$ = 0.01; p_{Site} = 0.75, Estimate$_{Site}$ = 0.02, Std.Error$_{Site}$ = 0.07).

Furthermore, when looking at total peering proportions, we found that most peering by infants is directed at adults and only very rarely at juvenile or infant role models (Figure 1.4). During late juvenility, however, other juveniles (i.e. peers) are the most frequent peering targets. Infants show a clear preference for related role models versus unrelated role models (Figure 1.5), although the interest in unrelated role models increases with age. Thus, familiar, related role models are preferred while the learner is young, whereas as they get older, less familiar, unrelated individuals become more attractive as peering targets, reflecting an increase in social competence and confidence, as well as the need for novel stimuli.

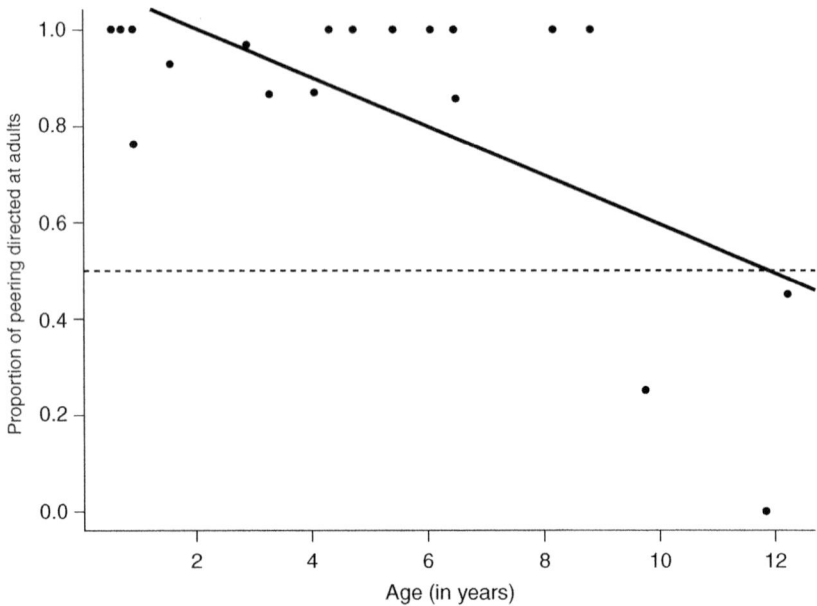

Figure 1.4 Peering preferences: age classes.
Note: The percentage of all peering events immatures at Suaq direct at adults and immatures (infants and juveniles). The percentage of peering directed at adult individuals decreases with age (Linear Mixed Effects Model: lmer (% Peering at adult individuals ~ Age + (1 | Focal)): p_{Age}< 0.001, Estimate$_{Age}$ = –4.99, Std.Error$_{Age}$ = 1.45).

In sum, while observing behaviour at Suaq (where these data have been collected systematically for the longest time period), immature orangutans peered at more than 191 different skills and knowledge elements, including 161 food species and techniques, 10 components of nesting behaviours, 2 moving habits (e.g. biting through lianas to then use them to sway across tree gaps), 8 different social behaviours, 5 tool use variants and 2 other behaviours. This suggests that immatures acquire their skill sets (ranging from basic subsistence skills to complex behaviour patterns) through socially mediated learning.

1.2   Discussion

New-borns of highly encephalized species such as great apes are born almost as naïve as human children. Immatures have to acquire virtually all their behaviour patterns and skills, including moving or nest building, diet and food processing and social skills. In other words,

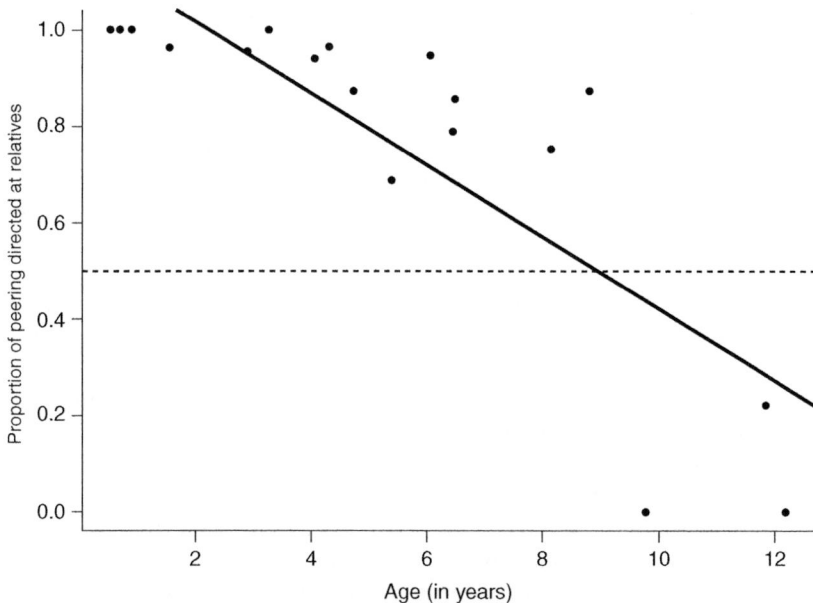

Figure 1.5 Peering preferences: relatedness.

Note: The percentage of all peering events immatures at Suaq direct at related versus unrelated individuals. The percentage of peering directed at related individuals decreases with age (Linear Mixed Effects Model: lmer(% Peering unrelated individuals ~ Age + (1| Focal)): $p_{Age} < 0.001$, Estimate$_{Age}$ = -7.34, Std.Error$_{Age}$ = 1.22).

most of their behaviour is not instinctive, but rather learned. This drawn-out learning process lasts years. Most importantly, however, it is socially mediated, through the peering-practice cycle, in which peering is followed by attempts to engage in these same behaviours. As individuals mature, an individual's selective attention gradually shifts from the mother to other trusted role models, including non-relatives.

This process of socially mediated learning declines toward adulthood. This pattern is not unique to orang-utans, but also found in chimpanzees (Humle, Snowdon, & Matsuzawa, 2009; Lonsdorf, 2006), gorillas (Corp & Byrne, 2001) and capuchin monkeys (Perry, 2009), and to some extent also in Japanese monkeys (Tarnaud & Yamagiwa, 2008), marmosets (Schiel & Huber, 2006) and bottlenose dolphins (Sargent & Mann, 2009), and to a lesser extent in brown lemurs (Tarnaud, 2004). Similar patterns may be found in birds (M. Griesser pers. com.). In short, in all species characterized by parent–offspring association, we see at least some level of socially mediated skill acquisition, although it may reach its apogee in the more highly encephalized lineages.

Socially mediated skill acquisition requires young learners to decide at numerous instances whether to pursue their own activities or attend to the behaviour of a role model (engage in social learning). In other words, when functional theories predict maturing individuals should have a preference for social learning (van Schaik, Graber, Schuppli, & Burkart, 2017) and specify the contexts in which they should deploy their social behaviour rather than pursue their own activities (Lehmann, Wakano, & Aoki, 2013), they assume there are decision mechanisms at work that produce these optimum decisions. ASL may be part of the bundle of mechanisms that lead to this "optimized" social learning in maturing apes.

The detailed behavioural observations on infant orang-utans indicate that social learning, or perhaps better, socially induced selective exploration and practice, is the default mode of learning in orang-utans. The question here is whether this social learning is to be called affective. There is virtually no evidence for active engagement on the part of the role model, let alone teaching, in chimpanzees (but see Boesch, 1991) or orang-utans (this study), despite researchers' close attention. In fact, the overwhelming impression is that role models, most often mothers, simply go about their business as usual, and leave it up to the learning individual to capture the relevant information.

However, in the absence of any discretely displayed emotion, the emotional engagement of the role model may be on a much more subtle level. Some degree of *joy* or *happiness* may result from having found a food source, even if it is an ordinary one. Building a nest might be connected to the *anticipation* of getting to lie down and rest soon. Complex foraging tasks (e.g. tool use) may come along with a certain *excitement* about getting to eat a particularly tasty or satiating food item. These emotions (or temporary affective states) of the role model may be enough to elicit an emotional engagement in the learning individual. And, on an even more general level, manipulating food items, nest material or any other object is always connected to some degree of *interest* in the object. If this interest can be called an emotion, or some form of affective state, ASL may be very common among socially learning species. The main difficulty becomes how to prove the presence of these affective states or emotions as the more subtle they are, the more difficult it becomes to verify their existence.

The ASL framework builds upon the transmission of the emotional engagement of the role model on to the learner. In non-human animals, the emotional reaction of the learner may be easier to capture than the emotional engagement of the role model, as the learner shows a change in behaviour upon attending to the information while the role model appears to simply complete its everyday tasks. Indeed, the variation in the learner's response at the same activity depending on its own knowledge state strongly suggests no emotional signalling by the role model in performing these routine subsistence skills. However, irrespective of what aspect of the role model's behaviour is the exact cause, the orangutan peering data suggests that the everyday behaviour of trusted role models does lead to the emotional involvement of the learner. Using the data we have collected, we will first summarize the evidence for the emotional engagement of the learning immatures and then ask if this engagement is sufficient evidence for one of the levels of the ASL continuum.

Our orang-utan data shows that immatures are oriented towards others' behaviour, and that they modify their behaviour accordingly, apparently becoming highly motivated to attend to the same object or even to perform the same action with the same stimuli as the role model. Role models seem to guide immature orang-utans' attention towards relevant aspects of the environment by attending to these same aspects. Infant orang-utans sometimes seem positively eager to approach mothers or others doing unusual things. They suddenly perk up and approach more quickly than normal, even from remarkable distances, suggesting that some form of arousal is motivating them. Moreover, these responses are highly selective. Initially, for example, an infant responds to a particular activity by the mother, say, eating some fruit of species x, with great curiosity, but will no longer do this after it has learned enough about this fruit to be able to confidently eat it independently. We see the same selectivity and changes in the choice of preferred role models with age. All of this suggests an emotional engagement on the part of the learner.

This emotionally regulated social attention is required because the alternative, cognitive regulation, is extremely unlikely. We cannot imagine that infants are aware of the fact that they are going to learn something. We also do not assume this for human infants and toddlers, yet they learn selectively as well. Thus, in terms of regulation, learning must involve reaching psychological goals that are very distinct from their functional goal. Accordingly, as described in the introductory chapter of this volume, affective observation is not about consciously obtaining information about the object per se, but rather about acquiring affective information concerning the object, the value. Watching others engage in activities and then practising these same activities must be intrinsically psychologically rewarding, or else the learner would not engage in it, given that there often is a delay until competence is achieved and thus some material reward is gained (see also Eibl-Eibesfeldt & Eibl-Eibesfeldt, 1975 on squirrels learning how to crack hazelnuts).

This self-rewarding element of watching a specific role model perform an activity is especially relevant in cases where acquiring the knowledge or skill takes many trials, and the functional reward (*knowing that*, or *knowing how to*) is not yet achieved. Indeed, the sustained effort required to maintain attention for so long, between attending to the object for the first time and mastering the observed skill of acquiring the displayed knowledge (i.e. and thus getting the physical reward), can only be explained if attending to the information is rewarding in itself. In great apes, these time gaps can take multiple years such as, for example, in the case of orang-utan tool use (Meulman, Seed, & Mann, 2013).

The orang-utan data also suggests that the class of role model (in terms of age and relatedness of the role model) that is most rewarding to watch changes over the different stages of development. In other terms, the relevant role model changes as new skills are developed. Whereas for young infants watching the mother must be especially rewarding, watching other role models seems to become more rewarding as the individuals mature. The ASL concept stresses that trust in the role model is an important precondition for all forms of ASL to work, with the possible exception of emotion contagion. A more detailed analysis of the peering practice data, where the effect of the class of role models on subsequent practice rates could be compared, would shed further light upon the trust dimension.

De Waal (2001, p. 231) refers to the process of non-human primate social learning as "BIOL", which stands for bonding- and identification-based observational learning. We posit that this BIOL may be the non-human primate equivalent of ASL. The main difference with ASL, as currently defined, is the focus on the emotional arousal of the learner. That the learner assigns high emotional valence to peering and practice is actually highly plausible. We acknowledge it may never be possible to prove the existence of subjectively experienced emotions in non-humans, but if we regard emotions as the experienced dimension of proximate mechanisms that can also objectively be described as motivations or as particular neuroendocrine states, we can plausibly ascribe emotions to infant orang-utans, even if one is not willing to ascribe to animals the subjective experiences that accompany them in humans (Aureli & Whiten, 2003). This position is especially plausible for intense emotions such as fear, where the neuroendocrine and physiological responses are well documented (Panksepp, 2004). But Panksepp (2004) also argues that the behavioural flexibility achieved by vertebrates is based on the "conscious dwelling on events" that are "guided by internally experienced emotional feelings" (p. 38). Thus, there is no compelling reason to deny the same link for various other, less well-studied emotions, although the nature of emotional regulation of learning remains largely unknown (Panksepp, 2004).

The likelihood that emotional arousal of the learner is important during social learning is also supported by the results of ghost-control experiments. In a ghost control, the agent is missing, but its actions and their results are simulated. Such studies with non-human primates failed to elicit learning beyond what was found in control conditions (Hopper, 2010), suggesting that an agent must be present to lend a particular context its emotional valence, consistent with the finding that it produces event memory (Howard, Wagner, Woodward, Ross, & Hopper, 2017). Likewise, common marmosets were only interested in actions they could observe if they interpreted them as intentional actions by agents (Burkart, Kupferberg, Glasauer, & van Schaik, 2012). Such highly selective attention requires some emotional reactivity to specific actions by specific agents.

All these results support the conclusion that social learning is clearly affective on the part of the learner. In wild primates, trusted role models' interest in an object during their everyday behaviour seems to elicit a high interest of the immature in the object, which would classify as affective observation. And this emotional reaction of the learner is plausibly caused by the affective state of the role model. The question remains whether this indirect evidence (without verifying the emotional engagement of the role model) is enough to confirm ASL. We are inclined to say yes, especially since the same processes that we see in orang-utan and chimpanzee infants are also seen in human infants (Legare & Harris, 2016), where ASL can be shown more directly.

In other words, the ASL concept (as currently defined) primarily stresses the importance of the role model, but if we can measure the affective state of the role model by the reaction it causes in the learner, it is perfectly applicable to non-human primates. To more clearly include the learner's emotional reaction in the ASL concept as a measure of the role model's emotional engagement would make it more measurable and provide evolutionary continuity as well as completeness for the human case.

Furthermore, the ASL concept currently stresses the valence of objects or activities (e.g. the presence of danger, playing sports together). That is surely relevant, but as we showed for great apes, social learning in nature mostly involves the learning of basic subsistence skills: learning to know what to do and how to do it. We have suggested that emotions are also involved there, albeit different ones. Moreover, an emotionally based social bond between learner and role model usually provides a critical backdrop to the social learning process (Aureli & Schaffner, 2002). This nicely coincides with the trust dimension of the ASL: trusted role models seem to elicit a different reaction from untrusted ones. Who young primates trust seems to change during different stages of development.

However, if ASL is also to cover the affective states and emotional experiences involved in the regular social learning of basic subsistence skills and knowledge, it will be more difficult to differentiate ASL from non-affective social learning. One could even argue that it is hard to conceive of any form of learning that is not emotionally mediated, at least in homeothermic vertebrates, turning ASL and social learning into synonyms. One could therefore argue that ASL serves to stress the affective dimension of a common, but critical process in the life of social vertebrates.

References

Aureli, F., & Schaffner, C. M. (2002). Relationship assessment through emotional mediation. *Behaviour, 139*(2), 393–420.

Aureli, F., & Whiten, A. (2003). Emotions and behavioral flexibility. *Primate Psychology*, 289–323.

Boesch, C. (1991). Teaching among wild chimpanzees. *Animal Behaviour, 41*, 530–532.

Burkart, J. M., Kupferberg, A., Glasauer, S., & van Schaik, C. P. (2012). Even simple forms of social learning rely on intention attribution in marmoset monkeys (Callithrix jacchus). *Journal of Comparative Psychology, 126*(2), 129–138.

Burkart, J. M., & van Schaik, C. P. (2010). Cognitive consequences of cooperative breeding in primates. *Animal Cognition, 13*, 1–19. doi:10.1007/s10071-009-0263-7

Cacioppo, J. T., Tassinary, L. G., & Berntson, G. (2007). *Handbook of psychophysiology*. New York, NY: Cambridge University Press.

Cheney, D. L., & Seyfarth, R. M. (1990). *How monkeys see the world: Inside the mind of another species*. Chicago, IL: University of Chicago Press.

Clutton-Brock, T. H. (2002). Breeding together: Kin selection and mutualism in cooperative vertebrates. *Science, 296*(5565), 69–72. doi:10.1126/science.296.5565.69

Corp, N., & Byrne, R. (2001). Sex difference in chimpanzee handedness. *American Journal of Physical Anthropology, 123*, 62–68.

de Waal, F. B. M. (2001). *The ape and the sushi master: cultural reflections of a primatologist*. New York, NY: Basic Books.

Eibl-Eibesfeldt, I., & Eibl-Eibesfeldt, I. (1975). *Ethology, the biology of behavior*. New York, NY: Holt, Rinehart & Winston.

Gergely, G., & Csibra, G. (2013). Natural pedagogy. In M. R. Banaji & S. A. Gelman (Eds.), *Navigating the social world: What infants, children, and other species can teach us* (pp. 127–132). New York, NY: Oxford University Press.

Hardus, M. E., Lameira, A. R., Singleton, I., Morrogh-Bernard, H. C., Knott, C. D., Ancrenaz, M., … Wich, S. A. (2009). A description of the orangutan's vocal and sound repertoire, with a focus on geographical variation. In S. A. Wich, S. S. Utami-Atmoko, T. Mitra Setia, & C. P. van Schaik (Eds.), *Orangutans: Geographic variation in behavioral ecology and conservation* (pp. 49–64). New York, NY: Oxford University Press.

Hopper, L. M. (2010). "Ghost" experiments and the dissection of social learning in humans and animals. *Biological Reviews, 85*(4), 685–701.

Howard, L. H., Wagner, K. E., Woodward, A. L., Ross, S. R., & Hopper, L. M. (2017). Social models enhance apes' memory for novel events. *Scientific Reports, 7*, 40926.

Humle, T., & Snowdon, C. T. (2008). Socially biased learning in the acquisition of a complex foraging task in juvenile cottontop tamarins, *Saguinus oedipus*. *Animal Behaviour*, *75*, 267–277.

Humle, T., Snowdon, C. T., & Matsuzawa, T. (2009). Social influences on ant-dipping acquisition in the wild chimpanzees (Pan troglodytes verus) of Bossou, Guinea, West Africa. *Animal Cognition*, *12*, S37–S48. doi:10.1007/s10071-009-0272-6

Jaeggi, A. V., Dunkel, L. P., van Noordwijk, M. A., Wich, S. A., Sura, A. A. L., & van Schaik, C. P. (2010). Social learning of diet and foraging skills by wild immature Bornean orangutans: Implications for culture. *American Journal of Primatology*, *72*(1), 62–71. doi:10.1002/ajp.20752

Legare, C. H., & Harris, P. L. (2016). The ontogeny of cultural learning. *Child Development*, *87*(3), 633–642.

Lehmann, L., Wakano, J. Y., & Aoki, K. (2013). On optimal learning schedules and marginal value of cumulative cultural evolution. *Evolution*, *67*, 1435–1445.

Lonsdorf, E. V. (2006). What is the role of mothers in the acquisition of termite-fishing behaviors in wild chimpanzees (Pan troglodytes schweinfurthii)? *Animal Cognition*, *9*, 36–46.

Maestripieri, D. (2009). The past, present and future of primate psychology. In D. Maestripieri (Ed.), *Primate psychology* (pp. 1–17). Cambridge MA: Harvard University Press.

Martins, E. M. G., & Burkart, J. M. (2013). Common marmosets preferentially share difficult to obtain food items. *Folia Primatologica*, *84*(3–5), 281–282.

Matsuzawa, T., Biro, D., Humle, T., Inoue-Nakamura, N., Tonooka, R., & Yamakoshi, G. (2008). Emergence of culture in wild chimpanzees: education by master-apprenticeship. In T. Matsuzawa (Ed.), *Primate origins of human cognition and behavior* (pp. 557–574). Tokyo, Japan: Springer.

Meulman, E. J. M., Seed, A. M., & Mann, J. (2013). If at first you don't succeed … Studies of ontogeny shed light on the cognitive demands of habitual tool use. *Philosophical Transactions of the Royal Society B*, *368*(1630), 20130050.

Panksepp, J. (2004). *Affective neuroscience: The foundations of human and animal emotions*. New York, NY: Oxford University Press.

Perry, S. (2009). Social influence and the development of food processing techniques in wild white-faced capuchin monkeys (Cebus Capucinus) at Lomas Barbudal, Costa Rica. *American Journal of Primatology*, *71*, 99–99.

Rapaport, L. G. (2011). Progressive parenting behavior in wild golden lion tamarins. *Behavioral Ecology*, *22*(4), 745–754.

Sargent, B., & Mann, J. (2009). From social learning to culture: Intrapopulation variation in bottlenose dolphins. In K. N. Laland & B. G. Galef (Eds.), *The question of animal culture* (pp. 152–173). Cambridge, MA: Harvard University Press.

Schiel, N., & Huber, L. (2006). Social influences on the development of foraging behavior in free-living common marmosets (*Callithrix jacchus*). *American Journal of Primatology*, *68*(12), 1150–1160.

Schuppli, C., Forss, S. I. F., Meulman, E. J. M., Atmoko, S. U., Noordwijk, M., & van Schaik, C. P. (2017). The effects of sociability on exploratory tendency and innovation repertoires in wild Sumatran and Bornean orangutans. *Scientific Reports, 7*(1), 15464.

Schuppli, C., Forss, S. I. F., Meulman, E. J. M., Zweifel, N., Lee, K. C., Rukmana, E., ... van Schaik, C. P. (2016). Development of foraging skills in two orangutan populations: Needing to learn or needing to grow? *Frontiers in Zoology, 13*(43), 1–17.

Schuppli, C., Meulman, E. J. M., Forss, S. I. F., Aprilinayati, F., van Noordwijk, M. A., & van Schaik, C. P. (2016). Observational social learning and socially induced practice of routine skills in immature wild orang-utans. *Animal Behaviour, 119*, 87–98.

Silvia, P. J. (2008). Interest: The curious emotion. *Current Directions in Psychological Science, 17*(1), 57–60. doi:10.1111/j.1467-8721.2008.00548.x

Snowdon, C. T., & Boe, C. Y. (2003). Social communication about unpalatable foods in tamarins (Saguinus oedipus). *Journal of Comparative Psychology, 117*(2), 142–148.

Tarnaud, L. (2004). Ontogeny of feeding behavior of Eulemur fulvus in the dry forest of Mayotte. *International Journal of Primatology, 25*(4), 803–824. doi:10.1023/b:ijop.0000029123.78167.63

Tarnaud, L., & Yamagiwa, J. (2008). Age-dependent patterns of intensive observation on elders by free-ranging juvenile Japanese macaques (Macaca fuscata yakui) within foraging context on Yakushima. *American Journal of Primatology, 70*(12), 1103–1113. doi:10.1002/ajp.20603

Tomasello, M. (2008). *Origins of human communication*. Cambridge, MA: MIT Press.

van Schaik, C. P. (2016). *The primate origins of human nature*. Hoboken, NJ: John Wiley & Sons.

van Schaik, C. P., & Burkart, J. M. (2010). Mind the gap: Cooperative breeding and the evolution of our unique features. In P. M. Kappeler & J. B. Silk (Eds.), *Mind the gap: Tracing the origins of Human Universals* (pp. 477–496). Berlin, Germany: Springer.

van Schaik, C. P., Graber, S., Schuppli, C., & Burkart, J. M. (2017). The ecology of social learning in animals and its link with intelligence. *Spanish Journal of Psychology, 19*(e99), 1–12.

Whiten, A., Horner, V., Litchfield, C. A., & Marshall-Pescini, S. (2004). How do apes ape? *Learning & Behavior, 32*, 36–52.

Wich, S. A., Krützen, M., Lameira, A. R., Nater, A., Arora, N., Bastian, M. L., ... van Schaik, C. P. (2012). Call cultures in Orang-Utans? *PLoS One, 7*(5), e36180.

CHAPTER 2

Affective social learning and the emotional side of cultural learning in primates

Thibaud Gruber and Christine Sievers

Primates are social beings and this has many consequences for their behaviour (Cheney & Seyfarth, 1990). On the one hand, evidence for social learning, particularly concerning their material knowledge, has accumulated over the last few decades, leading to claims of cultural behaviour in some species (Hobaiter, Poisot, Zuberbühler, Hoppitt, & Gruber, 2014; van Schaik et al., 2003; Whiten et al., 1999); on the other hand, both classic and more recent studies have described complex communication systems (Seyfarth, Cheney, & Marler, 1980), with a particular focus on intentional communicative behaviour production in recent research (Liebal, Waller, Burrows, & Slocombe, 2014; Townsend et al., 2016). The burgeoning literature on intentional communicative behaviour in animal communication, centred on the idea of goal-directed behaviour, is particularly important to discuss issues of emotion in communication in non-humans. A long-held assumption has indeed been that primate vocalizations are merely emotional reflections of the internal state of their producers, which goes directly against the idea of any sort of control over production, but gives emotions a prominent role over the life and behaviour of a given animal (Owren & Rendall, 2001; Tomasello, 2008). Nevertheless, interestingly, branding primate vocalizations as 'emotional' has not led to a breakthrough in the still controversial debate concerning the very existence of emotional lives in animals (Clay & de Waal, 2013).

Clément and Dukes (2017) have recently argued for the existence of affective social learning (ASL), a type of social learning that concerns the social transmission of values, and how they are influenced by emotions, and more generally, affect. We believe that ASL as envisioned by Clément and Dukes provides a useful template to analyse the emotional side of social learning in non-human primates. Clément and Dukes describe four stages: emotional contagion, affective observation, social

TG was supported by the Swiss National Science Foundation during the writing of this chapter (Grants no. CR13I1_162720/1 and P300PA_164678). We thank Daniel Dukes and Fabrice Clément for useful comments in an earlier draft of the chapter.

referencing – the latter two constituting social appraisal – and natural pedagogy, all of which may develop ontologically and evolutionarily. In this chapter, we will analyse cases in non-human primates (NHPs) that may constitute examples of the various categories outlined by Clément and Dukes (2017). Because our expertise mainly lies with chimpanzees (*Pan troglodytes*), we will mostly focus on this species, although we will also use examples coming from other primate species when needed. Subsequently, we will discuss the various cognitive processes that may underpin the four stages of ASL. We will argue that the later stages require flexible access to one's own and to others' mental representations, which may preclude NHPs from displaying the complex processing needed to engage in natural pedagogy (in line with Csibra & Gergely, 2009).

2.1   A primate's view on emotions and social learning

Social learning has become one of the most discussed topics in recent primate (and animal) literature (Hobaiter et al., 2014; Laland & Galef, 2009; Whiten, McGuigan, Marshall-Pescini, & Hopper, 2009). However, early claims of 'cultural' behaviour in Japanese monkeys (*Macaca fuscata*) and chimpanzees date back to as early as the 1960s (Goodall, 1964, 1973; Kawai, 1965). While there has been much debate regarding the precise social learning mechanisms at stake in primate behaviour (Nagell, Olguin, & Tomasello, 1993; Whiten et al., 2009), recent advances in data analysis, including the use of network-based analyses (Franz & Nunn, 2009; Hobaiter et al., 2014; Hoppitt & Laland, 2011) and field experiments (Lamon, Neumann, Gruber, & Zuberbühler, 2017; van de Waal, Renevey, Favre, & Bshary, 2010) have led to general acceptance of the existence of social learning for (presumed) socially acquired traditions, particularly in the context of foraging. As such, they provide opportunities where ASL could theoretically occur in NHPs.

Emotions constitute another, more recent area of interest in primate research, which is somewhat more controversial due to questions about whether to ascribe feelings or emotions to non-human animals without knowing how they themselves feel (Briefer, 2012). Nevertheless, work on variation in personalities in primates (Koski et al., 2017; Uher, Addessi, & Visalberghi, 2013) has paved the way to discuss emotions as a viable scientific topic in non-humans. Interestingly, emotions themselves have been present for a long time in the primate literature (Jürgens, 1979), most prominently in an ongoing debate about the evolutionary precursors of human language, but often limited to the question of whether vocalizations should be seen as uncontrolled expressions of an animal's internal emotional state (Owren & Rendall, 2001; Wheeler & Fischer, 2012) or not (Gruber & Grandjean, 2017; Gruber & Zuberbühler, 2013;

Townsend et al., 2016), compared to the more flexible use of gestures (Tomasello, 2008).

While the largely supposed emotional content of primate vocalization has often prevented discussions of possible social learning, the recent focus on intentional behaviour in animal communication, including vocalizations, may be instrumental to discussions of ASL. Indeed, the ability to understand another individual as goal-directed and having oneself the ability to produce goal-directed behaviour appear mandatory to the later stages of ASL (see below). In particular, natural pedagogy requires the involvement of various complex cognitive processes (Csibra & Gergely, 2009). An individual must be able to recognize that another individual lacks knowledge and needs input to acquire said knowledge. The knower must adapt her own behaviour to highlight particular areas of interest, in order that the learner acquires the behaviour. Furthermore, the knower must provide the information to be learned through *ostensive intentional communication*, that is, she overtly produces the information *for the learner* (directedness to learner, through ostensive signals) and the learner must be capable of grasping that the information was provided *for her*. Crucially, there has been no convincing proof up to now of such teaching in wild animals, particularly primates, unless a functional approach (where a 'knowledgeable model' loses efficiency concurrently to a 'naïve learner' acquiring novel behaviour) is taken (Caro & Hauser, 1992), which is very different to how teaching is conceived of in developmental science.

The lack of reports of teaching in animals, however, may be in part due to how teaching is conceived. Perhaps the adoption of a continuum running from non-active teaching to natural pedagogy, as proposed by ASL, may help us to better compare the teaching and learning skills of primates and other animals to the teaching and learning skills of humans. NHPs may display cognitively simpler or more passive forms of teaching, which may be influenced by emotional input or information transmitted by more or less passive teachers. Nevertheless, if ASL is to be used as a continuum, it must be assessed based on the cognitive requirements of the various stages. For example, among the early stages of ASL, affective observation needs an individual to at least possess the ability to recognize emotions in another individual, compared to emotional contagion, which does not require any knowledge about the other or any cognized mental state (e.g. a human baby, watching all adults in the room laughing loudly, may start laughing without knowing why). The main question we will address in the following section is whether there is any evidence for more cognitively developed aspects of ASL than 'basic' emotional contagion in NHPs, which will subsequently lead us to discuss the various cognitive aspects involved in each stage.

2.2   Some examples of ASL applied to primates

2.2.1   *Emotional contagion and affective observation*

Emotional contagion may be most directly discussed by referring to the classic vervet monkey (*Chlorocebus pygerythrus*) vocalization examples, described by Seyfarth, Cheney and colleagues (e.g. Seyfarth et al., 1980). In one such example, young infants produce the eagle alarm call in response to anything coming from above (i.e. not only eagles, but also falling leaves, for example) and leopard alarm calls in response to any entities approaching from ground level, (i.e. not only in response to leopards, but also to warthogs that in fact pose no danger to them at all) (Seyfarth et al., 1980). The ability to distinguish between a predator coming from above and a predator being on the ground, seems then, to be innately and phylogenetically connected to particular calls, but the ability to detect specific predators appears to be learned, to be a product of ontogeny: over time, young vervets learn to only produce alarm calls in response to situations that are really dangerous. How does this refinement come about? One answer might be through ASL.

When a vervet infant is using the alarm call correctly, sometimes mothers or other adults respond by repeating the same call. It is important here to avoid drawing any cognitively loaded conclusions about a potential connection between the infant's correct use and the mother's repetition of the call, particularly with respect to potential active teaching or active reinforcement as the co-occurrence of the calls is not sufficient to claim that the knowledgeable individual actively reinforces the learner (Seyfarth & Cheney, 1986). Most likely, the mother engages with the object, the eagle or the eagle shriek, displaying a specific affective state (fear) through behavioural cues and the production of the alarm call. But this does not exclude the possibility of the existence of a learning process in which the infant learns from the passive influence of the mother. The infant may learn how to apply the call correctly, i.e. it refines its 'knowledge' about the call's use through passive reinforcement via the mother's repetition of the correct call. Young vervets learn when to produce an eagle alarm call due to mothers producing the alarm call in the correct context. Therefore, the young vervet only receives positive reinforcement in the case of the correct stimulus and will gradually only call for the relevant threats.

There has been much debate over the precise content of vervet calls and the debate is still ongoing, with several commentators questioning whether there is any real referential meaning associated with these calls and whether their production is at all intentional, arguing that the production may in fact be possibly only an expression of their inner emotional state, i.e. fear (Ducheminsky, Henzi, & Barrett, 2014; Price et al.,

2015). In a recent publication (Sievers & Gruber, 2016), we argued that reference may not only be analysed under a biological functional reference approach (that is, the call functions to refer to a given stimulus, see Macedonia & Evans, 1993), but may also be considered through an intentional paradigm, with reference being considered as the intentional production of an act of reference (that is, an animal produces a call because it has the intention to refer to something in its environment). If such an approach is possible, the young vervet will learn from the adults engaging in an intentional act of referring to the eagle, without the adults necessarily having to compute that the young vervet is actually extracting information from their call production. Additionally, it does not matter whether the call is functionally referential, nor whether there is a strong emotional base to the call, as the important factor is the intentional production of the call upon seeing the stimulus (see Sievers & Gruber, 2016, for a discussion of signaller's reference).

The notion that the eagle or leopard call reflects the inner state of the vervet – of how it *feels* – offers one explanation here. Proponents of such a view may argue that the eagle call is initially made indiscriminately by young vervets in response to falling leaves and eagles because they cannot discriminate that falling leaves and eagles do not represent the same level of threat – in other words, because they are equally scared of both. An unlikely alternative is that infants learn to call when the eagles are present and not call when the leaves are present, irrelevant of the threats posed by either of these, perhaps simply as a reaction to seeing them. However, given the behavioural reaction and varied reactions of the vervets that accompany such calls (e.g. run in the tree and look in the sky after an eagle alarm call; versus stand up on one's feet and scan the ground after a snake alarm call), it seems that the threats and calls are inextricably linked. Developing vervets will subsequently learn the value (in terms of threat) of leaves and eagles. In other words, they learn that eagles are dangerous and that leaves are neutral. Learning this individually would prove highly dangerous, as encounters with predators are likely to have lethal consequences. Whether or not mothers intend to teach, infants appear to learn from them about the affective nature of their environment – of how to value objects in terms of, in this case, threat. This would appear to provide an example of ASL.

In this example, even though we are inclined to describe it as ASL, it appears difficult to describe it either as an example of *emotional contagion* or *affective observation*. Indeed, while one can argue that in the first few days of its life, the young vervet may only call as a response to others calling, with no apparent association between the call and a potential stimulus, it is hard to decipher whether the process becomes that of affective observation if and when the vervet is able to compute the relationship between the stimulus (e.g. the predator or the call) and the reaction (e.g. the predator-specific behavioural reaction). The mother is not actively engaging with the offspring, but the nature of her affective state provides information about the correct application of the alarm call – namely being in a precise state of fear in relation to the approaching predator in the sky, and not being in this state when a leaf is falling. The teaching process lacks ostensive cues by the knower, and active engagement by the knower with the learner. What the knower provides though, is information about how to apply the call (and to behave) appropriately, and the learner focuses on this important information due to affective states displayed by the knower. The knower in this case is an individual whose affective testimony is of value and importance for the young one, namely the mother. In fact, if the young vervet truly uses the possible feedback of other group members to tune its own reaction to flying stimuli, and thus achieves the correct vocalization for the correct stimulus, the young vervet example appears more to be in the realm of affective observation than, the simpler, emotional contagion.

A similar example may be found in chimpanzees as they learn about the use of pant-grunts. Chimpanzees have a repertoire of several grunt types produced in different contexts, pant-grunts being one of the most distinctive (Goodall, 1986). This grunt is particularly important in chimpanzee societies as it expresses submission of an individual towards another one (Goodall, 1986), but only a few studies have described its ontogeny. Laporte and Zuberbühler (2011) looked at young chimpanzees' pant-grunting behaviour, describing the development of pant-grunt production from newly born individuals (infants: 0–4 years old) to adolescence (juveniles: 5–9 years old and subadults: 10–15 years old). They found undirected grunt-like signals already in newborns. From 2 months of age onwards, grunting became more and more socially directed, and around 7 months of age, the context-specificity of the use of the grunts increased until subadulthood, when chimpanzees produced most of their grunts in the appropriate context, that is, towards higher-ranking individuals. Interestingly, this increased appropriateness correlated with the mothers' pant-grunting in the given situation as well. In fact, youngsters had the tendency to also pant-grunt when mothers pant-grunted. Even though Laporte and Zuberbühler refrained from making assumptions with regard to social learning involved in pant-grunt production, youngsters appeared to learn one way or the other about the context in which a pant-grunt should be produced and might even have learnt this from following the example of their mothers. Furthermore, individuals appear to switch models during ontogeny, initially mirroring their mother's grunting behaviour before switching to other subadult individuals (Laporte & Zuberbühler, 2011). This example again suggests that emotional contagion may occur in the very early stages of infancy, with infants not realizing the purpose of the call and producing the vocalization as part of a fixed repertoire, with no understanding of its use. However, affective observation may be needed to clearly outline the appropriate use of the vocalization in a social context. Here again, it appears that socially important individuals serve as passive teachers. In early ontogeny, these socially important individuals are the mothers, in adolescence, it is rather the peers (see also Schuppli & van Schaik, Chapter 1, this volume).

Affective observation may also be crucial regarding the acquisition of food habits or social customs. An interesting case concerns emigrating chimpanzee females, who arrive in an already habituated community. Habituation refers to the long and painful process by which the mere presence of scientists becomes accepted by a community of wild primates. It may take at least five years for males, and often more than ten years for female chimpanzees to come to accept the presence of researchers on the ground with them, leading them to display their normal behaviour without stress (Reynolds, 2005). It is thus baffling for researchers to observe newly emigrated females becoming habituated to researchers in a matter of days or weeks (Gruber, personal observations). Recently, Samuni, Mundry, Terkel, Zuberbühler, and Hobaiter (2014) may have offered some evidence to explain this behaviour, by describing the reverse effect that habituated individuals had on non-habituated individuals in easing their habituation process. Adolescent females of the well-habituated Sonso community in Budongo Forest, Uganda, were found to have emigrated in the nearby Waibira community, which was under habituation at the time of Samuni et al.'s study. They found that the presence of these individuals heavily influenced the behaviour of other non-habituated chimpanzees, who allowed researchers to study them from a closer distance and for a longer time. In ASL terms, it appears that, in this case, as with the newly immigrating females, the non-habituated individuals inferred from the behaviour of the habituated chimpanzees that the researchers posed no threat. Once again, it is unclear whether this is pure emotional contagion (or rather 'lack' of emotional reaction towards the researchers) or a subtler type of affective observation, the object being the researchers themselves. In the third section of this chapter, we will discuss the different possibilities and argue that the specific classification will depend on whether the learner is actively looking for information or not.

2.2.2 Social referencing

The ability to carry out social referencing appears to necessitate a cognitive jump compared to emotion contagion and affective observation. Indeed, subjects actively seek out emotional information to make sense of an event and the referent (e.g. the mother) gives ostensive clues about the event. As such, the knower engages actively with the learner. The paradigmatic case described by Clément and Dukes (2017) is the one of the visual cliff experiment, originally designed by Gibson and Walk (1960) and adapted to affective research by Campos and colleagues (e.g. Klinnert, Campos, Sorce, Emde, & Svejda, 1983). In this paradigm, a child must decide whether she wants to cross a glass floor covering a cleft. Studies have found that children will base their decision upon the information provided by their mother or someone they trust (see Clément & Dukes, Introduction, this volume). In an unfortunate turn of events, it appears that wild chimpanzees are themselves subjects to a 'real' visual cliff experiment, under the form of road-crossing, due to ever growing human encroachment in their habitats (Cibot, Bortolamiol, Seguya, & Krief, 2015; Hockings, Anderson, & Matsuzawa, 2006). Hockings and colleagues (2006) found that Western chimpanzees were able to evaluate the danger of a road by comparing other chimpanzees' behaviour between a non-dangerous road mostly used by pedestrians, and a dangerous road with high traffic use. In addition, the behaviour of the dominant individuals varied depending on whether the group crossed the dangerous road compared to the less dangerous road, with dominant individuals either taking the lead, or the rear guard, during crossing. Cibot and collaborators found that out of 122 individual crossings of a similarly dangerous road in Uganda, 20 per cent involved checking and waiting behaviour between individuals (see Figure 2.1). Therefore, we propose that social referencing may occur in the context of road-crossing in wild chimpanzees.

Other examples of social referencing may occur in the context of social play and greetings in primates. Indeed, these contexts necessitate disambiguation between partners in a possibly tense situation. For example, individuals must communicate whether their intention is to fight or to play, particularly in the case of rough play. To do so, they must acquire a social understanding of the outcome of their behaviour. Fröhlich and collaborators (2017) showed that the size of the gestural repertoire and the frequency of gestures in developing chimpanzees depended on the number of interactions with conspecifics other than their mother, and that chimpanzee youngsters with more social mothers enjoy access to a larger choice of communicative means compared to youngsters with less social mothers. Given the fact that youngsters use other individuals as references for signal uses, this suggests that these knowers have a value for the learners, i.e. they may matter as a point of reference. The existence of back-and-forths between individuals appears indeed an important avenue of research for the development of social referencing in NHPs and the ontogenetic aspect unearthed by Fröhlich and collaborators suggests

Figure 2.1 Road-crossing in wild chimpanzees provides a real-world application for studying social referencing (photo by Jaqueline Rohen, Bulindi Chimpanzee and Community Project).

that some learning might occur in this context as well. For social referencing, ostensive displays of intention by individuals may be mandatory as learners are required to actively request information. If, for instance, the road-crossing examples do have a learning effect on unexperienced road-crossers, we would expect a gaze directed to the knower at the very least, before it could be argued that social referencing had occurred. Such a gaze might then be interpreted as seeking information from a more experienced individual. The knower does not necessarily have to reply with explicit ostensive cues, but perhaps waiting behaviour, also seen in other contexts suggestive of intentional behaviour (Crockford, Wittig, Mundry, & Zuberbühler, 2012; Gruber & Zuberbühler, 2013), combined with ascribing value to the action through confidently crossing the road, is enough for social referencing to occur in a communicative context in NHPs.

Finally, social referencing may occur in the context of tool-use learning. In the Sonso community of Budongo Forest, chimpanzee females have been observed actively taking sticks out of the hands of their offspring (Gruber, personal observation), perhaps, at least, as a signal that they are unworthy of further attention, or, in other words, uninteresting. This community is known for its limited material culture, and particularly for its lack of tool use (Gruber, Muller, Reynolds, Wrangham, & Zuberbühler, 2011; Gruber, Muller, Strimling, Wrangham, & Zuberbühler, 2009). Despite extensive experimental exposure to sticks over the last decade

(Gruber, Zuberbühler, & Neumann, 2016), the Sonso chimpanzees have never developed stick use, experimentally or naturally. Interestingly, analysis of developmental data suggests that, while chimpanzees in Sonso handle sticks from a young age onward, they stop this behaviour by age 10 (Lamon, Neumann, & Zuberbühler, 2018). This suggests that mothers preventing their offspring from handling sticks has the long-term consequence of making chimpanzees less interested in sticks during their development, resulting in the absence of stick handling by age 10. Whether this represents a case of social referencing or affective observation is debatable. Indeed, the mother is actively providing feedback to her offspring, but it is unclear whether the infant itself requests feedback from its mother. This may thus constitute a case of passive learning, halfway between social referencing and affective observation, and suggesting additional steps in ASL. Alternatively, this may be a case of natural pedagogy, with the mother actively providing information in a socialization process, in this case by interfering with the building of a relationship between the learner and the stick. However, while we do not exclude this possibility, this appears unlikely to us for reasons explained below.

2.2.3   Natural pedagogy

There are only a few claimed cases of 'teaching' in chimpanzees. The only cases that come close to the phenomenon referred to by developmental psychologists took place in the Taï Forest in Ivory Coast and were described by Boesch (1991), with mothers apparently 'actively shaping' the learning of their offspring, either through replacing a nut in the correct place on an anvil, or by demonstrating the correct movement of the hand for the learner. However, these rare cases have not been observed since in Taï, and no other field researcher has ever reported such cases in any other chimpanzee community. Therefore, teaching, if it exists, appears to be incredibly rare in chimpanzees. In general, it is hard to document any case in NHPs or non-human animals where one cannot provide an adequate alternative explanation. In line with other theorists, we will argue here that full-blown teaching requires meta-representational abilities and that despite recent experimental evidence for theory of mind, particularly in the context of helping (Buttelmann, Buttelmann, Carpenter, Call, & Tomasello, 2017), it is unclear whether this case, as well as other cases in the primate literature, truly corresponds to the natural pedagogy described by Csibra and Gergely (2009). In fact, because there does not seem to be any active engagement from the mother towards the offspring in a triadic way with respect to the tool (apart from the cases described by Boesch), it seems more likely to be some kind of social appraisal.

As of now, it seems that there is much evidence for social appraisal in NHPs, both under the form of affective observation and social referencing, but no real evidence for the fourth stage of ASL, despite interesting data that may suggest the existence of some kind of 'proto-pedagogy'. In the following section, we dissect the cognitive mechanisms necessary for the different stages of ASL and discuss their presence or absence in NHPs.

2.3   Cognitive bases of ASL

The different examples we have provided above suggest that several cognitive processes are involved in the different stages of ASL. We will discuss them here, and a summary of these processes, and how they characterize each ASL step, can be found in Table 2.1.

2.3.1   Social learning

It is self-evident that the capacity for social learning is, in itself, a requirement for ASL. There has been much debate about the social learning capacities of non-human animals over the last two decades (Heyes & Galef, 1996; Laland & Galef, 2009). Social learning processes are usually sorted from the cognitively less demanding (e.g. local or stimulus enhancement, when the mere presence of a conspecific will drive the interest of an observant to a location or a stimulus), to the more cognitively demanding such as emulation, when an individual learns about the goal of an action; or imitation, when the individual learns the means by which the goal of the action is reached. There has been much debate on whether non-humans, particularly primates, are able to imitate, with a long-held tradition suggesting that they can only engage in emulation, but not imitation (Nagell et al., 1993). A more nuanced position may be that certain primates, in particular chimpanzees, are able to engage in limited forms of imitation, although not nearly as many as humans (Gruber, 2016; Whiten et al., 2009).

While there has been much work on social learning of technique, there has been much less work with respect to learning of vocalizations, or generally communicative means, possibly because of the long-held view of vocalizations as hardwired emotional productions over which the individual has little control (Tomasello, 2008). However, we would argue that there is no theoretical ground to oppose emotional content and intentional production (Gruber & Grandjean, 2017) and that despite a possible large genetic base, it may still be possible to isolate social learning effects, such as in bird tool use (Kenward, Rutz, Weir, & Kacelnik, 2006). For example, a young vervet may learn how to employ the alarm call through observing its mother's signalling behaviour. Whether it grasps the mother's goal here or not, i.e. whether either goal emulation was

Table 2.1 Summary of the cognitive processes required for the different steps of ASL

ASL step cognitive process	Emotion contagion	Affective observation	Social referencing	Natural pedagogy
Interaction	No (no direct interaction with object or teacher)	Dyadic (attending to teacher with the object)	Triadic (interaction with object and teacher)	Triadic (interaction with object and teacher)
Representations of object	No, or primary	Primary	Re-representations	Meta-representations
Goal-directedness	No	Learner	First learner engages, before knower becomes active	Teacher starts teaching
Ostensive behaviour	No	No	Yes	Yes

present or whether stimulus enhancement is enough to explain how it acquires the signal, remains to be investigated.

There may only be a difference in degree between all observational learning types in how far information is gained by learners observing knowers engaging with, for instance, an object, or producing a signal. Given the non-arbitrary nature of animal signal systems, stimulus enhancement or emulation learning might be a way of acquiring novel uses of signals and of grasping meaning refinements, particularly if some form of passive influencing by knowers is instantiated to help learners focus on the important or relevant features involved in the novel or refined signal use. ASL thus can account for how young vervets learn to use signals appropriately: by attending to socially important individuals who passively ascribe value to the correct use of the signal. Overall, it is unclear whether particular steps of ASL occur through particular social learning processes. A learner could well engage in imitation during affective observation, with the knower being oblivious to the very fact of being imitated. We will therefore not ascribe social learning mechanisms to ASL steps, although we will do so for the other cognitive capacities we discuss.

2.3.2   Interactions

Another important process is the relationship between the learner, the teacher and the object of learning influenced by emotions.

Indeed, emotional contagion does not appear to require the learner to draw any hypothesis about the cause of a given emotional reaction. Following the example described by Clément & Dukes (Introduction, this volume), a chimpanzee in its enclosure in a zoo hearing its caretakers watching the same rugby match, does not need to issue hypotheses about the cause of their uproar, but it may learn to associate the sounds of the match or vocalizations of the keepers with the emotions it feels, for example when it becomes tense. Starting from there, the three next steps of ASL require NHP learners to draw inferences between an object and the knowers. During affective observation, NHPs must carefully observe how the knower is engaged with a particular object (see Schuppli & van Schaik, Chapter 1, this volume). However, affective observation does not require NHPs to engage in any form of common ground (Tomasello, Carpenter, Call, Behne, & Moll, 2005), that is, they do not have to represent the fact that the knower and themselves have a particular relationship towards the same object of interest (Table 2.1): this only needs to be represented during social referencing and requires, we believe, the ability to engage in joint attention and its corollary, triadic interactions. Indeed, joint interactions are often apparent in behaviour due to the geometrical 'triadicness' observed between the individuals and the object of interest. Additionally, individuals engaged in joint attention display key behavioural features such as gaze alternation between social partners, sensitivity to their mutual attention state and persistence in signalling or use of new signals (elaboration) when initial attempts to communicate fail (Leavens & Bard, 2011). Nevertheless, researchers have proposed different definitions for joint attention, and whether one favours one or the other will determine whether a researcher grants joint attention (and triadic interactions) to NHPs or not. In particular, Tomasello and colleagues have favoured a definition of joint attention that supposes a degree of 'togetherness' whereby individuals know they are engaged together in a given interaction, leading to the concept of shared intentionality (Carpenter & Call, 2013; Tomasello et al., 2005) and this is the one favoured by Clément and Dukes (2017)when they first outlined ASL. Shared intentionality is particularly complex for animals because it supposes that individuals think through a we-mode rather than an I-mode (Bratman, 1992; Gilbert, 1989; Searle, 1995). In contrast, others have favoured leaner behavioural rather than cognitive approaches allowing bringing human and non-human primate development closer to one another (D'Entremont & Seamans, 2007; Gómez, 2007). For authors more inclined to adopt the second position, triadic interactions are within the realm of possibilities for NHPs, particularly in great apes (Gómez, 2010; Gruber, 2013b; Leavens & Bard, 2011; Pika & Zuberbühler, 2008), suggesting that this particular cognitive requirement for ASL is fulfilled. Nevertheless, the fourth stage of ASL, natural pedagogy, may require the shared intentionality and togetherness advocated by Tomasello and colleagues, and it remains controversial whether NHPs are able to access this level of representation.

2.3.3   Representations

The topic of mental representations appears as a most fundamental – and still under-discussed – aspect of NHPs' minds and has implications for discussions of ASL (Table 2.1). We believe it is mandatory for an ASL approach to analyse whether NHPs and other animals are able to represent objects, as well as the relationship between themselves and the object. In effect, emotional contagion does not require a learner to identify a change (see Clément & Dukes, Introduction, this volume), or even precisely what happened. A flight reflex, for example, does not require a non-human (or a human) animal to represent the threat that is causing the flight. It is evolutionarily adaptive to flee with the others. Because there seems to be little cognitive treatment during emotional contagion with respect to ASL, we suggest that there is no additional need for conscious treatment. In other words, animals do not need to access their representations or to reorganize them (Gruber, Zuberbühler, Clément, & van Schaik, 2015).

During affective observation, individuals must, at least, represent the relationship between the knower and the object of interest (Table 2.1). For example, the individual must represent that the knower is afraid of something. However, this may not require a treatment of the representation. In other words, so-called associative processes, which occur often in learning for animals (Heyes, 2012; Shettleworth, 2010), may also explain learning during affective observation. One animal may observe another animal having a good experience, represent the relationship between the stimulus and the learner and itself learn about the good experience provided by the stimulus. However, this process may occur without the learner having to reflect upon the relationship that unfolded in front of it. In other words, we believe that a direct treatment of the information by the learner relying on primary representations is enough to explain affective observation: the learner represents an aspect of the world (in this case, the experience of the knower with the stimulus).

Primary representations, however, may not sustain social referencing or natural pedagogy. In particular, more complex levels of representations are found under the broad category of meta-representations. Meta-representation is a mixed-bag term, most often used to refer to representations of representations. However, the mental complexity associated with the term depends on the authors. For example, some authors, such as Perner, require that, to engage in meta-representation, an individual must be aware of the fact that the representations it represents are representations (that is, meta-representations are representations of representations *as* representations) (Perner, 1991). Others, such as Leslie, more simply consider meta-representations to be representations of representations, without the need for the individual to know about their representational nature (Leslie, 1987). Perner calls such meta-representations secondary representations. They have also been described as re-representations (Karmiloff-Smith, 1992). We believe this level of representation is particularly relevant for research in NHPs and young children, because it is less cognitively demanding (Gruber et al., 2015) and could perhaps sustain social referencing. For example, Carpenter and Call (2013) suggest that NHPs may engage in parallel rather than true joint attention. Adopting even such a limited approach to triadic interactions for ASL requires that the learner must be able to represent not only the relationship between the knower and the object, but also its own relationship with the object; and this must occur in parallel (at the same time) in its mind. To do that, the learner must be able to relate these two representations, that is, to mentally juggle between the two representations and compare them ('how is my own experience with this stimulus', and 'how is her own experience with the stimulus'). To do so, we argue that it must rely on re-representations but does not need to reach the level of meta-representation (in the Perner sense). In other words, an individual can actively seek information from a knower because it knows the knower has a relationship with a given object of common interest, but it does not need to draw hypotheses about the mental state of this individual with regards to the object of interest. Such complex thoughts do however appear at the level of natural pedagogy, where the interaction between the knower and learner becomes that of a teacher and a pupil. The teacher knows that the learner should form knowledge about the object of interest and the learner knows that the teacher can transmit this knowledge. The ability to represent this knowledge about the object as knowledge requires, we believe, full-blown meta-representative abilities.

2.3.4   *Goal-directedness*

Goal-directedness is another key factor in ASL. As discussed above, discussions about intentional behaviour in NHPs have often tended to discuss goal-directedness from a behavioural perspective, rather than explore its cognitive bases (Sievers, Wild, & Gruber, 2017). A similar cognitive approach can be used for ASL. Emotional contagion does not require any goal-directedness, whether from the learner's or the knower's perspective. In fact, even though the knower might produce a given call in a goal-directed way, as exemplified in the vervet example, this is not a requirement. Contagion implies that the 'learner' might even simply 'catch' something from another 'learner', who happened to be before them in the line of propagation. In contrast, affective observation suggests that the 'knower' could be at the beginning of the line. In practice, the knower produces behaviour in response to a stimulus, which the learner picks up, as previously discussed. A different way of analysing the situation starting from affective observation onward is that the reaction of the knower is 'about something', joining a more traditional philosophical approach to intentionality (Brentano, 1874/1973; Dennett, 1983). Following on from this, social referencing appears to necessitate goal-directedness from both the learner and the knower. In the visual cliff experiment, the learner is directly analysing the behaviour of the knower towards an object of interest. Similarly, the knower knows that the behaviour of the learner is about the object of interest. Finally, in natural pedagogy, the behaviour of the learner and the knower is not only directed towards the object of interest, but also aims to upgrade the learner's knowledge. It is unclear whether such goal-directedness occurs in animal teaching at all. For example, arguably one of the best-known knowledge increases in animals is when young meerkat pups learn how to kill scorpions. The adult meerkats provide progressively unharmed (and therefore more dangerous) scorpions for the pups to practice on, giving them the chance to increase their knowledge progressively (Thornton & McAuliffe, 2006). Playback experiments that broadcast calls of pups of various age classes, showed that these calls were the main determinant of the state of the prey brought by adults (rather than say, the adults' knowledge of the age of the pups). This suggests that the progressive offering of prey is genetically based rather than explained by cognitively loaded reasons, in particular compared to the goal-directed teaching found in humans. In general, as of now, we find no conclusive evidence of natural pedagogy in the animal literature for which no alternative cognitively less demanding explanations can be proposed.

2.3.5   Ostensive behaviour

Finally, the ability to display ostensive behaviour is also key to the ASL framework (Dukes & Clément, 2017). Ostensive behaviour occurs when an individual makes it overt (explicit) to the audience that he or she is providing information *for* the receiver (Sperber & Wilson, 1995). The respondent, on the other hand, can infer from the provided evidence (i.e. the ostensive signal produced by the signaller) that this is the case. Ostensive behaviour thus appears as the basis for fully developed communication, as an act of open sharing of information, and is expressed by reacting appropriately to a change of behaviour in the communicative partner, that is by displaying behavioural flexibility (Sievers et al., 2017). As with goal-directedness, ostensive behaviour is not required for emotional contagion. Indeed, the knower does not make it overt to others that she is reacting in a particular way to a stimulus; it is simply 'reacting' with no further motives. Similarly, the learner will not infer that the knower intends for her to extract information, she simply does. Regarding affective observation, once again, there is no intended ostensive behaviour displayed by the learner, and we would also argue that there is no such expectation in the learner either. On the contrary, both social referencing and natural pedagogy appear to require some kind of ostensive behaviour, either from the learner or the knower, because they are entering active communication with one another. During social referencing, for example in the case of the visual cliff (or the chimpanzee equivalent of road-crossing), one individual will overtly make public the fact that it is undecided on whether to cross or not. The knower, in response to this, will overtly show that it is safe or unsafe to cross the road. With respect to natural pedagogy, ostensive communication is a constitutive element, as the actors are engaged in a flexible back-and-forth where the knower must make it overt that what he or she is doing contains the information that the learner has to learn, and the learner must also make overt the fact that the transmitted information is sufficient, or, on the contrary, not enough, for him or her to learn.

Whether the capacity to communicate overtly is present in non-human primates is widely discussed. Moore (2016) argues that eye gazing towards a conspecific in combination with gestures are indicators of the presence of overt communication of goals, while Scott-Phillips (2015) argues against evaluating gazing behaviour in intentional communication as an indicator for producing a signal *for someone*, i.e. overtly. He claims that monitoring the recipient alone does not give sufficient clues for an intention to overtly inform someone about a goal. Nevertheless, the point made by Scott-Phillips must be extended to non-verbal infants, who are yet to develop a full-blown theory of mind, and therefore to be full-blown ostensive intentional communicators, unless one accepts that the understanding of ostensive cues is innate for natural pedagogy to occur (Csibra & Gergely, 2009).

2.4   Future applications of ASL for comparative research

Our review of possible cases of ASL in non-human primates is by no means exhaustive and was not intended to be to begin with. Rather, we aimed in this chapter to highlight areas of research in comparative studies where a framework of ASL appears possible and might be useful. While the long-held view that instinctive behaviour drives every move of every non-human species is long gone, many authors nonetheless seem to refer to emotions or internal states to explain animal behaviour, with little discussion of how this may occur from a cognitive point of view. As such, emotions remain this uncontrollable state of mind that makes animals do things, in contrast to possibly more interesting intentional behaviour, which has become something of a hot topic in current animal research. This contrast is not warranted, as a dichotomy between intentional and emotional behaviour is theoretically flawed (Gruber & Grandjean, 2017). We therefore welcome Clément and Dukes' ASL framework in providing a way to bind social learning and emotions. We particularly welcome the idea of a continuum from stages with possibly little cognition involved in stages where our dissection of cognitive processes appears to require, at times, possibly uniquely human features. This allows cases to be identified where, although not reaching the level of natural pedagogy, non-humans still display strong evidence of ASL. As with other areas of research, the ultimate goal of comparative research is not to single out humans among all other species, but rather to isolate areas where possibly unique traits might have evolved, often as the combination of more ancient traits shared with other species (Gruber & Clay, 2016). We believe ASL will prove instrumental for at least two areas of comparative research: the acquisition of culture and the ontogeny of signal learning.

2.4.1   Comparative cultural learning

Debates on cultural learning in animal behaviour over the last few decades have often revolved around the social learning mechanisms at the origin of social spreads (Hobaiter et al., 2014; Laland & Galef, 2009; Nagell et al., 1993; Whiten et al., 2009), neglecting other aspects, such as the impact of ecology on cultural behaviour (Gruber et al., 2012; Laland & Janik, 2006; Sanz & Morgan, 2013) or mental representations of culture in non-humans (Gruber et al., 2015). This is problematic because culture is too complex to be reduced to social learning mechanisms, ecological influence or cognitive processes on their own, with each factor likely to be more influential than the others at certain times during the finite life-time of a cultural trait. For example, certain ecological conditions, both under the form of ecological opportunities and necessities, can lead to the emergence of a given foraging behaviour (Gruber et al., 2016; Rutz & St Clair, 2012). At this stage, emotional factors, mostly acting as a basis for variation in personality in animals, may already be acting in selecting a potential innovator (Gruber, 2016). The spread and maintenance of the behaviour in the community will depend on a mix of factors, including an ecological pressure to keep the behaviour in the repertoire, as well as the opportunities, both social and ecological, to express this behaviour (Gruber, 2013a).

Emotions, through ASL, also have a major role to play in the mainten-ance of a given behaviour in the community. One may consider interest or lack of interest as a potential outcome of ASL. If a given generation does not show interest in a visible resource (for example, because other equally or more advantageous resources become available, or the current one becomes too dangerous to acquire), the knowledge about exploiting this particular resource may become extinct because of this lack of interest, leading to the absence of affective observation or social referencing for the following generations. It is up to researchers in comparative cultural science to integrate emotions in the debate, similar to the work done by developmental or social scientists, particularly through discussions of irrational behaviour in humans when it comes to socially transmitted information. One major cause for over-imitation, the imitation of useless behaviour even when it is not needed for the completion of a task, appears indeed to be a drive for affiliation with others (Frick, Clément, & Gruber, 2017; Over & Carpenter, 2012). Similarly, humans continuously express the motivation to belong to their community by displaying sometimes non-adaptive behaviour (Baumeister & Leary, 1995). It remains to be seen whether similar processes occur in animals, with chimpanzees being a prime species to investigate such questions.

2.4.2 The role of ASL in the ontogeny of signal learning in non-human primates

Very often the hypothesis that young non-human primates ontogenetically learn communicative signals is a priori rejected, based on a comparison with human children's language acquisition, particularly as vocalizations are considered to be phylogenetically hardwired in their uses (Tomasello, 2008). This conclusion may be spurious for two reasons. First, while non-human primate vocal and gestural repertoires are not remotely comparable to human language in terms of combinatorial flexibility, there may still be a developmental dimension to signal learning. As great apes are capable of combining both gestures and vocalizations cross-modally to get different messages across (Genty, Neumann, & Zuberbühler, 2015), we may assume a certain degree of flexibility with regard to their uses. This is still a far leap from human combinatorial uses of language and other ostensive signals in interaction, and it might thus not be necessary for individuals to display imitation learning or complex forms of teaching for young individuals to learn signal uses in ontogeny. Instead, other steps of ASL may help shed light on potential learning of signal uses.

Second, as opposed to word meanings of human language, gesture and vocalization meanings in non-human primates are not arbitrary. For instance, Owren and Rendall (2001) claim that the acoustic features of monkey alarm calls (short with an abrupt onset) are specifically tuned to immediately grab the audience's attention in situations of predation and will serve the groups' survival. The use of an alarm call as an alarm call is in that sense not arbitrary, because its acoustic features serve its function to set conspecifics into alert mode through a 'startle effect' (but see Crockford, Gruber, & Zuberbühler, 2018, for cases where the acoustic structure may not predict urgency of situation). Some great ape gestures, being abbreviations of the behaviours they stand for, may not be arbitrary either[1] (i.e. they are not cognitively opaque). Given this and the fact that their uses are phylogenetically predisposed to a certain degree (for instance to be used as alarm calls), the ability to use signals correctly may not require elaborate learning processes (such as, active teaching for learners) to understand the appropriate application of a signal with the appropriate goal in mind. This does not imply though, that the uses of these non-arbitrary and phylogenetically predisposed signals cannot be, in part, learned and shaped during ontogeny. There is indeed evidence for some refinement of use occurring in the ontogeny of several non-human primate species. We have discussed two cases above: meaning refinement in ontogeny in the vervet monkey alarm call system and pant-grunt development in chimpanzees.

While mind reading and any other explicit reference to mental states of the other is most likely unnecessary for the passive teaching process to be successful, ASL can still account for these findings. The framework explains in particular why members of a community would attend to an individual's use of a particular signal: by using the signal in a certain way over and over again while simultaneously displaying a particular affective state, the socially important individual ascribes value to that particular signal use. Affective states thus replace the need for the active teaching of correct signal uses. Non-human primate signal learners already have a scaffold of what a signal means through phylogeny, i.e. the non-arbitrary character of the signals. Refinement and further flexibility in a signal use can be attained through observational learning in combination with simple forms of ASL. The occurrence and use of a signal are thus determined by several elements: phylogeny, i.e. selection processes, determines how a signal is used to a certain extent, but social learning capacities in the youngster and affective input by socially important individuals such as peers or adults, as well as ecological relevance (e.g. the presence of eagles as predators), determine and influence a signal's use altogether.

---

[1] Leaf-clipping in chimpanzees may be a special case. Chimpanzees pick leaves and then tear strips from these leaves with their teeth. None of the leaves used are eaten. Leaf-clipping is used in the courtship context (Hobaiter & Byrne 2014) in some chimpanzee communities, such as the Sonso community of Budongo Forest in Uganda. A non-arbitrary value to serve the function of signalling a certain message or eliciting a certain response is far less clear to see: any other signal might have served the purpose as well. Such signals may raise the question as to how far we can even possibly render a universal verdict on non-human animal signalling. Leaf-clipping appears more arbitrary, for instance, than monkey alarm calls.

2.5   Conclusion

ASL appears to be a very valid and useful approach to social learning of both material and communicative knowledge in non-humans, as well as humans. In particular, we hypothesize that it bridges social learning processes across species, and social appraisal may be a valid candidate for some possible type of proto-teaching, existing without the need to rely on language. There is much evidence that human social learning overwhelmingly relies on teaching and a natural capacity to adapt to others' minds, a phenomenon described as natural pedagogy. Natural pedagogy, as described in humans, may be too cognitively complex for non-humans, but also for non-verbal infants. ASL thus provides a useful framework both phylogenetically and ontogenetically to explore a dimension of learning that should no longer be ignored in comparative research.

References

Baumeister, R. F., & Leary, M. R. (1995). The need to belong: Desire for interpersonal attachments as a fundamental human motivation. *Psychological Bulletin, 117*, 497–529.

Boesch, C. (1991). Teaching among wild chimpanzees. *Animal Behaviour, 41*, 530–532.

Bratman, M. (1992). Shared co-operative activity. *Philosophical Review, 101*, 327–341.

Brentano, F. (1874/1973). *Psychologie vom empirischen Standpunkt, Duncker & Humblot, Leipzig. engl. Translation: Psychology from an Empirical Standpoint.* London, UK: Routledge and Kegan Paul.

Briefer, E. F. (2012). Vocal expression of emotions in mammals: Mechanisms of production and evidence. *Journal of Zoology, 288*(1), 1–20.

Buttelmann, D., Buttelmann, F., Carpenter, M., Call, J., & Tomasello, M. (2017). Great apes distinguish true from false beliefs in an interactive helping task. *PLoS One, 12*(4), e0173793. doi:10.1371/journal.pone.0173793

Caro, T. M., & Hauser, M. D. (1992). Is there teaching in non-human animals. *Quarterly Review of Biology, 67*(2), 151–174.

Carpenter, M., & Call, J. (2013). How joint is the joint attention of apes and human infants? In S. Terrace & J. Metcalfe (Eds.), *Agency and joint attention* (pp. 49–61). New York, NY: Oxford University Press.

Cheney, D. L., & Seyfarth, R. M. (1990). *How monkeys see the world: Inside the mind of another species.* Chicago, IL: Chicago University Press.

Cibot, M., Bortolamiol, S., Seguya, A., & Krief, S. (2015). Chimpanzees facing a dangerous situation: A high-traffic asphalted road in the Sebitoli area of Kibale National Park, Uganda. *American Journal of Primatology, 77*(8), 890–900. doi: 10.1002/ajp.22417

Clay, Z., & de Waal, F. B. M. (2013). Development of socio-emotional competence in bonobos. *Proceedings of the National Academy of Sciences, 110*(45), 18121–18126.

Clément, F., & Dukes, D. (2017). Social appraisal and social referencing: Two components of affective social learning. *Emotion Review, 9*(3), 253–261.

Crockford, C., Gruber, T., & Zuberbühler, K. (2018). Chimpanzee quiet hoo variants differ according to context. *Royal Society Open Science, 5*, 172066.

Crockford, C., Wittig, R. M., Mundry, R., & Zuberbühler, K. (2012). Wild chimpanzees inform ignorant group members of danger. *Current Biology, 22*, 142–146.

Csibra, G., & Gergely, G. (2009). Natural pedagogy. *Trends in Cognitive Sciences, 13*, 148–153.

D'Entremont, B., & Seamans, E. (2007). Do infants need social cognition to act socially? An alternative look at infant pointing. *Child Development, 78*, 723–728.

Dennett, D. C. (1983). Intentional systems in cognitive ethology: The 'Panglossian paradigm' defended. *Behavior and Brain Sciences, 6*, 343–355.

Ducheminsky, N., Henzi, S. P., & Barrett, L. (2014). Responses of vervet monkeys in large troops to terrestrial and aerial predator alarm calls. *Behavioural Ecology, 25*, 1474–1484.

Dukes, D., & Clément, F. (2017) Author reply: Clarifying the importance of ostensive communication in life-long, affective social learning. *Emotion Review, 9*(3), 267–269.

Franz, M., & Nunn, C. L. (2009). Network-based diffusion analysis: A new method for detecting social learning. *Proceedings of the Royal Society B: Biological Sciences, 276*(1663), 1829–1836.

Frick, A., Clément, F., & Gruber, T. (2017). Evidence for a sex effect during overimitation: Boys copy irrelevant modelled actions more than girls across cultures. *Royal Society Open Science, 4*(12). doi: 10.1098/rsos.170367

Fröhlich, M., Müller, G., Zeiträg, C., Wittig, R. M., & Pika, S. (2017). Gestural development of chimpanzees in the wild: The impact of interactional experience. *Animal Behaviour, 134*, 271–282.

Genty, E., Neumann, C., & Zuberbühler, K. (2015). Complex patterns of signalling to convey different social goals of sex in bonobos *(Pan paniscus)*. *Scientific Reports, 5*, 16135.

Gibson, E. J., & Walk, R. D. (1960). The 'visual cliff'. *Scientific American, 202*, 67–71.

Gilbert, M. (1989). *On social facts*. Princeton, NJ: Princeton University Press.

Gómez, J.-C. (2007). Pointing behaviors in apes and human infants: A balanced interpretation. *Child Development, 78*, 729–734.

Gómez, J.-C. (2010). The ontogeny of triadic cooperative interactions with humans in an infant gorilla. *Interaction Studies, 11*, 353–379.

Goodall, J. (1964). Tool-using and aimed throwing in a community of free-living chimpanzees. *Nature, 201*, 1264–1266.

(1973). Cultural elements in a chimpanzee community. In E. Menzel (Ed.), *Precultural primate behavior* (pp. 138–159). Basel, Switzerland: Karger.

(1986). *The chimpanzees of Gombe: Patterns of behavior*. Cambridge, MA: Harvard University Press.

Gruber, T. (2013a). Historical hypotheses of chimpanzee tool use behaviour in relation to natural and human-induced changes in an East African rain forest. *Revue de Primatologie, 5*, document 66. doi: 10.4000/primatologie.1690

(2013b). Wild-born orangutans (Pongo abelii) engage in triadic interactions during play. *International Journal of Primatology*, 1–14. doi: 10.1007/s10764-013-9745-1

(2016). Great apes do not learn novel tool use easily: Conservatism, functional fixedness, or cultural influence? *International Journal of Primatology*, 37(2), 296–316. doi: 10.1007/s10764-016-9902-4

Gruber, T., & Clay, Z. (2016). A comparison between bonobos and chimpanzees: A review and update. *Evolutionary Anthropology*, 25, 239–252.

Gruber, T., & Grandjean, D. (2017). A comparative neurological approach to emotional expressions in primate vocalizations. *Neuroscience & Biobehavioral Reviews*, 73, 182–190.

Gruber, T., Muller, M. N., Reynolds, V., Wrangham, R. W., & Zuberbühler, K. (2011). Community-specific evaluation of tool affordances in wild chimpanzees. *Scientific Reports*, 1, 128. doi: 10.1038/srep00128

Gruber, T., Muller, M. N., Strimling, P., Wrangham, R. W., & Zuberbühler, K. (2009). Wild chimpanzees rely on cultural knowledge to solve an experimental honey acquisition task. *Current Biology*, 19, 1806–1810.

Gruber, T., Potts, K., Krupenye, C., Byrne, M.-R., Mackworth-Young, C., McGrew, W. C., ... Zuberbühler, K. (2012). The influence of ecology on chimpanzee cultural behaviour: A case study of five Ugandan chimpanzee communities. *Journal of Comparative Psychology*, 126, 446–457.

Gruber, T., & Zuberbühler, K. (2013). Vocal recruitment for joint travel in wild chimpanzees. *PLoS One*, 8(9), e76073. doi: 10.1371/journal.pone.0076073

Gruber, T., Zuberbühler, K., Clément, F., & van Schaik, C. P. (2015). Apes have culture but may not know that they do. *Frontiers in Psychology*, 6, 91. doi: 10.3389/fpsyg.2015.00091

Gruber, T., Zuberbühler, K., & Neumann, C. (2016). Travel fosters tool use in wild chimpanzees. *eLife*, 5:e16371. doi:10.7554/eLife.16371

Heyes, C. M. (2012). Simple minds: A qualified defence of associative learning. *Philosophical Transactions of the Royal Society B Biological Sciences*, 367, 2695–2703.

Heyes, C. M., & Galef, B. G. (Eds.). (1996). *Social learning in animals: The roots of culture*. San Diego, CA: Academic Press.

Hobaiter, C., & Byrne, R. (2014). The meanings of chimpanzee gestures. *Current Biology*, 24(14), 1596–1600.

Hobaiter, C., Poisot, T., Zuberbühler, K., Hoppitt, W., & Gruber, T. (2014). Social network analysis shows direct evidence for social transmission of tool use in wild chimpanzees. *PLOS Biology*, 12(9), e1001960.

Hockings, K. J., Anderson, J. R., & Matsuzawa, T. (2006). Road crossing in chimpanzees: A risky business. *Current Biology*, 16(17), R668–R670.

Hoppitt, W., & Laland, K. N. (2011). Detecting social learning using networks: A users guide. *American Journal of Primatology*, 73, 834–844.

Jürgens, U. (1979). Neural control of vocalizations in non-human primates. In H. D. Steklis & M. J. Raleigh (Eds.), *Neurobiology of social communication in primates* (pp. 11–44). New York, NY: Academic Press.

Karmiloff-Smith, A. (1992). *Beyond modularity: A developmental perspective on cognitive science*. Cambridge, MA: MIT Press.

Kawai, M. (1965). Newly acquired pre-cultural behavior of the natural troop of Japanese monkeys on Koshima islet. *Primates*, 6(1), 1–30.

Kenward, B., Rutz, C., Weir, A. A. S., & Kacelnik, A. (2006). Development of tool use in New Caledonian crows: Inherited action patterns and social influences. *Animal Behaviour, 72*, 1329–1343.

Klinnert, M. D., Campos, J., Sorce, J. F., Emde, R. N., & Svejda, M. J. (1983). Social referencing: Emotional expressions as behavior regulators. *Emotion: Theory, Research and Experience, 2*, 57–86.

Koski, S. E., Buchanan-Smith, H. M., Ash, H., Burkart, J. M., Bugnyar, T., & Weiss, A. (2017). Common marmoset (Callithrix jacchus) personality. *Journal of Comparative Psychology, 131*, 326–336.

Laland, K. N., & Galef, B. G. (Eds.). (2009). *The question of animal culture*. Cambridge, MA: Harvard University Press.

Laland, K. N., & Janik, V. M. (2006). The animal cultures debate. *Trends in Ecology and Evolution, 21*(10), 542–547.

Lamon, N., Neumann, C., Gruber, T., & Zuberbühler, K. (2017). Kin-based cultural transmission of tool use in wild chimpanzees. *Science Advances, 3*(4), e1602750.

Lamon, N., Neumann, C., & Zuberbühler, K. (2018). Development of object manipulation in wild chimpanzees. *Animal Behaviour, 135*, 121–130.

Laporte, M. N. C., & Zuberbühler, K. (2011). The development of a greeting signal in wild chimpanzees. *Developmental Science, 14*(5), 1220–1234. doi: 10.1111/j.1467-7687.2011.01069.x

Leavens, D. A., & Bard, K. A. (2011). Environmental influences on joint attention in great apes: implications for human cognition. *Journal of Cognitive Education and Psychology, 10*(1), 9–31.

Leslie, A. M. (1987). Pretense and representation: The origins of 'theory of mind'. *Psychological Review, 94*(4), 412–426.

Liebal, K., Waller, B. M., Burrows, A. M., & Slocombe, K. (2014). *Primate communication: A multimodal approach*. Cambridge, UK: Cambridge University Press.

Macedonia, J. M., & Evans, C. S. (1993). Variation among mammalian alarm call systems and the problem of meaning in animal signals. *Ethology, 93*(3), 177–197.

Moore, R. (2016). Meaning and ostension in great ape gestural communication. *Animal Cognition, 19*, 223–231.

Nagell, K., Olguin, R. S., & Tomasello, M. (1993). Processes of social-learning in the tool use of chimpanzees (*Pan troglodytes*) and human children (*Homo sapiens*). *Journal of Comparative Psychology, 107*(2), 174–186.

Over, H., & Carpenter, M. (2012). Putting the social into social learning: Explaining both selectivity and fidelity in children's copying behavior. *Journal of Comparative Psychology, 126*, 182–192.

Owren, M. J., & Rendall, D. (2001). Sound on the rebound: Bringing form and function back to the forefront in understanding non-human primate vocal signaling. *Evolutionary Anthropology, 10*, 58–71.

Perner, J. (1991). *Understanding the representational mind*. Cambridge, MA: Bradford books.

Pika, S., & Zuberbühler, K. (2008). Social games between bonobos and humans: Evidence for shared intentionality? *American Journal of Primatology, 70*(3), 207–210.

Price, T., Wadewitz, P., Cheney, D., Seyfarth, R., Hammerschmidt, K., & Fischer, J. (2015). Vervets revisited: A quantitative analysis of alarm call structure and context specificity. *Scientific Reports, 5*, 13220.

Reynolds, V. (2005). *The chimpanzees of the Budongo forest: Ecology, behaviour and conservation.* Oxford, UK: Oxford University Press.

Rutz, C., & St Clair, J. J. H. (2012). The evolutionary origins and ecological context of tool use in New Caledonian crows. *Behavioural Processes, 89*(2), 153–165.

Samuni, L., Mundry, R., Terkel, J., Zuberbühler, K., & Hobaiter, C. (2014). Socially learned habituation to human observers in wild chimpanzees. *Animal Cognition, 17*(4), 997–1005. doi: 10.1007/s10071-014-0731-6

Sanz, C. M., & Morgan, D. B. (2013). Ecological and social correlates of chimpanzee tool use. *Philosophical Transactions of the Royal Society of London B: Biological Sciences, 368*(1630). doi: 10.1098/rstb.2012.0416

Scott-Phillips, T. (2015). Meaning in animal and human communication. *Animal Cognition, 18*(3), 801–805.

Searle, J. (1995). *The construction of social reality.* New York, NY: Free Press.

Seyfarth, R. M., & Cheney, D. L. (1986). Vocal development in vervet monkeys. *Animal Behaviour, 34*, 1640–1658.

Seyfarth, R. M., Cheney, D. L., & Marler, P. (1980). Monkey responses to three different alarm calls: Evidence of predator classification and semantic communication. *Science, 210*, 801–803.

Shettleworth, S. J. (2010). Clever animals and killjoy explanations in comparative psychology. *Trends in Cognitive Sciences, 14*(11), 477–481.

Sievers, C., & Gruber, T. (2016). Reference in human and non-human primate communication: What does it take to refer? *Animal Cognition, 19*(4), 759–768.

Sievers, C., Wild, M., & Gruber, T. (2017). Intentionality and flexibility in animal communication. In K. Andrews & J. Beck (Eds.), *Routledge handbook of philosophy of animal minds* (pp. 333–342). London, UK: Routledge.

Sperber, D., & Wilson, D. (1995). *Relevance: Communication and cognition, second edition.* Malden, MA: Blackwell.

Thornton, A., & McAuliffe, K. (2006). Teaching in wild meerkats. *Science, 313*(5784), 227–229.

Tomasello, M. (2008). *Origins of human communication.* Cambridge, MA: MIT Press.

Tomasello, M., Carpenter, M., Call, J., Behne, T., & Moll, H. (2005). Understanding and sharing intentions: The origins of cultural cognition. *Behavioral and Brain Sciences, 28*(5), 675–735.

Townsend, S., Koski, S., Byrne, R., Slocombe, K., Bickel, B., Braga Goncalves, I., … Manser, M. B. (2016). Exorcising Grice's ghost: An empirical approach to studying intentional communication in animals. *Biological Reviews, 92*(3), 1427–1433. doi: 10.1111/brv.12289

Uher, J., Addessi, E., & Visalberghi, E. (2013). Contextualised behavioural measurements of personality differences obtained in behavioural tests and social observations in adult capuchin monkeys (Cebus apella). *Journal of Research in Personality, 47*, 427–444.

van de Waal, E., Renevey, N., Favre, C. M., & Bshary, R. (2010). Selective attention to philopatric models causes directed social learning in wild vervet monkeys. *Proceedings of the Royal Society B: Biological Sciences,* *277*(1691), 2105–2111.

van Schaik, C. P., Ancrenaz, M., Borgen, G., Galdikas, B., Knott, C. D., Singleton, I., … Merrill, M. (2003). Orangutan cultures and the evolution of material culture. *Science, 299*(5603), 102–105.

Wheeler, B. C., & Fischer, J. (2012). Functionally referential signals: A promising paradigm whose time has passed. *Evolutionary Anthropology, 21,* 195–205.

Whiten, A., Goodall, J., McGrew, W. C., Nishida, T., Reynolds, V., Sugiyama, Y., … Boesch, C. (1999). Cultures in chimpanzees. *Nature, 399*(6737), 682–685.

Whiten, A., McGuigan, N., Marshall-Pescini, S., & Hopper, L. M. (2009). Emulation, imitation, over-imitation and the scope of culture for child and chimpanzee. *Philosophical Transactions of the Royal Society B: Biological Sciences, 364,* 2417–2428.

PART II

On human development and affective social learning

CHAPTER 3

Affective social learning

From nature to culture

Paul L. Harris

Research on learning from verbal testimony has shown that children readily acquire beliefs about the physical, social and psychological world by trusting the claims of other people (Harris & Koenig, 2006). Indeed, even preverbal infants can learn about the location, identity and function of objects from the communicative gestures of others (Harris & Lane, 2014). Parallel studies of learning via imitation have shown that, on the basis of observation and faithful copying, infants and children also learn how to act, whether in the context of solving practical problems (Horner & Whiten, 2005; Lyons, Damrosch, Lin, Macris, & Keil, 2011) or acquiring ritualistic behaviours (Herrmann, Legare, Harris, & Whitehouse, 2013). Both of these streams of research show that children are social learners in the sense that they seek information about what to believe and what to do from other people (Harris, 2012a). Moreover, children are not indiscriminate when they look to others for guidance. They are especially prone to learn from individuals who are knowledgeable rather than poorly informed, from individuals who belong to their own group rather than an out-group, and from individuals who belong to a consensus rather than dissent from it. Thus, children can reasonably be described as cultural learners – they are budding anthropologists who are disposed to adopt the beliefs and behaviours of the surrounding community (Harris, 2012b; Legare & Harris, 2016).

Studies of social learning have devoted limited attention to the domain of emotion. This is surprising because research in the 1980s on the phenomenon of social referencing established that infants register the emotional reactions of other people to a given situation and calibrate their own reactions to that situation accordingly. For example, in an influential study, when 12-month-old infants came close to an apparent cliff, they either advanced or balked at doing so, depending on whether their mother produced a positive or negative facial expression when infants came close to the cliff (Sorce, Emde, Campos, & Klinnert, 1985).

Those early findings on social referencing have been followed up in several ways. We now know that infants are influenced by another person's emotional expression primarily when they can infer what that expression is referring to by noting, for example, what the person is looking at or attending to. When such referential cues are absent, infants are less receptive (Moses, Baldwin, Rosicky, & Tidball, 2001). We also know that other people's emotional signals can have a relatively enduring, and not just an immediate, impact on infants' reactions. When encountering a given situation, infants appear to remember how other people have reacted to that situation earlier because they display continuing behavioural signs of being influenced by those prior reactions even when their informants are no longer present (Hornik, Risenhoover, & Gunnar, 1987).

An important implication of these studies is that infants' emotional reactions to a variety of situations are not necessarily based on their own autonomous appraisal. Instead, they are guided by the situational appraisals supplied by other people via their emotional expressions. My goal in this chapter is to argue for an expanded focus with respect to this type of affective learning from other people. If I am right, the findings that have been identified through research on social referencing are best understood in terms of the wide-ranging disposition for social learning sketched above. In other words, children are social learners not just in the sense that they are receptive to the beliefs and behaviours of the surrounding community but also in the sense that they are receptive to the affective appraisals of the surrounding community (Clément & Dukes, 2017). More specifically, I will argue that in the course of becoming members of a given culture, infants and children have a variety of emotionally uncertain encounters. They learn how to appraise those encounters via the distinctive emotional lens of their own culture. In doing so, they are guided by those who are likely to be representative of that culture rather than misfits or deviants. Moreover, in so doing, they take note of other people's verbal as well as their non-verbal expressions of emotion.

3.1   Encounters with uncertainty

In an article published in the relatively new journal *Mind*, William James set out his influential answer to the question: 'What is an emotion?' (James, 1884). His most provocative claim was that our bodily reactions are of primary importance in our experience of emotions. Faced with a bear, it is our pounding heart that tells us that we are afraid and hence we run. Especially important for the thrust of this chapter is James' parallel claim that many of our emotional reactions are inbuilt, adaptive appraisals of what he described as pieces of 'the world's furniture'. For example, James noted that our fear of heights, of the dark and of an approaching bear serves to protect us from harm. The assumption that there are innate and universal emotional reactions to particular items of the world's furniture is also built into the influential (albeit controversial) experimental work conducted by Paul Ekman (Ekman, 1973; Ekman & Friesen, 1971). His research programme is typically interpreted as a claim about the universality of particular facial expressions, but it is also effectively a claim about the universality of emotional reactions to particular items of the world's furniture: fear in response to a snake, disgust in response to a rotting carcass, happiness in response to the arrival of a friend and so forth (Harris, 2017).

Research on social referencing has shown that, within certain limits, social learning can shape such allegedly inbuilt reactions. Recall that the pioneering study of social referencing showed that infants adjust their reactions to an apparent cliff depending on the emotional signal conveyed to them by their mother. Such adjustments are generally produced within the context of a zone of uncertainty, notably in reaction to an intermediate cliff – one that is not so shallow as to remove all cues to danger, nor so deep as to indicate inevitable danger. Similarly, if infants are confronted by a slope rather than a cliff, their mother's expressive signals can lead them to descend or to stay put but only when the incline of the slope induces uncertainty and not when it is a very steep descent or a mild slope (Tamis-LeMonda et al., 2008).

There are several lessons to be drawn from these findings. First, social referencing is unlikely to override infants' inbuilt and autonomous convictions about a situation. A steep slope provokes hesitation in young infants no matter what signals their caregivers may express. This is nicely compatible with the assumption of James – and of Ekman – that certain features of the natural world are cues to danger. Yet, even in such situations, the cues to danger may be equivocal. In such ambiguous circumstances, social referencing is effective in telling infants how to react. Indeed, once we move away from the 'world's furniture' – i.e. away from situations that, for evolutionary reasons, elicit strong emotional reactions – to consider instead the diverse range of encounters that children will have within any particular culture, it is easy to find ambiguous stimuli that provoke uncertainty. For example, within a given culture, there are many different kinds of artefacts, many different kinds of foods and many different kinds of persons. It would be maladaptive for infants to approach these diverse encounters with overriding emotional preconceptions. No doubt, within each type of encounter, there may be some that elicit widespread aversion – especially if they deviate sharply from prototypic exemplars of the category in question. But many encounters will arouse equivocal or mild reactions rather than strongly positive or negative reactions. Hence, we can expect infants to be receptive to social input – to reference other people for emotional guidance – in a variety of situations. By implication, social referencing is not just a learning mechanism by which infants fine-tune their pre-existing emotional reactions to naturally occurring items of the world's furniture, such as a dangerous cliff. It is also a learning mechanism that enables them to discern and acquire the emotional convictions of the surrounding culture toward a plethora of otherwise ambiguous stimuli.

3.2   Affective social learning: artefacts, foods and people

Below, I describe a variety of studies in support of the claim that affective social learning (ASL) can be seen as part of wide-ranging disposition to learn from others. I focus on children's affective learning about cultural artefacts, foods, and people. In each case, I note parallels with the way that children learn from other people about what to believe and what to do.

3.2.1   *Artefacts*

Kim and Kwak (2011) presented infants of 12 and 16 months with a variety of cultural artefacts, notably toys. Pre-testing confirmed that some of the toys elicited uncertain reactions from the infants. In line with earlier findings on social referencing, adults' emotional signals proved effective in altering infants' reactions to these ambiguous toys. Thus, both age groups were likely to turn to look at nearby adults when presented with one of the ambiguous toys and their emotional state shifted to reflect the emotional input they received – positive in the context of a happy expression but negative in the context of a fearful expression. Moreover, infants' subsequent behaviour toward the toys also shifted. They approached or retreated from the toys depending on the emotional input they received, with this differentiation being more evident among the 16-month-olds than the 12-month-olds.

It is tempting to think that infants will be especially likely to seek affective guidance from an attachment figure such as their mother. Indeed, in an early commentary on social referencing, Ainsworth (1992) underlined this possibility. However, Stenberg and her colleagues (Stenberg, 2009; Stenberg & Hagekull, 2007) found that 12-month-old infants did not necessarily seek guidance about an ambiguous toy from a familiar caregiver. They were prone to turn to, and accept emotional guidance from a relatively unfamiliar adult – such as the experimenter – rather than their mother.

Follow-up studies revealed that infants were sensitive to the degree of expertise displayed by this unfamiliar adult. In one study, 12-month-old infants were exposed to two experimenters, one who provided evidence of local expertise by greeting the mother and her infant, showing them into the laboratory area and explaining the study, and one who simply followed and remained silent. Subsequently, infants looked more toward the expert than the non-expert, and regulated their behaviour toward an ambiguous toy more in accordance with the affective information that she supplied (Stenberg, 2012). By implication, infants have some ability to gauge which person might be an appropriate guide when they encounter uncertainty – notably, someone who displays familiarity with, and competence in, the surrounding environment.

Subsequent research further highlighted the importance of apparent competence (Stenberg, 2013). Twelve-month-old infants were again introduced to two adults. One adult played competently with various artefacts (e.g. successfully fitted bricks into a corresponding aperture based on their shape, and correctly labelled the bricks in terms of their colour: 'Now I am taking the blue brick …'). The other adult, by contrast, played less competently (e.g. failed to fit the bricks into their corresponding apertures and labelled them generically: 'Now I am taking this one … '). When presented with an ambiguous toy, infants were likely to look toward the more competent adult, and to be guided by her emotional signals in deciding whether to approach or avoid it. This bias toward a more competent informant emerged whether the two adults were familiar or unfamiliar to the infants.

Summing up these experiments on the appraisal of artefacts, they imply that infants regard other people not just as sources of reassurance – as traditionally emphasized by attachment theory – but also as sources of affective guidance when they encounter an uncertain situation. Given that perspective, we can expect infants to seek out, and to be receptive to, affective information that is provided by competent informants – those who are likely to be knowledgeable or informative rather than ignorant or uninformative with respect to the uncertain situation. In the wake of such affective information, infants adjust their behaviour accordingly – they approach the situation after positive input but avoid it after negative input.

By the age of 12 months, infants use pointing, especially index finger pointing, to elicit information from nearby adults, especially with regard to the name or function of unfamiliar objects (Harris, in press). In doing so, they are apt to prefer some adults rather than others. When Begus and Southgate (2012) presented 16-month-old infants with a series of novel objects, the infants often pointed them out to a nearby female experimenter. However, they were less likely to do so if she had proven to be poorly informed. Thus, they pointed less if she had misnamed familiar objects during an earlier familiarization period and expressed uncertainty about the names of the novel objects. These findings suggest that infants draw up an 'epistemic profile' of a potential informant and direct their pointing gestures to someone whom they regard as knowledgeable.

Do infants also use pointing to seek information about the emotional valence of unfamiliar objects? And in doing so, do they point indiscriminately no matter who might supply information or do they prioritize particular individuals? Given the findings described so far, we may expect infants to seek affective guidance from informative individuals. Kovács, Tauzin, Téglás, Gergely, and Csibra (2014) showed 12-month-old infants a series of attractive puppets that prompted infant pointing. In the sharing condition, an adult responded to infant points with shared interest in the puppet but she provided no information about it. She simply smiled, nodded, said 'Uh huh', and looked back and forth between the child and the puppet. By contrast, in the informing condition, an adult offered emotionally valenced information about the puppet – via her affective vocalization (such as 'Wow' or 'Yuck') and accompanying facial expression. Infants pointed to the puppets more often in the informing condition, particularly on later trials. By implication, they built up a distinctive profile of the adults as more or less informative interlocutors depending on the condition. Thus, in line with the findings reported by Stenberg and her colleagues, infants treat the expression of emotion as a form of information. As such, they direct their interrogative pointing to adults who have reliably supplied affective information in the past.

Poulin-Dubois and her colleagues offer support for the proposal that infants favour not just those individuals who provide affective information as such but rather for those individuals who provide plausible affective information. Chow, Poulin-Dubois, and Lewis (2008) presented 14-month-old infants with either a conventional or an unconventional emoter. The conventional emoter expressed positive affect while looking inside a box that held a toy, whereas the unconventional emoter expressed positive affect while looking inside an empty box. Thus, it was reasonable for infants to construe the conventional emoter as providing valid or helpful information about the contents of the box and the unconventional emoter as providing invalid or unhelpful information. In line with this interpretation, when infants subsequently watched the same adults look behind a barrier they were more likely to follow the gaze of the conventional as opposed to the unconventional emoter.

A follow-up study indicated that infants prefer to learn a new behaviour from someone whose emotional reactions are appropriate rather than inappropriate (Poulin-Dubois, Brooker, & Polonia, 2011). After seeing an adult prove to be a conventional or unconventional emoter – using the procedure just described – infants watched the same adult engage in an unusual action: rather than pressing a light switch with her hand, she did so with her forehead. When given a chance to turn the light on, infants were more likely to engage in faithful copying – by using their forehead rather than their hand – if the adult had proven to be a conventional rather than an unconventional emoter.

Chiarella and Poulin-Dubois (2018) obtained additional evidence that infants monitor the appropriateness of an adult's emotional reactions. Eighteen-month-old infants watched as an adult responded with sadness either in appropriate circumstances (having been given the wrong tool to achieve a goal) or in inappropriate circumstances (having been given the right tool to achieve a goal). When this adult subsequently provided emotional 'advice' by responding with happiness to the contents of one container and disgust to the contents of another, infants tended to follow that advice – by choosing the 'happy' container – if it was produced by the 'appropriate' emoter but not if it was produced by the 'inappropriate' emoter.

Summing up these various studies, the emerging picture is of selective rather than indiscriminate receptivity. Infants keep track of an individual's prior behaviour and are more likely to be receptive to someone who has proven competent or well informed. They seek input from individuals who have provided affective information as compared to those who have remained neutral or non-committal and from individuals whose affective reactions have proven appropriate or typical rather than deviant. This set of findings bears notable similarities to the pattern that has emerged in more neutral domains – those that are less clearly charged with emotion. Thus, in learning about object names or functions, preschoolers and infants are prone to be selective in their trust. They are more receptive to individuals who have proven knowledgeable in the past and who have supplied accurate and appropriate rather than deviant information – for example, by naming familiar objects correctly or demonstrating their use in a standard, culturally accepted fashion (Harris & Corriveau, 2011; Harris, Koenig, Corriveau, & Jaswal, 2018).

3.2.2   Foods

Children possess several adaptive mechanisms that are likely to steer them toward a safe diet. Neonates are prone to reject sour and bitter foods and to prefer sweet ones; infants and young children readily form an aversion to foods associated with subsequent nausea; and beyond the period of infancy, children display a neophobic bias – they avoid trying novel, and potentially risky, foods (Aldridge, Dovey, & Halford, 2009; Birch, 1999). However, these mechanisms are not enough to ensure a safe, variegated and healthy diet. On the one hand, infants and toddlers do not systematically avoid potentially toxic substances and on the other hand, early neophobia is likely to unnecessarily narrow the range of children's diet. Hence, as argued by Shutts, Kinzler, and DeJesus (2013), it is plausible that children's emerging food preferences are shaped and differentiated in a social context – by observing and learning from the habits and preferences of other people. Indeed, several studies have shown that in choosing whether to eat a novel food, young children are influenced by what other people eat.

Harper and Sanders (1975) found that toddlers and preschoolers (ranging from 14 to 48 months) were more likely to eat a novel food if an adult (either the mother or a female visitor) did not simply offer the food to the child but ate some first before offering it. Indeed, when children saw the adult eating the food, they were likely to ask for some even before it was offered – whereas such requests were rare if the adult did not eat the food before offering it. Similar results emerged in a follow-up study in which the adult was either a male or female visitor who interacted with the child in the absence of the mother. Children were often willing to be guided by the stranger even in their mother's absence.

Still, it is important to note that although such modelling effects are intriguing, they do not, strictly speaking, show that children's evaluation of the foods shifted as a result of watching adults eat them. At most, we can say that the adults' consumption evoked a comparable desire to eat in the children who watched. Indeed, it is possible that adult consumption might provoke a desire to eat any food – not the particular food that the adult is eating. To assess these possibilities more directly, Addessi, Galloway, Visalberghi, and Birch (2005) presented preschoolers with three novel foods to eat – all three foods consisted of semolina but they differed in colour and taste. Children were presented with one food while an adult sat opposite them not eating anything; they were presented with a second food while the adult enthusiastically ate a different food, as indexed by its different colour; finally, they were presented with a third food while the adult enthusiastically ate that same food, as indexed by its identical colour. Each food presentation was separated by a period of at least a week to minimize transfer from one presentation to another. When the adult was eating the same novel food as they were, children were quicker to try it, spent more time eating it, and consumed more of it – as compared to when the adults were eating a different food or simply sitting with them. Indeed, these two latter conditions had an equally weak impact on children's behaviour. By implication, adult consumption of a given food – rather than adult consumption per se – prompted children to try that food and to persist in eating it.

Children are receptive not just to adults but also to their peers. In a pioneering study of peer influence, Duncker (1938) found that preschoolers (ranging from 2 to 5 years) were likely to emulate the particular food choices of another child. For example, left to their own devices, they might choose to eat grapes rather than nuts, but having observed another child opt for nuts, they were likely to do the same. This child-to-child influence was especially potent if the model was older than the observer. Was this influence restricted simply to behavioural imitation or was children's liking of a given food also impacted by the choices that other children made? Duncker obtained some evidence of a shift in liking. Thus, there was some indication of a shift in food preferences, rather than just behavioural emulation, because the shift persisted in follow-up trials when the model was no longer present.

Birch (1980) also reported evidence of a stable shift in food preferences. Preschoolers aged 2 to 4 years first indicated their preferences among nine different types of vegetables. Subsequently, target children were seated at a table with three or four other children and all the children at the table were invited to choose between two vegetables: one had been ranked first or second and one last or last but one by the target child. By contrast, the other children at the table had expressed the reverse preferences. This procedure was continued for four days in succession to assess whether target children would shift their choices toward those made by the other children at their table. Indeed, on the fourth day, the majority of target children had shifted in their preferred choice whereas very few of their tablemates had done so. By implication, social influence was exerted by the peer majority over the individual target child whereas the reverse influence did not occur. Some weeks after this procedure, children were again questioned about their preferences among the set of nine vegetables. Target children now ranked initially disliked foods higher and initially preferred foods lower whereas children who had served as tablemates showed no such change.

In summary, these studies underline the power of imitation to both expand and redirect children's food preferences. After observing an adult eat a relatively novel food, toddlers and preschoolers are likely to try that same novel food. After observing another child and especially after observing several others eat a food that they do not particularly like, children will do likewise and in the longer term they may express increased liking for that majority choice.

The emotional valence that is attached to a given food is likely to vary from one culture to another. Accordingly, it would be appropriate for children to attune to, and be guided by, the affective reactions of members of their own cultural group. Granted the importance of language as a signal for cultural membership (Kinzler, Dupoux, & Spelke, 2007), it is likely that children will be especially prone to learn about unfamiliar foods from adults who speak the same way as they do. Indeed, when learning about the functions of objects, English-speaking children are more receptive to demonstrations provided by an informant who is a native rather than a non-native speaker of English (Kinzler, Corriveau, & Harris, 2011).

Do children display a comparable sensitivity to an informant's language in acquiring affective information about food? To examine this issue, Shutts, Kinzler, McKee, and Spelke (2009) gave 12-month-old infants an opportunity to sample two types of food. Infants then watched as two women each ate one of the foods; one woman expressed positive affect in English as she ate whereas the other expressed positive affect in French. When subsequently given a choice between the two foods, most infants opted for the food liked by the English speaker. Arguably, the infants could decode the comment of the English speaker more effect-ively than the comment of the French speaker but given the very limited vocabulary of 12-month-olds, this is unlikely. A more plausible interpret-ation, consistent with the modelling effects mentioned above, is that the English speaker swayed infants' choices because they identified her as belonging to their own cultural group and followed her lead.

In all the studies discussed so far, children's responses to novel or disliked foods were influenced by direct observation of the food choices made by other people, be they adults or children. Is the impact of other people confined to such direct observation or are there other less direct routes? In another pioneering study, Duncker (1938) explored this latter possibility. Children in the experimental group listened to a story about a Native-American boy, Eaglefeather, who, with the help of a field mouse, discovers that although the bark of one type of tree in the forest tastes sour and disgusting, another tree, a maple, delivers a sweet syrup. After re-enacting the story in pairs, with one child playing the role of the field mouse and the other child the role of Eaglefeather, children were invited to choose between two unfamiliar foods, one introduced as coming from the sour-tasting tree and the other from the sweet-tasting maple. By design, the former actually tasted relatively sweet whereas the latter had a bitter coating. In effect, the experiment probed how far children would choose between the two novel foods in terms of their actual sweetness or in terms of their appeal as signalled in the story. These choices were repeated several times in the course of the next couple of weeks. After sampling both, most of the control children – who had not heard the story – preferred the food that was actually sweeter and did so consist-ently in successive tests. By contrast, in early tests many of the experi-mental children chose the food that was preferred in the story even if on later tests they too chose the objectively sweeter option. By implica-tion, children's social learning about food need not be restricted to direct observation. They will emulate – at least for a while – the choices of a story protagonist, even if those choices run counter to their gustatory preference.

DeJesus, Shutts, and Kinzler (in press) asked if 5- and 6-year-olds would be swayed by verbal information about the relative popularity of two foods. An adult introduced as a teacher told the children that the food in one bowl was popular with other children whereas the food in another bowl was not. After the teacher had left, children could sample the food in each bowl. They consumed more of the allegedly popular food. They also judged it to taste better even though the food in each bowl was actually identical. In a follow-up study, children were told that one of the foods was popular with children and the other with adults. Again, children's consumption was swayed by the verbal testimony. They consumed more of the food alleged to be popular with children and again tended to claim that it tasted better.

In a final experiment, children's taste judgements were probed more directly to assess how far they could be swayed by information about popularity. First, 5- and 6-year-olds were presented with a sweet serving of applesauce (containing 0 ml of lemon juice) and a sour serving (containing 5 ml of lemon juice). They heard each serving described appropriately as 'sweet' and sour' and they tasted both. Next children were presented with intermediate servings (containing 1 ml, 2 ml, 3 ml and 4 ml of lemon juice) and asked to designate each as either 'sweet' or 'sour'. Each type of serving was presented twice – in one case it was described as popular with other children and in the other case as unpopular. For the 1 ml and 4 ml servings (which were close in flavour to the initial servings of 0 ml and 5 ml), this information about popularity did not sway children's perception. Thus, most children judged the relatively sweet serving as sweet and the relatively sour serving as sour. However, testimony did impact children's perception of the two intermediate servings (2 ml and 3 ml). A greater percentage of children claimed that these servings were sweet when they were alleged to be popular rather than unpopular with other children. Thus, consistent with the findings from infants on social referencing, children were particularly receptive to the affective reactions of others when they concerned relatively ambiguous stimuli, i.e. those falling in the intermediate range of the sweet–sour continuum.

Taken together, these studies underline both the limits and the potency of verbal reports in changing young children's reactions to food. After hearing a story describing the choices made by a story protagonist, children were led to try a novel food and, at least temporarily, to express a liking for it, even if the food actually tasted somewhat bitter. Indeed, verbal reports of peer popularity shifted children's taste perception – at least when the stimuli in question were ambiguous in flavour.

3.2.3   People

Do infants look to others for guidance when they are uncertain how to respond to a stranger? And are they selective about whose guidance to accept? De Rosnay, Cooper, Tsigaras, and Murray (2006) had infants ranging from 12 to 14 months old watch while their mother interacted with two different strangers. She behaved toward one stranger in a positive fashion and to the other in an anxious fashion. Subsequently, infants' reactions were observed as each stranger approached them. Mothers busied themselves in reading a magazine during this approach so that they provided no emotional cues to their infants at this stage.

Nevertheless, infants expressed more fear at the approach of the stranger who had provoked anxiety in their mother. By implication, infants had taken their mothers' distinctive interaction with each stranger to indicate a positive or negative appraisal of them – which infants then remembered and used to calibrate their own reactions to the two strangers.

When they appraise a person that they have not met before, do children pick up on other people's non-verbal affective signals toward that person even when the people producing them are unfamiliar to the children – rather than attachment figures, such as their mother? Fusaro and Harris (2008) obtained suggestive evidence of such sensitivity. Four-year-olds watched as two women they had never met before named a set of unfamiliar objects. Standing behind these two women were two onlookers. These onlookers displayed positive non-verbal signals toward one woman – they smiled and nodded their heads in approval when she supplied a name for each of the unfamiliar objects – but negative non-verbal signals toward the other woman – they frowned and nodded their head when she supplied a different name. When children were asked what the various unfamiliar objects were called, they almost always endorsed the name supplied by the woman who had been the target of positive signals from the two female onlookers. Indeed, the impact of the bystander reactions was very potent. Children selected that name on about 90 per cent of the trials. Thus, in the wake of the onlookers' non-verbal reactions, children had a strong preference for the information supplied by the woman who had been greeted positively rather than negatively.

One possible interpretation of these findings is that children viewed the onlookers as providing corrective feedback – effectively saying 'Yes, that's right' to one proposed name and 'No, that's wrong' to the other. This interpretation is not implausible because, along with their smiles or frowns, the onlookers effectively expressed agreement by nodding or shaking their head. So, children may have used the onlookers' input to decide which proposed name was correct – without forming any view of the two women proposing the names.

To evaluate this interpretation, Fusaro and Harris (2008) investigated children's reactions in subsequent trials. In these follow-up trials, the onlookers were no longer present but the procedure was otherwise the same as before: The two women proposed different names for each of a series of unfamiliar objects and children were again asked for their choice. If they had viewed the onlookers as commenting only on the names, children should now think of each name as equally plausible because the onlookers were no longer present to supply feedback on each name. However, most children continued to endorse the name proposed by the woman who had received onlooker approval. This tendency was not as pronounced as when the onlookers had been present but it was still very systematic. By implication, in the wake of the onlookers' reactions, the children had come to view one of the women in a more positive fashion than the other – at least in terms of her trustworthiness as an informant.

Subsequent research has shown that children's appraisal of an unfamiliar person can be impacted along several dimensions by the non-verbal signals of other people. Skinner, Meltzoff, and Olson (2017) presented 4- and 5-year-olds with a video clip in which they saw two target females approached and greeted by two other women. These two other women displayed positive, non-verbal signals when interacting with one of the target females – they smiled, leaned in and used a warm tone of voice. By contrast, they displayed negative, non-verbal signals toward the other target female – they scowled, leaned away and used a cold tone of voice. After this introductory period, children were probed for their appraisal of the two target women. Children displayed a multi-faceted bias toward the woman who had been approached and greeted positively rather than negatively. In response to questions from the experimenter, children expressed greater liking for her. They were more likely to think that she should receive a gift. Finally, in a test of their willingness to learn from the two women, children proved more likely to endorse the names supplied by the woman who had been greeted positively – echoing the results of Fusaro and Harris (2008). In sum, the emotionally expressive displays of other people, including people that they do not know, can steer young children toward a positive or negative impression of an individual – an impression that leads them to favour or disfavour that individual over another on measures of liking, generosity and trust.

In a follow-up study, Skinner et al. (2017) asked if such impressions with respect to the target individuals would be generalized to people who were closely affiliated with those target individuals. The first part of the study proceeded as before. A group of 4- and 5-year-olds observed one target woman being approached in a positive manner and a second being approached in a negative manner by two others. Replicating the findings of the first study, children liked, were more generous toward and preferred to learn from, the target woman who had been positively approached. Extending those findings, children also displayed a bias with respect to two other people, each introduced as the best friend of one of the targets. In a measure of overall bias, children liked the person introduced as the best friend of the positively greeted target more than the person introduced as the best friend of the negatively greeted target.

Skinner, Olson, and Meltzoff (2018) asked if this type of affective learning can help to explain how children might acquire a positive or negative impression not just with respect to particular individuals or their friends, but also to individuals who happen to belong to the same group? As in the earlier studies, 4- and 5-year-olds observed videos in which two women displayed positive emotional signals toward one target female but negative emotional signals toward another. Confirming earlier findings, children were more positively disposed – as indexed by a composite measure of liking, generosity and trust – toward the positively greeted target. Children were then probed for their reactions to two additional women, each dressed like one of the target women in terms of shirt colour, and hence appearing to belong to the same groups as them. As predicted, children generalized the bias they had displayed toward the target women to these two additional women. As Skinner et al. (2018) emphasize, such learning could provide a powerful basis for the acquisition of bias or prejudice toward an entire group of individuals.

In line with the social referencing paradigm, the research described so far has focused on the way that young children engage in affective learning about individuals – and groups – by taking note of other people's non-verbal expressions of emotion. Because of the inspiration provided by Darwin and Ekman for the study of such non-verbal signals, we know less about children's receptivity to verbal expression of emotions. Yet, as we saw in discussing their appraisal of foods, children are guided by verbal reports of other people's likes and dislikes. Is the same true when children appraise newly encountered individuals or groups?

To explore this possibility, Lane, Conder, and Rottman (2017) exposed children from 4 to 8 years of age to a negative verbal report about an unfamiliar group. An adult told the children that people belonging to this unfamiliar group ('Gearoos') are bad people who eat disgusting food, wear weird clothes and have an ugly-sounding language. Control children received no such information. After the adult delivering this message had left, children were invited by another adult to say whether they thought Gearoos were good people and to indicate – via a drawing measure – how close or distant they felt toward Gearoos. Especially among the older children (6 years and older) there was a clear impact of verbal testimony. Children exposed to the negative testimony were more likely to claim that Gearoos were bad, to position themselves further away from a Gearoo in the drawing task and to express reluctance to learn their alphabet, try their food or try their clothes. In sum, a brief verbal message led children to adopt a negative and avoidant stance toward a group they had never met.

3.3   Conclusions

Classic research on the development of emotion has often focused on young children's apparently unlearned emotional reactions to particular encounters – for example, their fear or hesitation in response to an approaching stranger, an apparent cliff or a dark passageway. Early research on social referencing successfully showed that in the context of such encounters, affective guidance from other people can lead infants to adjust their approach or withdrawal. Recent findings have underlined the wide scope of this type of ASL. When they are faced with an unfamiliar artefact, food or person, infants and young children are often disposed to accept affective guidance from other people.

Two inter-related issues warrant more research in the future. As emphasized in this review, children are indeed alert to the observable actions and expressive behaviours that other people produce – consistent with earlier work on social referencing. Nonetheless, the scope of learning that takes place via social referencing is likely to be quite restricted. As noted in the introduction to this chapter, such learning ordinarily occurs only when the target of the other person's affect can be inferred from his or her gaze direction. This effectively means that via social referencing young children are certainly able to learn about other people's affective reactions toward targets that are present and visible. At the same time, it also means that they cannot easily learn about other people's affective reactions to absent or invisible targets. For example, via the classic mechanism of social referencing, it is impossible for young children to learn about a parent's affective reactions to an encounter that lies in the future – whether it is a visit to a relative, a holiday destination or the doctor. No matter how expressive the parent is in terms of producing facial or vocal cues that indicate his or her emotion, an infant or toddler will have difficulty in inferring the target of those cues if the relevant encounter lies in the future – or elsewhere.

The existence of this restriction highlights the importance of those studies described in the present review, which show that children can be swayed toward a positive or negative appraisal of a given encounter simply by hearing a verbal report of other people's affective reactions toward that encounter – or toward an encounter of the same type. These studies underline the possibility that social learning in the domain of emotion is likely to encompass many more phenomena than can be fitted into the relatively narrow paradigm of social referencing. Stated more positively, these studies of how children learn from reports of other people's affective reactions make it possible to situate research on ASL within the broader research programme studying young children's learning from other people's testimony about all kinds of phenomena, invisible as well as visible, absent as well as present (Harris, 2012a; Harris & Koenig, 2006).

The second, closely related issue was first raised by Duncker (1938) in his thoughtful discussion of how exactly other people's affective reactions might impact on a child – or indeed on an adult. One possibility is that those affective reactions provide a more or less dichotomous and valenced appraisal of a given encounter. In this view, children are effectively informed that a given artefact, food or person can be tagged as positive or as negative. Indeed, when children learn how to appraise a given encounter via social referencing or affective observation, such dichotomous tagging may be all that is needed to steer their behavioural reactions toward approach or avoidance. However, as Duncker noted, it is possible and indeed likely that social influence can have a more subtle impact. In particular, it is feasible that other people's affective reactions lead children to focus, not on the encounter in its entirety, but on particular elements of the encounter, especially those that are consistent with, and help to make sense of, other people's reactions to the encounter. In this view, the affective testimony that other people supply does not simply invite an endorsement of a positive or negative stance toward the encounter. Instead, it leads children to attend to and weigh particular features of the encounter such that the overall gestalt is shifted. It goes without saying that, as compared to the non-verbal expression of emotion, verbal reports of emotion lend themselves much more easily to such a nuanced identification of particular elements within an encounter. It remains to be seen whether studies of children's learning from the affective testimony of other people can pinpoint such subtler shifts in the pattern of appraisal.

References

Addessi, E., Galloway, A. T., Visalberghi, E., & Birch, L. L. (2005). Specific social influences on the acceptance of novel foods in 2–5-year-old children. *Appetite*, 45(3), 264–271. doi:10.1016/j.appet.2005.07.007

Ainsworth, M. D. S. (1992). A consideration of social referencing in the context of attachment theory and research. In S. Feinman & S. Feinman (Eds.), *Social referencing and the social construction of reality in infancy* (pp. 349–367). New York, NY: Plenum Press. doi:10.1007/978-1-4899-2462-9_14

Aldridge, V., Dovey, T. M., & Halford, J. G. (2009). The role of familiarity in dietary development. *Developmental Review*, 29(1), 32–44.

Begus, K., & Southgate, V. (2012). Infant pointing serves an interrogative function. *Developmental Science*, 15, 611–677.

Birch, L. L. (1980). Effects of peer models' food choices and eating behaviors on pre-schoolers' food preferences. *Child Development*, 51, 489–496.

    (1999). Development of food preferences. *Annual Review of Nutrition*, 19, 41–62.

Chiarella, S. S., & Poulin-Dubois, D. (2018). 'Are you really sad?' infants show selectivity in their behaviors toward an unconventional emoter. *Infancy*, doi:10.1111/infa.12230

Chow, V., Poulin-Dubois, D., & Lewis, J. (2008). To see or not to see: Infants prefer to follow the gaze of a conventional looker. *Developmental Science*, 11, 761–770.

Clément, F., & Dukes, D. (2017). Social appraisal and social referencing: Two components of affective social learning. *Emotion Review*, 9, 253–261.

DeJesus, J. M., Shutts, K., & Kinzler, K. D. (2017). Mere social knowledge impacts children's consumption and categorization of foods. *Developmental Science*, 21(5). doi:10.1111/desc.12627 de Rosnay, M., Cooper, P. J., Tsigaras, N., & Murray, L. (2006). *Behaviour, Research and Therapy, 44*, 1165–1175.

Duncker, K. (1938). Experimental modification of children's food preferences through social suggestion. *Journal of Abnormal & Social Psychology, 33*, 489–507.

Ekman, P. (1973). Cross-cultural studies of facial expression. In P. Ekman (Ed.), *Darwin and facial expression* (pp. 169–222). New York, NY: Academic Press.

Ekman, P., & Friesen, W. (1971). Constants across cultures in the face and emotion. *Journal of Personality and Social Psychology, 17*, 124–129.

Fusaro, M., & Harris, P. L. (2008). Children assess informant reliability using bystanders' non-verbal cues. *Developmental Science, 11*, 781–787.

Harper, L. V., & Sanders, K. M. (1975). The effect of adults' eating on young children's acceptance of unfamiliar foods. *Journal of Experimental Child Psychology, 20*, 206–214.

Harris, P. L. (2012a). *Trusting what you're told: How children learn from others.* Cambridge, MA: Belknap Press/Harvard University Press.

   (2012b). The child as anthropologist. *Infancia y Aprendizaje, 35*, 259–277.

   (2017). Emotion, imagination and the world's furniture. *European Journal of Developmental Psychology, 14*(6), 672–683.

   (2019). Infants want input. In V. Grover, P. Uccelli, M. L. Rowe, & E. Lieven (Eds.), *Learning through language: Towards an educationally informed theory of language learning.* Cambridge, UK: Cambridge University Press.

Harris, P. L., & Corriveau, K. H. (2011). Young children's selective trust in informants. *Proceedings of the Royal Society B, 366*, 1179–1190.

Harris, P. L., & Koenig, M. (2006). Trust in testimony: How children learn about science and religion. *Child Development, 77*, 505–524.

Harris, P. L., Koenig, M. A., Corriveau, K. H., & Jaswal, V. K. (2018). Cognitive foundations of learning from testimony. *Annual Review of Psychology, 69*, 251–273.

Harris, P. L., & Lane, J. D. (2014). Infants understand how testimony works. *Topoi: An International Review of Philosophy, 33*, 443–458.

Herrmann, P. A., Legare, C. H., Harris, P. L., & Whitehouse, H. (2013). Stick to the script: The effect of witnessing multiple actors on children's imitation. *Cognition, 129*, 536–543.

Horner, V., & Whiten, A. (2005). Causal knowledge and imitation/emulation switching in chimpanzees (*Pan troglodytes*) and children (*Homo sapiens*). *Animal Cognition, 8*, 164–181.

Hornik, R., Risenhoover, N., & Gunnar, M. (1987). The effects of maternal positive, neutral, and negative affective communications on infant responses to new toys. *Child Development, 58*, 937–944.

James, W. (1884). What is an emotion? *Mind, 9*, 188–205.

Kim, G., & Kwak, K. (2011). Uncertainty matters: Impact of stimulus ambiguity on infant social referencing. *Infant and Child Development, 20*, 449–463.

Kinzler, K. D., Corriveau, K. H., & Harris, P. L. (2011). Children's selective trust in native-accented speakers. *Developmental Science, 14*, 106–111.

Kinzler, K. D., Dupoux, E., & Spelke, E. S. (2007). The native language of social cognition. *PNAS, 104*, 12577–12580.

Kovács, A., Tauzin, T., Téglás, E., Gergely, G., & Csibra, G. (2014). Pointing as epistemic request: 12-month-olds point to receive new information. *Infancy, 19*, 543–557.

Lane, J. D., Conder, E. B., & Rottman, J. (2017). Effects of testimony on children's evaluation of novel social groups. Paper presented at the Biennial Meeting of the Society for Research in Child Development, Austin, Texas.

Legare, C. H., & Harris, P. L. (2016). The ontogeny of cultural learning. *Child Development, 87*, 633–642.

Lyons, D. E., Damrosch, D. H., Lin, J. K., Macris, D. M., & Keil, F. C. (2011). The scope and limits of overimitation in the transmission of artifact culture. *Philosophical Transactions of the Royal Society B, 366*, 1158–1167.

Moses, L. J., Baldwin, D. A., Rosicky, J. G., & Tidball, G. (2001). Evidence for referential understanding in the emotions domain at twelve and eighteen months. *Child Development, 72*, 718–735.

Poulin-Dubois, D., Brooker, I., & Polonia, A. (2011). Infants prefer to imitate a conventional person. *Infant Behavior and Development, 34*, 303–309.

Shutts, K., Kinzler, K. D., & DeJesus, J. M. (2013). Understanding infants' and children's social learning about foods: Previous research and new prospects. *Developmental Psychology, 40*, 419–425.

Shutts, K., Kinzler, K. D., McKee, C. B., & Spelke, E. S. (2009). Social information guides infants' selection of foods. *Journal of Cognition and Development, 10*, 1–17.

Skinner, A. L., Meltzoff, A. N., & Olson, K. R. (2017). 'Catching' social bias: Exposure to biased nonverbal signals creates social biases in preschool children. *Psychological Science, 28*, 216–224.

Skinner, A. L., Olson, K. R., & Meltzoff, A. N. (2018). Roots of prejudice: Observing other people's nonverbal bias can create prejudice in preschool children. Unpublished manuscript.

Sorce, J. F., Emde, R. N., Campos, J. J., & Klinnert, M. D. (1985). Maternal emotional signaling: Its effect on the visual cliff behaviour of 1-year-olds. *Developmental Psychology, 21*, 195–200.

Stenberg, G. (2009). Selectivity in infant social referencing. *Infancy, 14*, 457–473. (2012). Why do infants look at and use positive information from some informants rather than others in ambiguous situations? *Infancy, 17*, 642–671, (2013). Do 12-month-olds infants trust a competent adult? *Infancy, 18*, 873–904.

Stenberg, G., & Hagekull, B. (2007). Infant looking behaviour in ambiguous situations: Social referencing or attachment behaviour? *Infancy, 11*, 111–129.

Tamis-LeMonda, C. S., Adolph, K. E., Lobo, S. A., Karasik, L. B., Ishak, S., & Dimitropoulou, K. A. (2008). When infants take mothers' advice: 18-month-olds integrate perceptual and social information to guide motor action. *Developmental Psychology, 44*, 734–746.

CHAPTER 4

Natural pedagogy of social emotions

György Gergely and Ildikó Király

The aim of this chapter is twofold: Our first goal is to argue that evolved systems of emotion-based social learning and the capacity for ostensive communication have become intertwined in multiple ways during human evolution to serve the functions of social information exchange and cultural knowledge transmission during ontogenetic development. This allows human infants to communicate and learn *by* emotions as well as *about* emotions through ostensive communication and natural pedagogy. On the one hand, from very early on, human infants inquire, request, and convey information *by* emotion expressions through the system of natural pedagogy, which employs the ostensive use of emotion displays as informative communicative gestures to convey relevant information about referents, even before children acquire language. On the other hand, we shall argue that infants also learn *about* social emotions through the communicative exchange of emotion expressions with their caregivers relying on specialized 'teaching' mechanisms such as ostensive emotion-reflective interactions and social bio-feedback.

Our second goal is to expand a particular, evolutionary-based view of *social emotions* as special types of kind concepts that belong to the *culturally shared ontological kind categories* that humans possess and share with other social agents in their cultural community. This conceptualization of social emotions as dispositional kind categories (whose tokens are the specific dispositional states of individuals to whom the emotion is ascribed) implies a view of *dispositional essentialism* about the representation of categorical emotions in humans. According to this view, social emotions are represented in terms of *underlying causal dispositional states* that we infer and attribute to individual social agents to account for their

The research leading to this chapter has received funding from the European Research Council under the European Union's Seventh Framework Programme (FP7/2007–2013)/ ERC grant agreement no. 609819 SOMICS. We thank John S. Watson and Tibor Tauzin for their valuable comments on the manuscript.

emotion-based actions and expressions that they produce in different social and cultural contexts.

Finally, after explicating this dispositional approach to causal essentialism for representing social emotion concepts, we shall propose and elaborate the hypothesis that *ostensive communication* and *natural pedagogy* provide specialized social learning mechanisms, which play a central developmental role in the acquisition and cultural transmission of the complex – and in many regards culture-specific – set of relevant information that form the representational contents of the dispositional emotion categories that human social agents share, recognize, attribute, communicate, and reason about in relevant social, cultural, and normative contexts.

4.1   Social learning *by* emotions in humans

4.1.1   *Evolved emotion systems as social learning programmes*

We shall argue for the evolutionary emergence of human social emotion concepts by building on significant recent advances in emotion research that have uncovered the evolved design features and underlying neural mechanisms of a set of basic emotion-based systems that have been selected to function as social learning programmes (Blair, 2003, 2007). This body of research has identified certain core emotion displays that function in a referential and communicative manner and that have evolved to serve the social transmission of valence information about their referents to conspecific observers. Sensitivity to particular emotion expressions (such as disgust, fear, sadness, or anger) that display evaluative information about the external referents they are directed at and evoked by has evolved, in several social species, with the function of automatically transmitting valence information about unfamiliar referent objects to other conspecifics. The proposal that these core emotional expressions (triggered by particular types of referents, such as food or approaching predators) evolved to serve social and communicatory functions is based on the observation that they tend to be automatically activated, stimulus-driven behavioural displays that are triggered by largely prespecified stimulus events and are displayed primarily in the presence of social conspecifics (Blair, 2003, 2007). The propensity to display such referential emotion displays in social contexts has been selected to make relevant valence information about their referents available for social conspecifics. The evidence thus made available can then be vicariously acquired through social observational learning mechanisms, as a result of which the social observer will come to associate and represent the valence-related evaluative information displayed as a relevant property of the referent.

(It has also been reported that displaying referential affective signals such as predator-induced alarm calls in vervet monkeys may induce differential effects in social observers: when such affective alarm calls are produced by juvenile vervet monkeys, they induce with higher probability a behavioural reaction by the mothers than by other unrelated adult females in the social group present, see Cheney & Seyfarth, 1980). The central point of this evolutionary proposal is that these specific, emotion-based social learning systems have been selected to support the rapid and automatic transmission and spread of adaptive evaluative information about external referents among conspecific social agents (Blair, 2003, 2007).

Such emotion-based social learning systems are not human-specific adaptations, as they have been reported in other non-human primate species as well. For example, valence learning through social referencing (or, more likely, by affective observation, cf. Clément & Dukes, Introduction, this volume) has been claimed to be present in chimpanzees who observe their conspecific's automatic display of disgust towards novel food items, which the observer learns to avoid in the future (Russell, Bard, & Adamson, 1997). This has been observed in monkeys, too, who tend to avoid unfamiliar referents after having observed a caregiver's display of fear or disgust expression towards them (a phenomenon referred to as observational fear, Mineka & Cook, 1993). Evidence for cooperative signalling, i.e. active information donation through referential disgust reactions (Snowdon & Boe, 2003) or sentinel behaviour (Clutton-Brock, 2002) has been found in cooperative breeders such as callitrichid primates (see for reviews: Clément & Dukes, Introduction, this volume; Schuppli & van Schaik, Chapter 1, this volume). So, as cogently argued by Blair (2007), these core systems of emotion-based social observational learning are ancient adaptations that have evolved to support the spread of valence information about unfamiliar referents in several social animal species, including non-human primates as well as human infants.

4.1.2 Human-specific modifications in the communicative use of emotion-based social learning programmes

However, when comparing how the evolved referential emotion displays are produced and employed by human infants and how they fulfil their function in non-human primates, we find significant differences and modifications in the degree of intentional control over the production of emotion displays, a greater variety of their potential evoking conditions, and an increased scope of applicability and generalized referential domain.

Referential emotion displays in non-human primates tend to be automatic, stimulus-driven, and domain-specific responses, which are normally triggered by fixed and prespecified types of external referents and produced in the presence of social conspecifics. In particular, the activation of emotion displays in non-human primates does not appear to be voluntarily controlled and is not produced with the intention of conveying valence information to social conspecifics about their referents. Nevertheless, the evolved propensity to automatically activate such stimulus-driven referential emotion displays in the presence of social conspecifics is justly characterized as serving primary referential and communicative evolutionary functions, even if the emotion displays are not intentionally and voluntarily produced by the individual to fulfil these purposes. It seems, rather, that their communicatory and referential functions are automatically achieved as a consequence of the selected design features of social observational learning mechanisms. As a result, the third-person observation of referential emotion displays induces the social observer to associate and represent the displayed emotional valence-information as a property of the referent that the emotion expression is directed at. Certainly, such automatic production of referential emotion displays induced in the presence of conspecific partners does not imply, indicate, or justify the attribution to the non-human primate a communicative intention to manifest relevant information about the referent with the purpose of conveying it to the conspecific observer (see Schuppli & van Schaik, Chapter 1, this volume). This fact pinpoints an essential difference between the underlying mechanisms that are available for non-human primates on the one hand and human infants on the other – to realize the communicative function of valence-expressive referential emotion displays. As argued above, while non-human primates are able to rely on the emotional valence information referentially displayed by a conspecific to identify and represent it as a relevant valence property of the referent, they, nevertheless, don't seem to be able to actively and intentionally seek out, request, or offer such communicative emotion expressions as a source of relevant information about unfamiliar referents. In contrast, human infants appear to be able to do so from very early as, in fact, they tend to seek out others' referential emotion displays actively and intentionally – at least by the end of their first year of life. Recently, several studies on social referencing in humans have provided clear evidence showing that infants actively initiate communicative referential gestures, such as 'proto-interrogative' pointing (Southgate, van Maanen, & Csibra, 2007), ostensively addressed to knowledgeable social partners (caregivers as well as unfamiliar adults) in order to obtain relevant and new information about the indicated referent through the communicative emotion displays elicited from their addressee. Furthermore, it has also been demonstrated that human infants are more likely to selectively address such ostensive information requests to individuals who they represent as both competent and willing epistemic sources of relevant information concerning the referent about which they want to learn (Begus & Southgate, 2012; Kovács, Tauzin, Téglás, Gergely, & Csibra, 2014). By the end of their first year, infants also develop voluntary control over the intentional production of emotion displays to be used as ostensive gestures to communicatively address and inform their caregivers about valence-relevant properties of referents (Gergely, 2013; Gergely & Unoka, 2008).

4.1.3 *The role of ostensive communication and natural pedagogy in social learning by emotions in humans*

Here we shall argue that these human-specific modifications in the early functioning and intentional control of the emotion-based social learning programmes (including the increased scope of their possible eliciting conditions and the domain-generality of their referential application to manifest evaluative information about a broad variety of referents) reflect the important role that *ostensive communication* has come to play in social learning *by* emotions in humans. Humans have evolved species-unique cognitive adaptations for ostensive-inferential communication (Sperber & Wilson, 1986, 2002) and natural pedagogy (Csibra & Gergely, 2006, 2011; Gergely, Egyed, & Király, 2007) that have become selected to convey and exchange different kinds of relevant information about a broad scope of intended referents in various knowledge domains between cooperating social epistemic partners. Here we shall argue that these newly evolved human-specific systems for ostensive communication and mind reading that serve relevant information transfer have co-opted and put to modified (and extended) use the basic repertoire of referential emotion-expressive behavioural displays that had already been available as part of the more ancient adaptations for emotion-based social learning programmes. When employed in an ostensive communicative context, however, these emotion-expressive referential displays have become 're-used' in a modified manner (see Gergely, 2013) as intentionally produced, informative communicative gestures to ostensively manifest relevant (valence-related) information about the intended referent 'for' the addressee to infer and learn about.

Of course, the more ancient primary adaptations of emotion-based social learning systems continue to function automatically in humans as well, according to their original evolved design, whenever activated in a third-person – social and referential – observational context (similarly to the manner they are employed for affective valence-learning about novel food items through the disgust-based emotional learning system in non-human primates). However, as pointed out by Blair (2003), and as the social referencing studies with human infants discussed above indicate, it is significant that infants – apart from observing others' referential emotion displays from a third-person viewpoint (as is typically the case in affective valence learning about referents in other primate species) – are often presented with such valence-expressive referential displays in a second-person ostensive communicative interactive context. In such communicative and pedagogical contexts, infants are addressed by specialized ostensive gestures (such as establishing eye contact or being addressed in motherese, see Csibra, 2010; Csibra & Gergely, 2006, 2009), which express the other's communicative intention to convey to them relevant and new information (their informative intention) about an intended referent. When preceded or accompanied by ostensive signals, the motor display patterns of referential emotion expressions also tend to be intentionally modified and transformed in an ostensively 'marked' manner (see Gergely, 2013) to indicate their function as ostensive manifestations of relevant and new information about the referent 'for' the infant to infer and learn about.

In sum, our proposal is that, in humans, the referential emotion displays of the primary social learning programmes often appear hierarchically embedded in and recruited by the evolved system of ostensive inferential communication. When used in such second-person ostensive contexts, they serve as informative referential gestures that are produced intentionally and often in an ostensively marked manner in order to manifest and convey relevant new information or culturally shared knowledge for the addressee about various types of referents or referent kinds. This offers an explanation for the fact that the human-specific modifications allowing for the ostensive communicative use of emotion displays also led to a significant relaxation and flexible extension of the built-in constraints that characterize the primary functional use of communicative and referential emotion expressions in non-human primate species, which are restricted to automatically triggered displays induced in non-ostensive, third-person, social observational learning contexts.

Given this analysis, we are now in a better position to specify more precisely what we refer to when we speak about 'social emotions' as ontological dispositional kind concepts that humans assume to share with other social members of their cultural community. On the one hand, this conceptualization of social emotions refers to the kinds of underlying causal dispositional emotional states that humans infer and attribute to each other in order to account for and justify their emotion-induced actions and emotion displays during communicative social interactions. On the other hand, human social emotions are those kinds of dispositional emotion states that we intentionally express and voluntarily display as ostensive communicative gestures to realize our communicative and informative intentions towards our social partners. The goal of such ostensive uses of emotion displays is to influence and modify our social partners' motivational, emotional, and epistemic mental states, as well as their evaluative attitudes in relation to social and moral values, actions, and reputational concerns. Thus, human social emotions are considered to be communicatively employed emotional dispositional states that are ostensively manifested to convey relevant information with the intention to change our social partners' intentional mental states through the evolved mechanisms of ostensive communication and natural pedagogy. In other words, our social emotions are dispositional emotional kind states that we assume to share with other persons in our social and cultural community and that we can infer, recognize, label, display, and communicate about to justify and evaluate each others' emotion-induced actions and opinions within social and cultural interactive contexts.

4.1.4   *Evidence for social learning by emotions in ostensive communicative contexts*

We have proposed that when referential emotion displays are manifested in an ostensive communicative context, human infants are able to learn about relevant valence-related referent properties that they infer from the demonstrated valence information conveyed in relation to the referent object. In fact, in earlier work (Egyed, Király & Gergely, 2013; Gergely et al., 2007) we hypothesized that referential emotion expressions can provide two types of information for the infant as a function of the context in which they are observed. When such emotion displays are ostensively manifested in a second-person communicative context, infants interpret them in an 'object-centred' manner as conveying relevant valence-related information about their referent that is generalizable to other members of the referent kind as well. Furthermore, infants also assume that communicatively presented emotion expressions manifest shared cultural knowledge about their referent that is available to other individuals as well in their social and cultural community. However, when the emotion displays are observed in a third-person non-ostensive context, infants interpret them in a 'person-centred' manner as providing information about the person-specific disposition or subjective preference of the individual toward the referent object.

For example, in a violation-of-expectation looking time study with 14-month-olds, Gergely et al. (2007) demonstrated that when two models displayed emotion expressions with contrastive valence towards two different kinds of referent objects in an ostensive communicative context, infants encoded only which object was referred to as having a positive valence, and which object was referred to as negative, but they did not differentiate the models' contrastive preferences. So, when the emotion expressions were communicatively addressed to them, infants relied on an 'object-centred' interpretation and formed generalized expectations that all others will perform the same kind of object-directed actions that are appropriate given the objective valence quality of the referent. This evidence suggests that the referential valence information becomes part of the infant's newly formed object representation when it is presented ostensively.

In addition, in a further study in which object-directed emotion expressions were displayed either in communicative or non-communicative contexts, it was shown that 18-month-olds could flexibly assign either a person-centred preference interpretation or an object-centred valence interpretation to the referential emotion displays as a function of the kind of observation context in which they appeared. When a first model presented them with object-directed valence information in a second-person ostensive communicative manner (demonstrating contrastive emotional attitude expressions, e.g. joy/interest vs. dislike/disgust, towards two different kinds of referent objects respectively), infants were ready to use their newly learnt knowledge about object valence to respond to the communicative object-request addressed to them by a second, different person (who entered the scene after the first model had left) by handing her the object towards which the first model had expressed a positive emotional attitude (joy/interest). In contrast, in a non-communicative third-person observational condition where infants observed the first model's object-directed emotion displays without accompanying ostensive signals being addressed to them, they understood that the emotion expressions manifested person-specific preference information, which applied only to the individual who displayed them. This was shown by the finding that infants in this condition did not generalize the valence information expressed by the first model towards the objects when they responded to the second person's object-request (giving her one or the other object with equal likelihood). However, when the first model herself returned to ask for one of the objects, the infants could recall her previously expressed person-specific preference and gave her the object towards which she had initially expressed a positive emotional attitude. These findings indicate that infants are prepared to learn and generalize socially shared knowledge about object valences from non-verbal referential emotion displays at an early age as long as the object-directed emotion expressions are presented to them in an ostensive communicative manner, confirming the previous study. These studies, therefore, provide converging evidence demonstrating that referential emotion displays expressed in an ostensive communicative context convey an interpretation that the valence information expressed about the referent is generalizable to the referent kind and represents universally shared knowledge that is available to all individuals in one's social-cultural community (Egyed et al., 2013; Gergely et al., 2007).

4.2   Social learning *about* emotions in humans

4.2.1   *Why do we feel our emotions? Self-attribution of dispositional emotion states and emotional self-control*

Below we shall argue that social emotions are represented as inferred and attributed underlying dispositional state changes that contain various kinds of causally relevant information. These include the type of challenge that the emotion-evoking conditions represent (e.g. danger), the specific goals (e.g. removal of threat), and action tendencies induced (e.g. fight or flight), perceptual and attentional orientation, evaluative inferential and representational processes, and patterns of internal (visceral and proprioceptive) bodily changes characteristic of the dispositional emotion state (e.g. fear). The contents of the attributed set of causally relevant dispositional changes support inferences and predictions about the actions the person is likely to perform to cope with or resolve the challenge that the emotion-inducing conditions represent. Thus, we argue that the differential patterns of physiological and visceral bodily states that drive appropriate coping reactions form one of the central causal components of the underlying dispositional emotion states ascribed. One may, however, ask: what is the functional role of the person's introspective access and phenomenological subjective awareness of the specific bodily state changes that the emotion-triggering conditions induced in him? In other words: why do we 'feel' our dispositional emotional state changes, when these internal bodily reactions could (and sometimes apparently do) perform their adaptive causal function of generating appropriate coping responses even without the individual being consciously aware of them? Furthermore, do infants have similar introspective access and subjectively felt experience of their changed dispositional emotional states in the same way as adults who can verbally report detecting their categorical dispositional emotion states?

Gergely and Watson (1996, 1999; see also Gergely & Unoka, 2007, 2008) have proposed that the evolved adaptive function of such introspective access to one's own dispositional internal state changes serves the function of *self-attribution* of emotions by detecting, diagnosing, and ascribing to oneself one's own changed categorical dispositional states. This ability allows one to predict the reactions one is likely to produce in the emotion-inducing circumstances, which serves the vital function of *self-control* when the self's anticipated emotional reactions need to be inhibited or modified because of the possible negative consequences that they may induce in other social agents (or in the self as a consequence of other social agents negative reaction induced towards them) in the given social, cultural, and situational circumstances.

In this view, emotional self-control will become possible with the establishment of secondary representations and control structures that (a) introspectively monitor, detect, and evaluate the primary level dispositional emotional state changes induced in oneself; and (b) can inhibit or modify the self's anticipated emotional reactions that would be likely to be automatically induced by the dispositional state change and could be expected to induce negative reactions in others (consequently leading to negative outcomes for the self) in the given social and situational context.

Therefore, a precondition for the voluntary control and self-regulation of dispositional emotion states is that the meta-representational level of self-monitoring and self-attribution (that detects and represents one's own primary dispositional state changes) and the voluntary control processes it has access to, should be informed about the ongoing dispositional state changes that are induced in one's internal bodily states by the emotion-triggering conditions. Within this framework, consciously felt emotions can be conceived of as internal *signals* that inform the level of meta-representational processes that monitor the self's primary dispositional states about the automatic affective state changes that have been induced in the organism. As secondary representations of discrete dispositional state changes become established and can be ascribed to the self, they will be subject to a process of representational elaboration as a result of the learning processes linking emotion expressions with types of situations and characteristic behavioural outcomes. At this point, the dispositional contents of one's emotion states, which come to be encoded by one's second-order categorical emotion representations, become cognitively accessible and can serve as the basis for action prediction when the emotion state is attributed to the self or to the other.

Gergely and Watson (1996, 1999) also hypothesized that the infant in its initial state is not yet sensitive to the groups of internal state cues that are indicative of discrete changes in their dispositional emotion states: an introspective capacity, which forms a precondition for self-attribution of categorical emotion states and their changes to oneself. In this view, therefore, the set of internal (visceral as well as proprioceptive) cues that are activated when being in and expressing a dispositional emotion state are, at first, not detected or perceived consciously by the infant, or, at least, are not grouped together categorically in such a manner that they could be perceptually accessed by introspective monitoring as a distinctive dispositional emotion state that has been induced in oneself in the given context.

Neither do young infants appear to be able to exercise sufficient voluntary control over their automatic emotional reactions, as they seem to possess only rudimentary means of affective self-regulation at this early stage of development (such as turning away from over-arousing stimuli or thumb-sucking, see Demos, 1986; Malatesta, Culver, Tesman, & Shepard, 1989). In fact, the dominant, biosocial view of emotional

development holds that mother and infant form an affective communication system from the beginning of life (Bowlby, 1969; Fonagy, Gergely,
Jurist, & Target, 2002; Fonagy, Gergely, & Target, 2007; Hobson, 1993;
Stern, 1985; Trevarthen & Aitken, 2001; Tronick, 1989) in which the
caregiver plays a vital interactive and adaptive role in modulating the
infant's affective states (Field, 1994; Fonagy et al., 2002, 2007; Malatesta &
Izard, 1984; Tronick & Cohn, 1989). Mothers are normally rather efficient
at reading their infants' emotion displays and inferring their internal
dispositional state changes, and sensitive caregivers tend to attune their
own affective responses to modulate their infant's emotional states in an
adaptive manner (Malatesta et al., 1989; Fonagy et al., 2002, 2007; Gergely,
2007b; Tronick, 1989).

   Furthermore, Gergely and Watson (1996, 1999) hypothesized that at
the beginning of life, the perceptual system is set with a bias to attend
to and explore the external world, and builds representations primarily
on the basis of exteroceptive stimuli. According to this proposal, the
dispositional content of discrete emotions is learned first by observing
the affect-expressive displays of others and associating them with the
evoking situations and behavioural outcomes that accompany these
emotion expressions. In this view, while young infants may have some
initial awareness of the component stimuli that belong to the groups
of internal state cues, which are indicative of the onset of categorical
dispositional emotion states but only as part of the 'blooming, buzzing
confusion' (James, 1890/1950) of internal sense-impressions they may
experience. Such internal state cues may also contribute to the overall
(positive or negative) hedonic quality of the infant's awareness (and may
play important evolved reinforcing functions of the kind that Blair (2007)
hypothesized to mediate the learning effects of the core emotion-based
social learning programmes).

4.2.2   The social bio-feedback theory of emotion mirroring

But how does the infant develop awareness of and come to represent the
sets of internal state cues as indicative of categorically distinct emotion
states of the self? According to Gergely and Watson's 'social bio-feedback
theory', the species-specific human propensity for the facial and vocal
reflection of the infant's automatic emotion-expressive displays during
affect-regulative interactions plays an important role in this developmental process. It is proposed that the infant's repeated experience
with being presented with a contingent external reflection of his affect-
expressive displays in a given type of evoking context serves a 'teaching'
function that results in gradual sensitization to the relevant internal state
cues as well as to the identification of the correct set of internal stimuli
that correspond to the distinctive categorical emotion states that the baby

is in. As a result of this process, the infant will eventually come to develop an introspective attentional orientation and increasing awareness of the distinctive internal cues that in a given type of context are indicative of the categorical emotion states he is in, and will become able to detect, represent, and self-attribute his particular discrete dispositional emotion states.

Based on Watson's foundational work on infants' innate capacity for contingency detection and maximizing (see Watson, 1985, 1994, for a review), Gergely and Watson (1996, 1999) proposed that the hypothesized sensitization effects of parental emotion-reflective interactions are mediated by the same psychological mechanism that has been demonstrated in *bio-feedback training procedures* (e.g. Dicara, 1970; Miller, 1969, 1978). In such studies, continuous measurements are made of the ongoing state changes of some internal stimulus state to which the subject has no direct perceptual access initially (such as changes in blood pressure). The internal state changes registered are mapped on to an *external* stimulus equivalent, contingently presented and directly observable to the subject, the state of which co-varies with that of the internal stimulus. Repeated exposure to such an externalized representation of the internal state eventually results in *sensitization to* and in certain cases subsequent *control over* the internal state changes. Thus, the basic proposal is that contingent parental affect-reflecting responses provide a kind of *natural social bio-feedback training* for the infant (for details, see Gergely & Watson, 1996).

In this view, the parent who (unlike the infant) is able to read and interpret the baby's facial, vocal, or postural emotion-expressive behavioural displays will produce affect-modulating interactive behaviours, which will include the repeated production of contingent external reflections of the baby's internal emotional state changes. This interactive process can be conceived of as a case of intuitive instructed learning in which the 'teacher' function is played by the repeated presentation of the parent's affect-reflective emotion expression, which is contingent on the presence of the dispositional emotion-state changes that the infant is going through.

There are two central developmental functions of interest here that are served by the caregiver's contingent reflections of the infant's emotionally expressive behavioural displays. The first is *the sensitization function*: as a result of the contingent social bio-feedback training, the infant becomes able to detect and group together the sets of internal state cues that are indicative of his distinct dispositional emotion states that the parent attributes and reflects to them. The second is *the representation-building function*: by setting up separate representations for the parent's ostensively 'marked' emotion-reflective gestures that are contingent with the infant's emotion-expressive behaviours and refer to the discrete emotion state the baby is perceived to be in, the infant will establish secondary representations that become associated with his – originally non-conscious and procedural – dispositional emotion states. Importantly, these emotion-reflective parental displays also tend to be accompanied by the production of emotion-expressive *words* whose referential meaning will start to become established in this process as well as second-order representations of the primary dispositional emotion states they reference. These secondary representational structures will then provide the cognitive means for meta-representational introspective monitoring, accessing, and attributing discrete emotion states to the self, and will form the basis for the infant's emerging ability for voluntarily emotional self-control.

4.2.3   *Social bio-feedback as ostensive referential communication*

Elsewhere (Fonagy et al., 2002; Gergely, 2007b, 2013; Gergely & Watson, 1996, 1999; Gergely & Unoka, 2007, 2008), we have emphasized the functional importance of the fact that contingent empathic emotion-reflective displays tend to be executed in a saliently *marked* manner that perceptually clearly distinguishes them from the caregiver's corresponding realistic emotion expressions. Such 'marked' affect-reflecting displays are *saliently transformed versions* of the normative motor display patterns of the corresponding realistic emotion expressions of the caregiver. Some of the typical features of 'markedness' involve: (a) exaggerated, slowed-down execution of the spatial-temporal display pattern of the corresponding realistic, normative emotion expression; (b) schematic, sometimes abbreviated or only partial execution of the normative display pattern of the same emotion; and (c) accompanying the contingent emotion-reflective parental display by *ostensive communicative signals, emotion-expressive words and referential gestures*, including direct eye contact, referential gaze-direction at the emoting baby, eyebrow flashing, slightly tilted head, widely opened eyes, and so on (see Gergely, 2013).

Gergely and Watson's original interpretation of the function of this kind of distinctive 'marking' of parental affect-reflective emotion displays (Gergely & Watson, 1996) emphasized its importance as a cue signalling to the infant that the emotion display is 'not for real', and that its expressed emotional content should be decoupled from the caregiver. In other words, marked emotion displays indicate to the infant that the attribution of the expressed emotion as the real emotion state of the caregiver should be inhibited. This was considered especially important in cases when the caregiver's contingent emotion expression reflects a *negative* emotion display of the infant. When salient marking of the emotion mirroring display is absent in such cases, the infant could easily confuse the observed external emotional reaction with the corresponding normative emotion expression. This could lead to the attribution of the expressed emotion to the caregiver as her actual, realistic negative affect state. The consequent perception of the caregiver being in, and expressing toward the infant, a realistic negative emotion state could then induce traumatic escalation, rather than contingent emotion regulation of the baby's negative emotion state.

More recently (see Gergely, 2007b; Gergely & Unoka, 2007, 2008), this functional characterization of 'markedness' has been extended by generalizing it in two ways. First, it was proposed that ostensively framed, marked, emotion-reflective parental displays constitute a special kind of instance of the general class of ostensive referential communicative 'teaching' manifestations generated by the human-specific cultural learning system called *natural pedagogy* (Csibra & Gergely, 2009, 2011; Gergely, 2007b, 2013; Gergely & Csibra, 2005, 2006; Gergely et al., 2007). In particular, in this interpretation, ostensively communicated, marked, emotion-reflective displays can be conceived of as pedagogical teaching manifestations where the relevant cultural information being conveyed for the infant to learn is that his currently expressed dispositional emotion state (that is contingently reflected in a marked manner and is being referenced by emotion expressive words by the 'teacher') belongs to those categorical emotions that are socially shared by (and can be communicated to) other members of the cultural community that the infant belongs to.

This interpretation can also provide a more principled and generalized explanatory account of why the marked emotion-reflective displays of the caregiver are interpreted self-referentially by the infant, leading to their referential *anchoring* (in the form of internalized second-order representations) to those internal dispositional emotion states that the mirroring displays contingently reflect. Furthermore, this new interpretation of 'marked' emotion mirroring displays constitutes a form of ostensive pedagogical communication that referentially identifies and is 'about' the particular dispositional emotion state the infant is in. Such emotion-reflective interactions also convey relevant information about the socially shared categorical emotion kind that the infant's dispositional emotion state exemplifies. The ostensive communicative context of contingent emotion-reflective displays also provides an account of why the ostensive referential cues that include the features of 'markedness' of affect-reflecting expressions help to establish an introspective orientation of the infant's (initially externally biased) attentional processes. Considering marked affect-mirroring as a case of pedagogical communication referencing the infant's self-states also sheds further explanatory light on the consequent increase in sensitivity to internal subjective affective states and the contingent effects of their expression on the external social environment.

4.3   Social emotions as ontological kind concepts

In our view, social emotions in humans are special types of ontological kind concepts that form part of the culturally shared ontological kind categories that humans possess and (assume to) have in common with other social agents in their cultural community. This approach to social-emotional kind concepts, therefore, implies a version of dispositional causal essentialism for representing the kinds of social emotion categories we attribute to and share with other social agents in our cultural community. Essentialism is the idea that entities of various kinds have essential underlying causal properties, which are not directly observable but are causally responsible for the observable features of the entities that bear them (Kripke, 1972/1980; Putnam, 1975). Psychological essentialism is the view that essentialism underlies human children's conceptual development in various cognitive domains (Carey, 1995; Gelman, 2003; Kelemen & Carey, 2007; Medin, & Ortony, 1989). The assumed underlying essential property of a kind concept is represented in terms of a 'causal placeholder' representation (Carey, 2009; Gopnik & Nazzi, 2003) that may be empty or whose contents may be opaque to the child. Infants appear to assume that different words refer to different kind concepts, so, when learning the meaning of novel words, they open an 'empty causal place-holder' representation for the underlying abstract causal essence that they assume to be responsible for the observable properties of the particular referents that belong to the kind category the verbal label refers to. Young children have been argued to make essentialist assumptions not only about natural biological and material kinds (such as dogs or gold), but also about human-made artefact kinds (such as tools serving – and designed for – their essential proper function and characterized by their normative functional use) or social kinds (such as normative traditions or religious rituals) (Futó, Téglás, Csibra, & Gergely, 2010; Gergely & Jacob, 2012; Király, Csibra, & Gergely, 2013). Here we suggest extending this essentialist approach to the acquisition of dispositional emotion concepts and the meaning of emotion-expressive words as well.[1]

---

[1] Note that differentiating 'biological and natural' vs 'social and cultural' concepts is not a binary and mutually exclusive distinction when applied to essentialist kind concepts in humans. There can be biologically based but culturally specified ontological kinds as can be argued, for example, in the case of our conceptualization of different kinds of tools. The underlying causal essence of artefact kinds is represented in terms of the function they normatively serve and for which they had been designed (see Kelemen & Carey, 2007). While humans may have evolved an abstract kind concept of functional artefacts, they will need to acquire further culture-specific information to identify the specific functions and normative uses served by the particular kinds of artefacts that exist in our culture and that belong to the set of ontological kind categories shared by our social and cultural community. In this case biological and cultural factors appear to interact in determining the specific contents of our shared ontological kind categories.

We suggest that the kinds of social emotion categories we attribute to and assume to share with others refer to the specific type of changes in the underlying causal dispositional states and properties that are induced in an agent by emotion-triggering input conditions.[2] The dispositional changes so induced are assumed and represented to possess relevant causal power to generate the kind of adaptive coping reactions and emotion expressions the person is likely to perform to deal with or resolve the challenge represented by the emotion-inducing situations. Assuming that a set of normativity conditions apply (see Gergely & Jacob, 2012; Millikan, 1984, 1993; Neander, 1995; Prinz, 2004), we can then rely on the specific kind of dispositional changes attributed to the person to anticipate, account for, or justify his consequent actions in the given situation.

The social emotions we ascribe to others (or to ourselves) refer to specific kinds of dynamic and temporary dispositional states that an individual is inferred and represented to be 'in' currently or for some period of time due to the causal triggering conditions that induced the emotion state. (This dynamic and temporal aspect of the dispositional state changes that characterize a person's transient emotion states differentiates the emotional dispositions from the stable and enduring underlying causal dispositional and affordance properties that are represented and attributed as the causal essence of natural biological or material kinds, or physical artefact kinds, see Armstrong, 1968; Ryle, 1949; Watson, 1995). The view of dispositional essentialism for social emotion kinds outlined above represents the underlying causal 'essence' of the social emotion ascribed to a person as the set of relevant causal dispositional state changes that the emotion-triggering input conditions have induced in the agent. (Apart from characteristic changes in bodily arousal and visceral states, these also include changes in perceptual and attentional orientation, cognitive inferential processes, and consequent informational – e.g. evaluative – representational states as well.) The inferred dispositional state changes and properties attributed to the person are assumed to have relevant causal power or potential to bring about (or at least causally influence) the kinds of adaptive actions, reactions, and emotion-expressive

---

Our current proposal that social emotions are dispositional kind concepts that also belong to our socially and culturally shared ontological kinds is, therefore, a further extension of this essentialist conceptual framework. Emotion categories do have a biological core, but their representation as shared ontological kinds becomes enriched by learning about a set of further – and often culture-specific – relevant information that contributes to the numerous underlying causal factors, which determine the surface manifestations of specific dispositional emotion states such as their behavioural expressions or their expectable social consequences in various cultural contexts.

[2] Dispositional states refer here to transient emotional states causally induced at the moment while dispositional properties refer to (more) stable emotional (temperamental) traits that become causally activated: contrast 'he became irritated by the joke' vs 'his irritability became activated by the joke'.

communicative displays that the person is likely to perform to efficiently cope with the challenge represented by the triggering conditions that induced the emotion state in the first place.

4.3.1 Social emotion concepts and dispositional essentialism

The version of dispositional causal essentialism for social emotion kinds we propose is in clear contrast with the dominant (as well as classical) view of *biological essentialism* of emotions (that goes back to ideas of Aristotle, Descartes, and Darwin), which is currently represented by much influential research within the general framework of 'basic' or 'differential emotions theory' as developed by Tomkins, Ekman, Izard, and their followers (see for reviews e.g. Clément & Dukes, Introduction, this volume; Ekman, 1992). This classical view of biological essentialism assumes that emotions evolved as differential patterns of internal changes in physiological and visceral bodily states that are triggered by specific input conditions (e.g. stimuli representing danger trigger the basic emotion of fear). The primary adaptive and causal function of the evolved patterns of basic emotional bodily states induced by emotion-triggering stimuli is assumed to be the optimization of the body's readiness to engage in specific types of goal-directed action tendencies (such as fight or flight) in order to cope with the challenge of the environmental triggering conditions that evoked them (Ekman & Friesen, 1974). Within this framework, differential facial emotion expressions are considered to be additional, automatic causal consequences of the basic bodily emotion states induced by the particular emotion-triggering contexts (Ekman, 1992; Ekman, Levenson, & Friesen, 1983). As a result, the automatically induced differential emotion displays de facto manifest and provide externally detectable universal indicators of the internal basic emotion states the body is induced to be in. In this view, the specific pattern of physiological and visceral bodily state changes constitutes the *internal causal essence* of basic emotions whose evolved primary function is to prepare the agent's adaptive behavioural reactions to cope with the exigencies of the environmental triggering conditions that activated them. The specific facial and vocal emotion expressive displays, however, are considered only as causally induced automatic by-products that provide non-intentional but observable behavioural indicators of the basic emotional states that have been induced in the organism.

During the last decades, much empirical and cross-cultural work has focused on testing the central tenets of 'differential emotions theory' (Ekman, 1992; Ekman, Friesen, & Ellsworth, 1972; Ekman et al., 1983) with mixed and sometimes arguably negative results (e.g. Crivelli and Fridlund, 2018; Nelson & Russell, 2013; see also Clément & Dukes,

Introduction, this volume, for a review). These studies concentrated on testing two basic developmental propositions of differential emotions theory: (1) that there is an evolved and universal set of differentiable facial expressions of basic emotions detectable early in life, which are triggered by (2) the onset of identifiable, specific, and differential patterns of physiological and visceral bodily state changes that constitute the evolved set of basic emotions, which are automatically induced under specific input circumstances. These approaches and their critical findings rendered the theoretical proposals postulating an innate set of basic, differential, and universal emotion expressions, on the one hand, and the corresponding differential patterns of internal changes in physiological and visceral bodily states that constitute categorical emotions on the other, at least controversial, while some of the more radical critics went so far as to outright reject the evolutionary-based theory of basic emotions (Nelson & Russell, 2013; Russell, 2013).

Instead of providing an evaluative review of this complex critical literature (for that, see Barrett, 2006; Jurist, 2018; Russell, 2013), we shall argue that the scrutinized core assumptions of the view of biological essentialism represented by basic emotion theory are not vital elements of and have no direct consequences to the functionalist version of *dispositional essentialism* we are advocating for social emotion categories in humans. In fact, in our view, many of the recent criticisms that not only questioned the particular assumptions of the differential emotions theory they tested, but went further to reject all other essentialist construals of emotions in general (e.g. Crivelli, & Fridlund, 2018), make the mistake of throwing out the baby with the bathwater, as they end up unable to account for a number of significant properties of human social emotions that can be captured by (and call for) a theory of dispositional essentialism of social emotion concepts.

4.3.2   *The epistemic functions of dispositional essentialism about social emotions*

In contrast, according to the present proposal, the attributed dispositional state changes induced by the emotion-triggering conditions include all the relevant causal factors that are likely to influence the kinds of reactions, emotion displays, cognitive inferences, and evaluative processes that the person is likely to engage, in order to cope with the emotion-inducing situation. Therefore, the inferred and attributed causal dispositional state changes will support the observer's *informative inferences and predictions* about the individual's likely reactions, emotion expressive behaviours, cognitive inferences, and evaluative representations that he will produce to deal with the challenges that the given emotion-triggering context represents for him.

Furthermore, recent evolutionary arguments about the adaptive nature and evolutionary origins of the human capacity for reasoning have emphasized its central argumentative and justificatory functions in social interactions and cooperation (Mercier & Sperber, 2011, 2017). Within this framework, justifying one's actions by making reference to the causal emotional dispositional states that induced it can serve important social epistemic functions in persuasion, argumentation, and social reasoning about the (normative) appropriateness and degree of social acceptability of an agent's actions under particular social, normative, or moral contexts. Pointing at a given dispositional emotion state as a reason for one's behaviour functions to provide or at least to offer potential *justification for the person's actions* to be considered for social evaluation by others in socially relevant and typically normative interactive or moral situations (Mercier & Sperber, 2017). Therefore, inferring, ascribing, and normatively evaluating the causal dispositional emotion states that one is in and that one perceives and/or claims to drive one's actions have come to play a central justificatory and argumentative role in social, normative, and moral interactions and reputation management.

4.3.3   Social emotions are intentional mental states

Social emotions, therefore, are not reducible to differential patterns of physiological and visceral bodily states even though the dispositional state changes that they imply do involve – as a central causal component – such specific bodily state changes. When we infer and attribute social emotion states to others (or ourselves) we, in fact, ascribe specific kinds of intentional mental states to them, which are characterized by 'aboutness' and 'referentiality' that are defining properties of intentional mental states such as beliefs, desires, and other representational mental attitudes. That the social emotion states we infer and ascribe to persons, in fact, belong to the class of intentional mental states, is also shown by the fact that terms for emotions, like other 'intentional idioms', express propositional attitudes and, as such, are characterized by the semantic property of 'referential opacity' (Dennett & Haugeland, 1987; Quine, 1960). This refers to the fact that certain logical operations, such as the substitutability of terms with identical referents, break down in the case of expressions involving intentional relations such as 'x believes that p' or 'y desires that q'. Thus, while the statement 'Oedipus was angry about Laius' comments' is true, it does not follow that 'Oedipus was angry about his father's comments' is also true, even though 'Laius' and 'Oedipus' father' refer to the same individual (since Oedipus may not know or may have forgotten who his father is).

The social emotions we infer and attribute to others (or ourselves) as temporary *dispositional states or properties* are therefore special kinds of intentional mental states that show *'aboutness' in relation to some referent object or event*, and that involve *'evaluative'* dispositional attitudes 'about' and 'towards' their represented referent object or evoking condition. So, in this view, the social emotions ascribed to an individual are not simply sensations of visceral bodily states but are, as philosophers say, *intentional mental or dispositional states* with 'formal objects' that they are 'about' and that have the power of causally inducing them. Thus, the formal object of fear is a threatening object (or any conditions perceived, inferred or imagined that is evaluated as representing danger). As pointed out by Prinz (2004), this assumes a meaning-conferring causal relation between the kinds of emotions induced and the types of eliciting conditions that trigger them. This view also requires access and attention to certain normativity assumptions or 'conditions of correctness' under which the induction and attribution of specific emotional dispositional states take place and where the emotion-driven coping responses they cause can be considered 'appropriate' and adaptive within the given social cultural context.

4.4   Natural pedagogy and the transmission of socially shared cultural knowledge about kind concepts

The theory of natural pedagogy proposes a human-specific cognitive adaptation of mutual design that exploits humans' preparedness for ostensive-inferential communication (Sperber & Wilson, 1986, 2002) for the fast and efficient transmission of ontological kind categories and generic knowledge in various content domains that are shared by members of one's social and cultural community (Csibra & Gergely, 2006, 2011; Gergely, 2007a, 2013; Gergely & Csibra, 2005, 2006; Gergely et al., 2007).

Knowledgeable caregivers take a pedagogical attitude toward their naïve infant: as expert adults, they show a natural inclination to display ostensive communicative cues (such as eye contact or addressing the infant in motherese), together with marked forms of referential gestures and knowledge demonstrations. On the recipients' side, such ostensive pedagogical signals trigger a specific type of attentional orientation and a receptive learning attitude in the infants. Following Grice's pragmatic approach to inferential communication (Grice, 1975, 1989), according to relevance theory (see Sperber & Wilson, 1986, 2002), humans evolved a species-unique capacity to recognize communicative agency showing special sensitivity to cues of communicative exchange of relevant information (such as turn-taking exchange of variable signals, see Tauzin & Gergely, 2018). Even young preverbal infants exhibit a readiness to engage in ostensive-referential communication when being addressed by ostensive signals (such as eye contact or motherese), which induce them to attribute to the other an overt 'communicative intention' to manifest and convey new and relevant information about an intended referent (the communicator's 'informative intention') for them to infer and acquire. In addition, as proposed and evidenced by natural pedagogy theory (Csibra & Gergely, 2006, 2009, 2011; Gergely and Csibra, 2005, 2006, 2013; Gergely et al., 2007; Gergely & Jacob, 2012) evolved sensitivity to ostensive addressing cues induce in infants, not only an expectation that the other's communicative gestures will be referential, but also that they will manifest relevant information about the intended referent that can be generalized to the kind category the referent belongs to (e.g. Futó et al., 2010) and that conveys cultural knowledge of ontological kinds that are shared by other members of their social and cultural community (e.g. Egyed et al., 2013). Ostensive cues induce in infants an attitude of basic epistemic trust (Gergely et al., 2007) and a fast-mapping receptive learning attitude to acquire the shared ontological categories and generic cultural knowledge that are manifested to them and that they assume all members of their social and cultural community possess. The types of new and relevant cultural knowledge that are typically transmitted through pedagogical communication include new words and gestural symbols (Gergely & Csibra, 2005, 2006; Vouloumanos and Waxman, 2014), artefact kinds, their normative functions and stereotypic use (Futó et al., 2010; Gergely, Bekkering, & Király, 2002; Király et al., 2013), valence-related information about object kinds (Egyed et al., 2013; Gergely et al., 2007), culturally habitual manners of actions (Gergely et al., 2002; Király et al., 2013), opaque rituals, and traditions. Here we propose to add to this list the transmission of culture-specific information about socially shared emotion kinds.

4.5 Conclusion: natural pedagogy as a mechanism for social learning of the dispositional contents of culturally shared emotional kind concepts

We have argued that recognizing, attributing, learning, and reasoning about the kinds of social emotions we share and ascribe to others (or to ourselves) in our social community can be best conceptualized as represented in terms of the specific type of changes in the underlying causal dispositional states that we infer to have been induced by particular types of emotion-triggering input conditions. The set of (temporal and dynamic) changes in the relevant dispositional emotion states inferred is represented as the underlying causal essence of the social emotion category that is ascribed to individuals and that is assumed to be shared by all social agents in one's cultural community.

The underlying causal essence of the kind of social emotions attributed to and shared by others must involve the representation of a complex set of relevant cultural and normative information. This includes information about the range of emotion-triggering input conditions and their socially shared significance, normative social expectations about the situational contexts for expressing (or inhibiting) the communicative displays of the emotion states induced, the kinds of internal bodily state changes and their level of experienced intensity, the social consequences of acting on and/or communicatively displaying the induced emotional states in various cultural contexts, and other, often rather culture-specific conditions. Recognizing, attributing, representing, and adaptively reasoning about social emotions, therefore, presupposes the acquisition of a variety of relevant information about the range of culturally acknowledged causal evoking conditions, cognitively often opaque and highly normative social display rules that specify the cultural contexts under which displaying an emotion is socially acceptable, discouraged, or required, and learning about the culture-specific social consequences of emotion-based actions that lead to evaluative appraisal of the self and influences its moral reputation.

As a striking example of the significant culture-specific differences in the various causal factors that constitute the underlying dispositional state changes that characterize specific social emotions such as anger, aggression, and shame, we can refer to the case of so-called honour cultures like the one found among Whites in the contemporary South of the United States, which has been investigated in detail by the social psychologists Nisbett and Cohen (1996). In laboratory studies, these authors showed that southern US college students were more likely than northern college students to respond with anger and act aggressively when they were insulted. The insult involved an unfamiliar person bumping into the participant as he was walking down the hallway who then insulted the participant verbally. Southern students were more than twice as likely as northern students to become visibly angry at the insult (85 per cent vs. 35 per cent). They showed surges in their levels of testosterone (a hormone associated with aggression, competition, and dominance) and cortisol (a hormone associated with stress and arousal) after the bump. They were also more cognitively primed for aggression, completing scenarios with more violent endings. Additionally, southerners also became more aggressive as they subsequently walked down the hallway and encountered another individual (who was 6 feet 3 inches tall and weighed 250 pounds). In a culture of honour, a person (usually a man) feels obliged to protect his reputation by answering insults, affronts, and threats through the use of violence. Even small insults function as sufficient causal triggering conditions that induce a high degree of anger as they are interpreted to represent severe threats to one's (and one's family's) reputation leading to the culturally expected normative response of anger and violence in order to restore the threatened reputation. Failing to react with aggression, even to small (and in other cultures trivial and often non-consequential) insults, induces shame and embarrassment, and frequently leads to being shunned or expelled from one's family and social community.

Given the complex, normative, often cognitively opaque, and in many cases highly culture–specific conditions that constitute shared knowledge of social emotion categories, we have argued that they must be (and can only be fully) acquired from knowledgeable epistemic sources through ostensive communication, epistemic exchange, and pedagogical knowledge demonstrations. Therefore, in this chapter, we have proposed that the dispositional contents of the social emotion categories we share, infer, ascribe, name, communicate, and reason about when interacting with our social partners can only be adequately mastered through active social communicative exchange and epistemic inquiry, which exploit human-specific cognitive adaptations for ostensive communication. In particular, we have proposed that a central role is played in this affective social learning (ASL) process by the communicative learning mechanism of natural pedagogy that is specialized for manifesting and transmitting generic and often opaque categorical knowledge shared by the social and cultural community in a variety of ontological domains including dispositional emotion kinds.

References

Armstrong, D. M. (1968). *A materialist theory of mind*. New York, NY: Humanities Press.

Barrett, L. F. (2006). Emotions as natural kinds? *Perspectives on Psychological Sciences, 1*, 28–58.

Begus, K., & Southgate, V. (2012). Infant pointing serves an interrogative function. *Developmental Science, 15*(5), 611–617.

Blair, R. J. R. (2003). Facial expressions, their communicatory functions and neuro-cognitive substrates. *Philosophical Transactions of the Royal Society of London. Series B, Biological Sciences, 358*, 561–572.

 (2007). The amygdala and ventromedial prefrontal cortex in morality and psychopathy. *Trends in Cognitive Sciences, 11*(9), 387–392. doi: https://doi.org/10.1016/j.tics.2007.07.003

Bowlby, J. (1969). *Attachment and loss. Vol. 1: Attachment*. London, UK: Hogarth Press and the Institute of Psychoanalysis.

Carey, S. (1995). The growth of causal understandings of natural kinds. In D. Sperber, D. Premack, & A. J. Premack (Eds.), *Causal cognition: A multidisciplinary debate* (pp. 263–291). Oxford, UK: Clarendon Press.

 (2009). *The origin of concepts*. New York, NY: Oxford University Press.

Cheney, D. L., & Seyfarth, R. M. (1980). Vocal recognition in free-ranging vervet monkeys. *Animal Behaviour, 28*, 362–367.

Clutton-Brock, T. H. (2002) Breeding together: Kin selection, reciprocity and mutualism in cooperative animal societies, *Science, 296*, 69–72.

Crivelli, C., & Fridlund, A. J. (2018). Facial displays are tools for social influence. *Trends in Cognitive Sciences, 22*(5), 388–399.

Csibra, G. (2010). Recognizing communicative intentions in infancy. *Mind & Language, 25*, 141–168.

Csibra, G., & Gergely, G. (2006). Social learning and social cognition: The case of pedagogy. In M. H. Johnson & Y. M. Munakata (Eds.), *Processes change in brain and cognitive development: Attention and performance XXI* (pp. 249–274). Oxford, UK: Oxford University Press

(2009). Natural pedagogy. *Trends in Cognitive Sciences, 13*(4), 148–153.

(2011). Natural pedagogy as evolutionary adaptation. *Philosophical Transactions of the Royal Society of London. Series B, Biological Sciences, 366*, 1149–1157.

Demos, V. (1986). Crying in early infancy: An illustration of the motivational function of affect. In T. B. Brazelton & M. W. Yogman (Eds.), *Affective development in infancy* (pp. 39–73). Norwood, NJ: Ablex.

Dennett, D., & Haugeland, J. C. (1987). Intentionality. In R. L. Gregory (Ed.), *The Oxford companion to the mind* (pp. 383–386). Oxford, UK: Oxford University Press.

Dicara, L. V. (1970). Learning in the autonomic nervous system. *Scientific American, 222*, 30–39.

Egyed, K., Király, I., & Gergely, G. (2013). Communicating shared knowledge in infancy. *Psychological Science, 24*, 1348–1353.

Ekman, P. (1992). Facial expressions of emotion: New findings, new questions. *Psychological Science, 3*(1), 34–38.

Ekman, P., & Friesen, W. V. (1974). Detecting deception from body or face. *Journal of Personality and Social Psychology, 29*, 288–298.

Ekman, P., Friesen, W. V., & Ellsworth, P. (1972). *Emotion in the human face.* New York, NY: Pergamon Press.

Ekman, P., Levenson, R. W., & Friesen, W. V. (1983). Autonomic nervous system activity distinguishes between emotions. *Science, 221*, 1208–1210.

Field, T. (1994). The effects of mother's physical and emotional unavailability on emotion regulation. *Monographs of the Society for Research in Child Development, 59*(2–3), 208–227.

Fonagy, P., Gergely, G., Jurist, E., & Target, M. (2002). *Affect-regulation, mentalization, and the development of the self.* New York, NY: Other Press.

Fonagy, P., Gergely, G., & Target, M. (2007). The parent–infant dyad and the construction of the subjective self. *Journal of Child Psychology and Psychiatry, 48*(3–4), 288–328.

Futó, J., Téglás, E., Csibra, G., & Gergely, G. (2010). Communicative function demonstration induces kind-based artifact representation in preverbal infants. *Cognition, 117*, 1–8.

Gelman, S. A. (2003). *The essential child.* Oxford, UK: Oxford University Press.

Gergely, G. (2007a). Learning 'about' versus learning 'from' other minds: Human pedagogy and its implications. In P. Carruthers, S. Laurence, & S. Stich, (Eds.). *The innate mind: Foundations and the future* (pp. 170–198). Oxford, UK: Oxford University Press.

(2007b). The social construction of the subjective self: The role of affect-mirroring, markedness, and ostensive communication in self-development.

In L. Mayes, P. Fonagy, & M. Target (Eds.), *Developmental science and psychoanalysis* (pp. 45–88). London, UK: Karnac.

(2013). Ostensive communication and cultural learning: The natural pedagogy hypothesis. In H. S. Terrace & J. Metcalfe, (Eds.), *Joint attention and agency* (pp. 139–151). New York, NY: Oxford University Press.

Gergely, G., Bekkering, H., & Király, I. (2002). Rational imitation in preverbal infants. *Nature, 415*, 755.

Gergely, G., & Csibra, G. (2005). The social construction of the cultural mind: Imitative learning as a mechanism of human pedagogy. *Interaction Studies, 6*(3), 463–481.

(2006). Sylvia's recipe: The role of imitation and pedagogy in the transmission of cultural knowledge. In S. Levenson & N. Enfield (Eds.), *Roots of human sociality: Culture, cognition and human interaction* (pp. 229–255). Oxford, UK: Berg.

(2013). Natural pedagogy. In M. R. Banaj & S. A. Gelman (Eds.), *Navigating the social world: What infants, children, and other species can teach us* (pp. 127–132). Oxford, UK: Oxford University Press.

Gergely, G., Egyed, K., & Király, I. (2007). On pedagogy. *Developmental Science, 10*(1), 139–146.

Gergely, G., & Jacob, P. (2012). Reasoning about instrumental and communicative agency in human infancy. *Advances in Child Development and Behaviour, 43*, 59–94.

Gergely, G., & Unoka, Z. (2007). The development of the unreflective self. In F. N. Bush (Ed.), *Mentalization: Theoretical considerations, research findings, and clinical implications* (pp. 57–102). Hillsdale, NJ: Analytic Press.

(2008). Attachment, affect-regulation and mentalization: The developmental origins of the representational affective self. In C. Sharpe, P. Fonagy, & I. Goodyer (Eds.), *Social cognition and developmental psychology* (pp. 305–342). Oxford, UK: Oxford University Press.

Gergely, G., & Watson, J. S. (1996). The social bio-feedback theory of parental affect mirroring: The development of emotional self-awareness and self-control in infancy. *International Journal of Psychoanalysis, 77*, 7–31.

(1999). Early social-emotional development: Contingency perception and the social bio-feedback model. In P. Rochat (Ed.), *Early social cognition* (pp. 101–137). Hillsdale, NJ: Erlbaum.

Gopnik, A., & Nazzi, T. (2003). Words, kinds and causal powers: A theory theory perspective on early naming and categorization. In D. H. Rakison & L. M. Oakes (Eds.), *Early category and concept development: Making sense of the blooming, buzzing confusion* (pp. 303–329). New York, NY: Oxford University Press.

Grice, H. P. (1975). Logic and conversation. In P. Cole & J. Morgan (Eds.), *Syntax and semantics*. New York, NY: Academic Press.

(1989). *Studies in the way of words*. Cambridge, MA: Harvard University Press.

Hobson, R. P. (1993). *Autism and the development of mind*. Hove, UK: Lawrence Erlbaum.

James, W. [1890] (1950). *The principles of psychology*. New York, NY: Dover.

Jurist, E. (2018). *Minding emotions*. New York, NY: Guilford Press.

Kelemen, D., & Carey, S. (2007). The essence of artifacts: Developing the design stance. In E. Margolis & S. Lawrence (Eds.), *Creations of the mind: Theories of artifacts and their representation* (pp. 212–230). Oxford, UK: Oxford University Press.

Király, I., Csibra, G., & Gergely, G. (2013). Beyond rational imitation: Learning arbitrary means actions from communicative demonstrations. *Journal of Experimental Child Psychology 116*(2), 471–486.

Kovács, Á. M., Tauzin, T., Téglás, E., Gergely, G., & Csibra, G. (2014). Pointing as epistemic request: 12-month-olds point to receive new information. *Infancy, 19*(6), 543–557.

Kripke, S. (1972/1980). *Naming and necessity.* Cambridge, MA: Harvard University Press.

Malatesta, C. Z., Culver, C., Tesman, R. J., & Shepard, B. (1989). The development of emotion expression during the first two years of life. *Monographs of the Society for Research in Child Development, 54*, Serial No. 219.

Malatesta, C. Z., & Izard, C. E. (1984). The ontogenesis of human social signals: From biological imperative to symbol utilization. In N. A. Fox & R. J. Davidson (Eds.), *The psychobiology of affective development* (pp. 161–206). Hillsdale, NJ: Lawrence Erlbaum Associates.

Medin, D. L., & Ortony, A. (1989). Psychological essentialism. In S. Vosniadou & A. Ortony (Eds.), *Similarity and analogical reasoning* (pp. 179–195). Cambridge, UK: Cambridge University Press.

Mercier, H., & Sperber, D. (2011). Why do humans reason? Arguments for an argumentative theory. *Behavioral and Brain Sciences, 34*, 57–111.

(2017). *The enigma of reason.* Cambridge, MA: Harvard University Press.

Miller, N. E. (1969). Learning visceral and glandular responses. *Science, 163.* 434–445.

(1978). Bio-feedback and visceral learning. *Annual Review of Psychology, 29*, 373–404.

Millikan, R. G. (1984). *Language, thought and other biological categories.* Cambridge, MA: MIT Press.

(1993). *White queen psychology and other essays for Alice.* Cambridge, MA: MIT Press.

Mineka, S., & Cook, M. (1993). Mechanisms involved in the observational conditioning of fear. *Journal of Experimental Psychology: General, 122*, 23–38.

Neander, K. (1995). Misrepresenting and malfunctioning. *Philosophical Studies, 79*, 109–141.

Nelson, N. L., & Russell, J. A. (2013) Universality revisited. *Emotion Review, 5*, 8–15.

Nisbett, R. E., & Cohen, D. (1996). *Culture of honor: The psychology of violence in the South.* Boulder, CO: Westview.

Prinz, J. (2004). Embodied emotions. In R. C. Solomon & L. C. Harlan (Eds.), *Thinking about feeling: Contemporary philosophers on emotion*, Oxford, UK: Oxford University Press.

Putnam, H. (1975). The meaning of meaning. In K. Gunderson (Ed.), *Language, mind, and knowledge.* Minneapolis, MN: University of Minnesota Press.

Quine, W. V. (1960). *Word and object.* Cambridge, MA: MIT Press.

Russell, C. L., Bard, K. A., & Adamson, L. B. (1997). Social referencing by young chimpanzees (Pan troglodytes). *Journal of Comparative Psychology, 111*, 185–193.

Russell, J. A. (2013). *Agency: Its role in mental development*. London: Psychology Press.

Ryle, G. (1949). *The concept of mind*. London, UK: Hutchinson.

Snowden, C., & Boe, C. (2003). Social communication about unpalatable foods in tamarins (Saguinus oedipus). *Journal of Comparative Psychology, 117*, 142–148.

Southgate, V., van Maanen, C., & Csibra, G. (2007). Infant pointing: Communication to cooperate or communication to learn? *Child Development, 78*, 735–740.

Sperber, D., & Wilson, D. (1986). *Relevance: Communication and cognition*. Oxford, UK: Blackwell.

(2002). Pragmatics, modularity and mindreading. *Mind and Language, 17*, 3–23.

Stern, D. N. (1985). *The interpersonal world of the infant*. New York, NY: Basic Books.

Tauzin, T., & Gergely, G. (2018). Communicative mind-reading in preverbal infants. *Scientific Reports, 8*(9534).

Trevarthen, C., & Aitken, K. J. (2001) Infant intersubjectivity: Research, theory, and clinical applications. *Journal of Child Psychology and Psychiatry, 42*, 3–48.

Tronick, E. Z. (1989). Emotions and emotional communication in infants. *American Psychologist, 44*, 112–119.

Tronick, E. Z., & Cohn, J. F. (1989). Infant–mother face-to-face interaction: Age and gender differences in coordination and the occurrence of miscoordination. *Child Development, 60*, 85–92.

Vouloumanos, A., & Waxman, S. R. (2014). Listen up! Speech is for thinking during infancy. *Trends in Cognitive Sciences, 18*, 642–646.

Watson, J. S. (1985). Contingency perception in early social development. In T. M. Field & N. A. Fox (Eds.), *Social perception in infants* (pp. 157–176). Norwood, NJ: Ablex.

(1994). Detection of self: The perfect algorithm. In S. T. Parker, R. W. Mitchell, & M. L. Boccia (Eds.), *Self-awareness in animals and humans: Developmental perspectives* (pp. 131–148). New York, NY: Cambridge University Press.

(1995). Mother–infant interaction: Dispositional properties and mutual designs. In N. S. Thompson (Ed.), *Perspectives in ethology. Vol. 11. Behavioral design* (pp. 189–210). New York, NY: Plenum Press.

PART III

On the mechanics of affective social learning

CHAPTER 5

Calibrating emotional orientations

Social appraisal and other kinds of relation alignment

Brian Parkinson

Other people's emotions provide information about their relational orientations to objects, events, and other people. For example, finding out that someone is angry about something implies that they did not want it to happen and attribute the fact that it did to some external agency. We may conclude that what happened was unfair or that the angry person is predisposed to direct blame externally, specifically for this kind of event or more generally. These inferences depend on our knowledge of associations between discrete emotions and appraisal patterns (e.g. Elfenbein, 2007; Hareli & Hess, 2010; Parkinson, 1996). We extract the implications of an encapsulated emotional meaning. In other words, other people's specific emotions can explicitly teach us about person–environment transactions.

But there are also other, less explicit forms of interpersonal emotional influence. We may simply follow someone else's lead when orienting to a new event, e.g. by automatically sharing an ally's anger at any perceived provocation from our mutual enemy. We may adjust to unfolding relational processes in real time before any coherent emotional meaning consolidates, as happens when we melt into someone else's embrace. We may be attuned to the interpersonal affordances of the developing emotions of co-actors or interaction partners, falling into reciprocal states of communion or rapport. In each of these cases, our orientation towards other people changes in response to other people's oriented movements and signals. We sometimes come to terms with one another at an emotional level without explicitly registering those terms.

This chapter maps out some of the possible processes whereby emotions exert social influence leading to explicit and implicit learning relating to events, people, and the relations between them. As a result of these processes, learners may acquire new facts, attitudes, norms, skills, habits, and dispositions, or may change their existing beliefs or practices in response to other people's emotions. I focus specifically on triadic situations where two people calibrate orientations to something

117

or someone in their shared environment. When addressing these situations, most psychological research has focused on explicit inferential processes that lead to interpersonal effects on interpretation and evaluation of the emotion's intentional object, so I will consider ways in which existing paradigms might be extended to accommodate a broader range of processes and outcomes. My conclusion will be that emotions acquire their explicit meanings and implications as a consequence of developmentally earlier and conceptually prior processes of implicit relation alignment.

5.1   Extending the referencing paradigm

Interpersonal emotional influence starts right at the beginning of life when infants respond to the movements, sensations, and secretions that penetrate the womb. However, its paradigmatic manifestation is found in a situation of relatively weaker social dependence, one where toddler and caregiver are placed at a relatively greater physical and mental distance from one another, namely the social referencing scenario (see Clément & Dukes, Introduction, this volume).

The toddler is placed at the edge of a visual cliff, uncertain whether the glass surface above the drop is safe to cross (Sorce, Emde, Campos, & Klinnert, 1985). A questioning glance towards mum is met by a smile or a simulated gasping face intended to convey fear. The smile usually encourages forward crawling. The fear face never does.

A number of interrelated processes may contribute to this robust effect. Smiles provide incentives encouraging increased interpersonal closeness. Wide eyes directed at novel objects signal threat or uncertainty. They conflict with the toddler's expectation that the caregiver should offer a more affiliative response to their tentative request for engagement. They are not the usual interpersonal approach behaviours.

These possibilities suggest that social referencing effects might work without toddlers making inferences about appraisals based on the categorization of an emotion that is being explicitly communicated to them. However, the latter inferential explanation is the one that has gained most credence in the literature. The toddler requests information about the ambiguous object of the visual cliff, by looking in turn at the object, then the caregiver. The caregiver responds with clarificatory emotional information. The smile provides reassurance that the cliff is safe, whereas the mouth-gaping, wide-eyed "fear" face warns that it is dangerous. The toddler draws the intended conclusion and either behaves or stops behaving accordingly. In other words, the toddler not only registers the relation between the emotional object and their caregiver's orientation to it, but also changes their own behaviour in ways that imply sensitivity to the emotion's specific relational meaning.

Debates persist about the extent to which social referencing effects depend on differentiated inferences about appraisal rather than more directly detected approach or avoidance tendencies or valence displays (e.g. Walle, Reschke, Camras, & Campos, 2017). However, it seems clear that socialized humans acquire knowledge of typical appraisal-emotion connections at some stage of development, and that this knowledge ultimately becomes explicit. In principle, most adults are certainly capable of making inferences about other people's specific orientations to objects, events, or people on the basis of information about their supposed discrete emotions (e.g. Parkinson & Manstead, 1993; Smith & Lazarus, 1993). It would be surprising if they never applied this knowledge in order to draw conclusions and develop expectations about any of these things (e.g. Hareli & Hess, 2010). People certainly can learn something when they perceive other people's emotional orientations. But should we see these inferential processes of affective social learning (ASL) as prototypical and paradigmatic of social appraisal and triadic relation alignment more generally? Does the point at which humans develop this kind of emotional understanding of others represent a genuine developmental hinge-point or simply an overlapping stage of a more extended and complicated process? In the following sections, I consider more as well as less articulated ways in which emotions may exert social influence and induce affective learning, starting with those that have been investigated most intensively.

5.2   Social appraisal

The idea of social appraisal corresponds to the most common interpretation of social referencing effects. Indeed, Campos and Stenberg (1981) first used the term to describe "appraisal of how another individual is reacting emotionally to the event" (p. 275; see also Clément & Dukes, Introduction, this volume). In Manstead and Fischer's (2001) subsequent formulation, social appraisal covers the various ways in which personal appraisals incorporate the perceived appraisals of other people as picked up from their apparent emotional orientation to what is happening. Thus, toddlers may appraise their mother's fear as implying that they are facing a threatening situation, thereby clarifying the practical significance of the emotional object. Someone else's emotional orientations can also provide a guide to the normative appropriateness of a potential emotional response to an object, as happens when we refrain from laughing at an off-colour joke when our companion appears to be disgusted by its content (Manstead & Fischer, 2001). In both cases, we change our own appraisal to bring it more into line with the appraisal of another person. Correspondingly, picking up an enemy or opponent's emotional reaction may lead to divergent appraisals, as can happen when we gloat about a rival football team's misfortune on the basis of their supporters' apparent distress (e.g. Leach, Spears, Branscombe, & Doosje, 2003).

Like appraisal more generally (e.g. Leventhal & Scherer, 1987), social appraisal may be instantiated by a variety of different processes operating at different stages. However, most research has focused on a limited subset of these possible processes, specifically emphasizing emotion attribution and appraisal inferences. In the following subsections, I draw distinctions between these and other possible processes based on how the other person's emotion is apprehended and how information about its meaning then affects the appraisals and emotions of the person who is responding to the resulting social influence. For simplicity's sake, I refer to the person whose emotions are doing the influencing as the *source* and the person whose appraisals are influenced as the *target*, thus aligning the present analysis with more general social psychological accounts of social influence and attitude change (e.g. Latané & Wolf, 1981; Petty & Cacioppo, 1986). It is worth noting that the "target" need not be someone who is targeted by a specific influence attempt, but instead should be seen as the target of any influence that might happen for any reason (even incidentally). Thus, the term is broadly equivalent to the term "learner" in the ASL process (see Clément & Dukes, Introduction, this volume) and the term "receiver" in models of non-verbal communication (e.g. Buck, Savin, Miller, & Caul, 1972).

To count as social appraisal, the influence process must involve the source presenting an emotion or emotional information in a way that can be registered by the target, and the target responding to this registered emotion or emotional information by changing their orientation to the object at which the source's emotion appears to be directed. This means that some of the processes whereby a source's emotions might influence the target's behaviour would not count as social appraisal because they are not mediated specifically by a change in the target's orientation to the perceived object of the source's emotion and therefore do not involve appraisal (even broadly construed). Thus, the putative phenomenon of primitive emotion contagion (Hatfield, Cacioppo, & Rapson, 1994) is distinct from social appraisal because it does not depend on the object orientation of the source's emotion (Parkinson, 2011).

Other cases of interpersonal emotional influence can be distinguished from social appraisal because the source is oriented to a different object, event, or person from the target, allowing no direct social calibration of object-directed appraisals. For example, becoming emotional about another person's emotional orientation (interpersonal meta-emotion, e.g. Elfenbein, 2007; Parkinson & Simons, 2012) is distinct from social appraisal because the target's appraisal is directed at the source's appraisal, rather than calibrated against it. Having set out these parameters, I will now consider some of the possible ways in which social appraisal processes might operate.

5.3   Reverse engineering

The most articulated (and most commonly investigated) form of social appraisal involves the target drawing explicit inferences about how to appraise what is happening based on their categorization of the source's emotion. A related attribution-based process was first proposed by Weiner, Russell, and Lerman (1979; see also Hareli, 2014). However, the subsequent incorporation of appraisal principles is developed in most detail by Hareli and Hess' (2010) reverse-engineering model (see also Elfenbein, 2007, on "backtracking"; de Melo, Carnevale, Read, & Gratch, 2014, on "reverse appraisal"; van Kleef, 2009, on "Emotions as Social Information (EASI)"). Reverse engineering involves the target working backwards from information about the source's emotion to draw conclusions about how the source must have been appraising the situation in order for the emotion to occur in the first place. Thus, the target's knowledge about what appraisals usually go with which emotions helps them work out what the situation means to the source on the basis of their emotional reaction to it. This inferred situational meaning in turn changes the target's own appraisal of what is happening (see Figure 5.1). For example, if I notice that you are angry, I may conclude that you are directing blame externally, and that something potentially blameworthy must have happened.

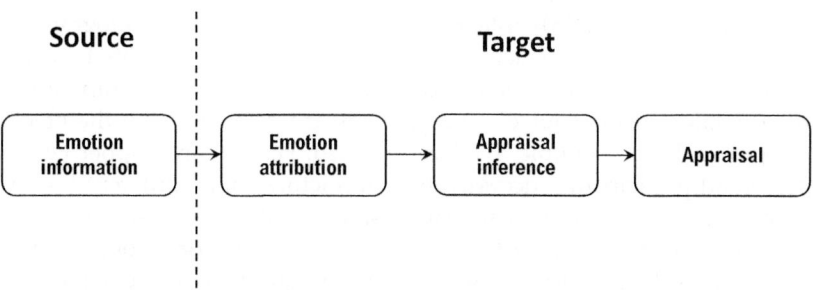

Figure 5.1 Reverse-engineering process (based on Hareli & Hess, 2010).

Note: This figure sets out the four stages implied by Hareli and Hess' (2010) reverse engineering model of social appraisal. The source provides emotion information which leads the target to attribute an emotion, then draw inferences about the source's appraisal based on that emotion attribution, which in turn affect the target's own appraisal of what is happening or has happened.

A number of studies have demonstrated that reverse engineering provides a viable explanation of effects of information about a source's emotion on the target's judgements about objects and events. For example, van Doorn, van Kleef, and van der Pligt (2015) asked participants to imagine that a friend had been involved in a car accident. When this friend was described as expressing anger while talking about this accident, participants tended to infer that someone else was responsible, but when the friend described as expressing regret, participants tended to see them as personally responsible. In other words, participants (as targets) based their conclusions about what had happened on the appraisal implications of the source's described emotions.

Hess and Hareli (2018) manipulated information about the source's emotion using photographs of facial expressions rather than explicit written instructions. Pictures of faces were presented next to pictures depicting scenes intended to induce disgust, pride, fear, or happiness. For example, a smiling face was presented alongside a photo of flies crawling over a cake (disgust) or a picture of hands holding a trophy (pride). Participants were told that the face was showing the person's reaction to the simultaneously presented scene even when the usual emotional interpretations of the face and scene did not match. Hess and Hareli found that participants adjusted their appraisals of the depicted objects and events to bring them more into line with the intended emotional implications of the faces. For example, a nose-scrunching "disgust" face tended to reduce the appraised pleasantness of associated happy and proud scenes and a gasping "fear" face tended to increase appraisals of their suddenness.

Hess and Hareli (2018) explicitly told participants that the photographed facial expressions were reactions to the simultaneously presented scenes. Other investigators have obtained comparable effects by manipulating the direction of the source's eye gaze toward or away from the object of appraisal. For example, Bayliss, Frischen, Fenske, and Tipper (2007) presented participants successively with pictures of 36 different household objects (e.g. saucepans, spanners, and kettles) alongside pictures of nose-scrunching "disgust" faces or smiles. In one condition, the eyes on the source's face turned towards the simultaneously presented object immediately before the expression changed from neutral to the relevant emotion giving the impression that the source was reacting to the target object. In another condition, the source's eyes turned away from the object before the emotion was expressed.

Participants subsequently reported liking objects that had been presented in association with "disgust" expressions significantly less than those that had been associated with smiles, but only when the source's eyes had turned towards the object rather than away from it. In other words, it was not the simple association between the emotional signal and the object that produced the effect on judgement, but the fact that the source's emotional orientation seemed to be directed at the object.

Mumenthaler and Sander (2012; see also Chapter 6, this volume) assessed how similarly animated facial stimuli affected perceptions of the emotion expressed on a second animated face. The source's face either turned its gaze towards or away from the second face (object of appraisal) while each face showed a dynamic emotion expression. Perceptions of the emotion expressed by the second face were influenced more by the first face's expression when its eyes turned towards that second face. For example, an "angry" face turning its gaze toward a second "fear" face increased participants' perceptions of expressed fear, probably because fear is a more likely reaction from someone at whom anger is directed.

These studies suggest that gaze direction coupled with facial expression produces comparable effects on object perception and judgement to more explicit information about an emotion's orientation. Does that mean that the same explicit inferential process of reverse engineering operates in these cases too? In other words, did participants consciously infer an appraisal from the source's expressed emotion and use gaze cues to work out that this appraisal was about the object at which gaze was directed (household object or second face) before changing their own appraisal of that object? Two findings call this interpretation into question. First, in Bayliss and colleagues' (2007) research, participants seemed unaware that the presented facial expressions had influenced their ratings of the household objects. Indeed, the experimental instructions encouraged them to focus on categorizing the objects and to ignore the faces. Second, Mumenthaler and Sander (2015) found that even subliminally presented facial expressions were capable of altering immediate interpretations of simultaneously presented facial stimuli. The implication therefore seems to be that gaze-cued social appraisal can operate without any explicit inferential process. One possible interpretation is that appraisal inferences based on facial expression become automatic over the course of development, allowing the reverse-engineering sequence to run below the level of conscious awareness. Another is that people are capable of perceiving object-directed appraisals directly from facial expressions without first needing to decode their emotional meaning (cf. Scherer, Mortillaro, Rotondi, Sergi, & Trznadel, 2018).

Emotion-related information can convey information about the source as well as about the object to which the source is oriented. For example, Hareli and Hess (2010) asked participants to imagine that they were evaluating a candidate for employment after reviewing their account of being blamed by colleagues for a failed project in a previous job. The key manipulation concerned the candidate's reported emotional reaction to interpersonal blame, which was described as angry, sad, or calm. Participants judged the angry candidate as having a more dominant and less warm personality than the sad or calm candidate. These effects were mediated by participants' inferences about the candidate's appraisals. Thus, participants perceived angry candidates as appraising the event as more urgent, and their inferences about urgency in turn seemed to lead to their conclusion about dispositional dominance.

Arguably the most direct form of information provided by a source's object-directed facial expression concerns their relational orientation towards the object (e.g. Frijda, 1986) rather than either the person or object in isolation. For example, smiling about something tends to imply that it is concordant with your current motives and goals.

De Melo and colleagues (2014) specifically investigated targets' inferences about a source's motives by manipulating the facial responses of a computer-animated male avatar with whom participants played an online Prisoner's dilemma game. The avatar showed different possible facial expressions depending on its own behaviour following the participant's cooperation. In the "expressively cooperative" condition, the avatar smiled after mutual cooperation and showed a face conveying regret after defecting. In the "expressively competitive" condition, the avatar showed the opposite pattern of expressive reactions (i.e. smiling after defection and showing regret after mutual cooperation). In other words, the avatar's apparent emotions were linked to the outcomes of each round and conveyed appraisals of those outcomes. For example, regret expressed after mutual cooperation implied self-blame for receiving a motivationally incongruent outcome, whereas expressed happiness implied that mutual cooperation was the desired outcome.

Participants ended up cooperating more with the expressively cooperative avatar even though it did not smile more often than the expressively competitive avatar across all trials. In other words, the effects depended on the events to which the avatar's expressions were oriented and not purely on the expressions themselves. Regret about mutual cooperation and regret about defection conveyed different messages about the avatar's motives.

In a follow-up study, participants reported their impressions of the avatar's appraisals immediately before deciding whether or not to cooperate. As predicted, regret expressions led participants to perceive the avatar as blaming himself more for defecting, and smiles led them to believe that the outcome was consistent with the avatar's motives. Further, these inferred appraisals mediated effects of the avatar's emotion expressions on participants' reported intentions to cooperate, supporting the reverse-engineering account.

In a further study, de Melo and colleagues replaced the avatar's facial expressions with explicit verbal communications about appraisals. Participants were asked to imagine that they had just played a round of the game, and that the other player had typed a message conveying their appraisal of what had happened using a computer chat system. For example, instead of showing a regret face, the other player wrote: "I do not like this outcome and I blame myself for it" (de Melo et al., 2014, p. 83). The appraisal messages had similar effects to the emotion expressions, again suggesting that the faces used in the earlier studies had affected participants' cooperation levels by communicating appraisals.

The research reviewed in this section shows that presenting information about a source's emotions can influence a target's judgements of the object of the emotion, the source, and the source's orientation towards the emotion's object. Many of these effects also seem to depend on the kinds of explicit inference implied by the reverse-engineering model. In other words, targets sometimes work backwards from emotion information to draw conclusions about the source's appraisal of relational meaning. However, demonstrating that emotion information *can* activate reverse-engineering processes does not prove that reverse engineering explains all possible forms of social appraisal. Indeed, the kinds of emotion information manipulated in studies demonstrating reverse engineering may specifically encourage this kind of inferential process. The issue then arises of whether similar processes also operate when methodological constraints are relaxed.

5.4   Emotion-independent appraisal information

Studies demonstrating reverse engineering and social referencing presuppose that the social appraisal process starts with the source's expression of an intact discrete emotion. Participants are told or shown that someone is experiencing distinctive states such as anger, disgust, or happiness and the effects of this explicit emotional information are then assessed. These procedures maximize the probability that participants base their judgements on specific categorical emotional meanings implying patterned appraisals. Explicitly presenting targets with information intended to convey the source's emotion strongly encourages them to use this information when making subsequent judgements.

Even in these restrictive contexts, however, the active ingredient of the experimental manipulations may not always be an integrated emotional meaning. For example, de Melo and colleagues (2014) showed that directly communicating verbal information about appraisals (e.g. "I do not like this situation and blame myself for it", p. 83) produced equivalent effects to facial expressions of emotions associated with these appraisals. Perhaps, then, participants bypassed emotion categorization and extracted information about appraisal and orientation more directly from presented facial and gaze cues (e.g. Sander, Grandjean, Kaiser, Wehrle, & Scherer, 2007; Scherer et al., 2018; see also Figure 5.2). Maybe the avatar's contextualized facial display simply indicated whether he

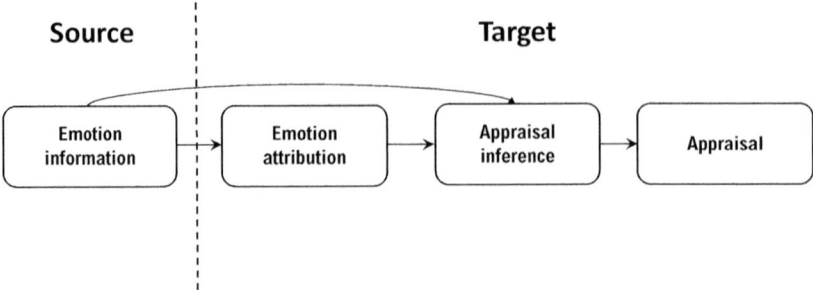

Figure 5.2 Social appraisal bypassing emotion inference.
Note: Intended manipulations of information about the source's emotion may directly provide information about the source's appraisal, thereby influencing the target's appraisal independent of any attribution of emotion to the source. In other words, the social appraisal process might bypass one of the stages implied by Hareli and Hess' (2010) reverse-engineering model (as presented in Figure 5.1).

was favourably or unfavourably disposed to the unfolding transaction. Indeed, the findings of studies that simply compare effects of one specific negative and one specific positive emotion (e.g. Bayliss et al., 2007) are susceptible to explanations in terms of simple attributions of valence or desirability rather than any more articulated appraisal pattern.

What happens in situations where no explicit verbal or facial emotional information is communicated either by source or experimenter? What if sources are neither displaying preselected canonical expressions of discrete emotions (e.g. Scherer et al., 2018) nor telling targets what kind of emotion they are experiencing? The cues that targets respond to in these circumstances are likely to depend on a range of factors relating both to current task demands and targets' own emotional orientations to what is happening. Even when the target automatically categorizes the source's emotion, not all interpersonal effects are necessarily mediated by detected categorical meaning. Targets may also pick up the source's directed stare, their leaning towards or away from something, or any other of their signals or movements that suggest evaluation, direction of attention, muscular tension, and so on. Each of these emotion-related responses may convey a component of appraisal that shapes the target's own orientation. Although the target may often piece together the components into a coherent pattern of appraisal or categorical emotional meaning, this does not seem to be a necessary precondition for the exertion of interpersonal influence. It may be that each separate aspect of the source's orientation independently influences the target's own separate responses.

A number of studies have shown that dissociable components of patterned facial expressions carry lower-level meanings relating to specific appraisals. For example, Frijda and Philipszoon (1963) correlated separate facial muscle movements with perceivers' judgements of pleasantness, submissiveness, control, and passivity (see also Smith & Scott, 1997). More recently, Scherer and colleagues (2018) used animated avatars to generate specific facial movements and asked participants to make judgements about the appraisals that they conveyed. Manipulated combinations of facial action units reliably led to perceptions of appraisals. For example, lowered brows and narrowed eyes were perceived as indicating scrutiny, whereas raised brows and widened eyes were perceived as indicating suddenness. Attributions of emotion were less consistent than attributions of appraisals, making it unlikely that the latter depended on the former.

The research reviewed in this section suggests that the active ingredient of social appraisal manipulations need not be an intact emotional meaning, but rather componential (or "sub-emotional") information about specific appraisals that may or may not be integrated into an emotional pattern. Future research should separately manipulate these lower-level appraisal and meaning components in order to determine their dissociable effects on targets' orientations, actions, and emotions in addition to their more established effects on interpersonal perceptions of the source's appraisals (e.g. Scherer et al., 2018).

When targets pick up appraisal information from the source's verbal communications or non-verbal displays without registering any particular discrete emotion, no reverse-engineering process is necessary. The target already knows what the source's appraisal is without having to work backwards from the source's perceived emotion. However, to the extent that the source's emotion influences the target's appraisal before inducing any emotional reaction, the process would still qualify as social appraisal. In the next section, I consider cases where the source's orientation to an emotional object might affect a target's responses without any separate process of prior appraisal.

5.4.1 Orientation cues and movements

In the previous section, I argued that inferences based on emotion information need not be mediated by either emotion categorization or attribution. But do interpersonal effects of facial displays necessarily require inference or transmission of appraisal information at all? Perhaps some aspects of a source's orientation are more directly perceptible from low-level stimulus features. Perhaps orientation cues even nudge target responses without needing to be categorized in appraisal or emotional terms.

Lee, Susskind, and Anderson (2013) showed that participants were better able to detect gaze direction from schematic pictures of eyes taken from a canonical "fear" expression, than from pictures of "neutral" or "disgusted" eyes. The main reason is that "fearful" eyes widen, with the consequence that the sclera becomes more visible. Inversion of these eye stimuli reduced participants' perceptions of their emotionality but did not interfere with detection of gaze direction. In other words, gaze could be tracked more accurately from widened eyes, independent of their perceived fearfulness. Lee and colleagues did not assess participants' perceptions of the appraisals associated with inverted "fear" eyes, but it also seems unlikely that the effects were mediated by appraisal inferences.

Widened eyes also improved discrimination of peripheral stimuli appearing in places where their gaze was directed. These results suggest that components of facial expressions can induce interpersonal attention-orienting effects in addition to conveying appraisals. These effects, like those on appraisal perceptions (Scherer et al., 2018) do not seem to depend on targets attributing discrete emotion to the source.

Taken alone, interpersonal effects of eye-widening on attentional activity do not fully qualify as social appraisal because they only influence one aspect of the target's orientation, which would not in itself qualify as appraisal. However, it is possible that dynamic patterns of eye gaze that are attuned in real time to unfolding situations produce more articulated interpersonal effects. Further, if the source's widened eyes direct the target's attention to emotionally relevant aspects of an object or event, they may bring additional consequences for appraisal further downstream. Indeed, the perceived relation between the source's orientation movements and the event towards which they are oriented may itself carry emotional significance (e.g. Adams & Kleck, 2005; Sander et al., 2007).

In addition to gaze cues, other aspects of the source's emotional orientation may also induce adjustments in targets. For example, dynamically articulated movements sometimes entrain the movements of other people so that they attain a common rhythm and tempo (e.g. McGrath & Kelly, 1986). Thus, sources engaged in smooth or jerky transactions with environmental objects may tend to solicit correspondingly relaxed or agitated movements from co-actors or interactants. Combining direction of attention with entrainment of movement may facilitate mutual alignment of emotion-related orientations towards objects (see Figure 5.3). Further informational contributions from interpersonal displays and signals may help to consolidate a more articulated emotional experience involving patterned appraisals. In principle, at least, it seems possible that social appraisal processes could consolidate from combined lower-level adjustments, and that information transfer need not be the only driving force behind the resulting interpersonal influence.

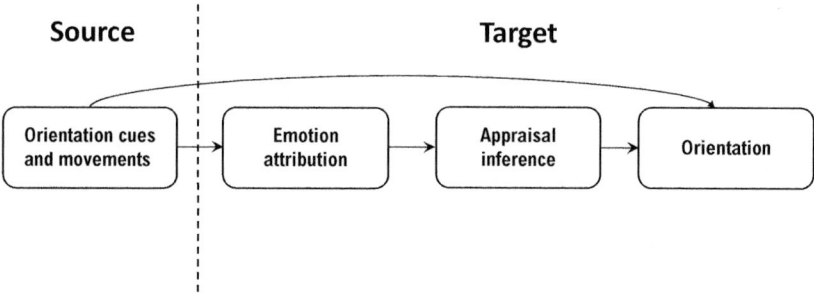

Figure 5.3 Orientation-based effect.
Note: Some interpersonal effects of the source's facial and bodily movements and cues may bypass both emotion attribution and appraisal inference and influence aspects of the target's orientation more directly.

5.5 Relation alignment

The kinds of interpersonal calibration implied by dynamic gaze-tracking and mutual adjustment of bodily posture and movement stretch the concept of social appraisal beyond its original boundaries. In these cases, the source does not explicitly provide appraisal information and the target makes no inferences about appraisal. Any consequences for the target's interpretation and evaluation of objects or events happens further downstream. The more direct effects operate on the target's embodied relation to the object of the source's emotion, and any ASL is implicitly manifested in this changed relational orientation rather than explicitly registered as new knowledge. For all these reasons, the more general term "relation alignment" seems to accommodate these processes more accurately (Parkinson, 2017).

Most emotions function to align relations between a person and an object or other person (e.g. Frijda, 1986), or between two or more people's orientations to the same object or person. Sometimes this process involves direct object-oriented movements without any directly interpersonal aspects. Often, it also involves signalling and communication. More active and strategic attempts at self-regulation or interpersonal regulation may play a role too. In my view, social appraisal covers some of these kinds of relation alignment but not others. The following subsections present examples of processes that calibrate people's object orientations in ways that cannot be fully explained by the operation of social appraisal.

5.5.1 Ostension and emotion regulation

Social appraisal often happens unintentionally when onlookers simply register the source's emotional orientation to what is happening, much in the same way as we tend to divert our gaze in the direction that other people are looking when we pass them on the street. However, in many circumstances, sources attempt to direct the target's attention, appraisal, and emotional orientation more strategically. In the classic social referencing studies, caregivers attune their expressions to eye contact from toddlers and explicitly direct attention to the expressed emotion's object (i.e. the visual cliff, Sorce et al., 1985). Indeed, a caregiver's goal in communicating their relational orientation may be precisely to encourage or discourage particular forms of behaviour towards an attended object using ostensive means (e.g. Clément & Dukes, 2017). This means that the source specifically regulates their emotion communication so that it is tailored to the target's perceived capacities and perspective.

How might the source's ostensive intentions affect the process of emotional influence? First, they make it more likely that the target receives explicit information relating the source's appraisal to its object. Indeed, the source is likely to continue or intensify the influence attempt until the target appears to register their relational orientation, thus introducing an element of interpersonal feedback to the transaction (see below). Second and correspondingly, ostension makes it more likely that the active ingredient of the source's presentation is the relational orientation to the object, taking the form of a regulated, object-directed, emotion presentation. Third, the source's tailored presentation reduces the target's own need to engage in complicated inference processes in order to pick up the source's appraisal. Fourth, implications of the source's appraisal for the target's own orientation and appraisal are more straightforward because the target simply has to decide whether or not to conform to the recommendation.

Taken together, these considerations imply that ostensive social referencing partly bypasses some of the same stages of emotional influence as the kinds of unregulated orientation cuing considered in the previous section (see Figure 5.3). In both cases, the source's orientation specifically encourages a corresponding orientation from the target with relatively little need for mediation by inference or calibration of appraisal. The difference is that the interpersonal process is explicitly regulated by the source rather than being incidental, thus allowing flexibility in achieving intended effects.

If the source's central intention is to encourage the target to appraise an object in a particular way, why does the influence attempt need to involve emotion at all? One answer is that the non-verbal signals associated with emotion communication can track events and targets' reactions to those events in real time, permitting a more dynamically attuned form of interpersonal influence (e.g. Stern, Hofer, Haft, & Dore, 1985). Another is that emotionality adds emphasis and focuses the target's attention. Finally, emotion communication introduces incentives to the influence process.

It warns of potential costs or signals potential rewards that will ensue from action or inaction. Some of these costs and rewards depend on the object that the emotion is about, while others depend on the source's anticipated reactions to failure to comply. In either case, it is important to remember that emotion communication does not simply involve the interpersonal transmission of appraisal information, but also more coercive motivational processes. Sometimes the point of getting emotional about something is to push or pull other people in certain directions, and not simply to provide them with knowledge about facts or values.

5.5.2   Reciprocal emotional influence

The interpersonal processes considered so far in this chapter have mainly involved one-way interpersonal influence running from sources to targets. The source provides or presents cues, nudges, or more articulated forms of information, and the target responds by inferring emotional implications or making more direct interpersonal adjustments. However, in many situations outside the laboratory, interactants and co-actors send information backwards and forwards to one another and mutually adjust their developing orientations to what is happening. Does this reciprocal relationality make a difference to the processes involved in emotional influence and ASL?

Most of the experimental paradigms used in social appraisal studies systematically exclude the possibility of reciprocal influence to avoid complicating interpretation of underlying mechanisms. However, as we have seen, social referencing studies often do put sources and targets into relatively direct contact with one another, permitting some forms of bidirectional exchange of information and mutual calibration of orientations.

For example, toddlers and their mothers apparently participated in a constrained form of non-verbal dialogue across the visual cliff in Sorce and colleagues' (1985) classic study. Although some form of social appraisal was probably involved, it is less likely to have depended on unidirectional reverse engineering. That would imply that the toddler first worked out that their mother was afraid, inferred that she appraised the visual cliff as dangerous, then reached the conclusion that the cliff represented a personal threat too, before finally deciding not to risk crossing on to the glass. More plausibly, the toddler adjusted their own prior orientation in response to interpersonal feedback from the regulating caregiver. They were likely already attuned to the potential barrier to crawling presented by the visual cliff, and to their mother as a potential source of comfort and information at the other side before responding to any emotional influence. The toddler's tentative movements then adjusted to the mother's widening eyes and gasping mouth, which the mother was probably regulating responsively in attunement to the toddler's developing orientation. Thus, both parties may be seen as interlocking parts of a dynamic system of forces and counterforces, and not simply separate providers or receivers of appraisal information. Both mother and toddler serve as both source and target of emotional influence.

This does not mean that emotional influence always operates to an equal degree in both directions. In Sorce and colleagues' (1985) research, the mother was the authority figure with greater experience of how the world works. The toddler had less capacity to function independently, especially when confronting an unfamiliar and potentially threatening situation. It was the mother who did most of the teaching, and the toddler who did most of the ASL. However, the toddler's questioning glances and looks of puzzlement still made a difference to when and how the mother provided interpersonal feedback and thus partly determined how the interaction unfolded.

Interpersonally distributed processes play an even greater role in consolidating orientations when interactions involve agents with less pronounced differences in power or status. Few studies have directly investigated these processes, but some researchers have explored what happens when fully competent adults face emotionally relevant events together.

Schachter's (1959) social affiliation research suggested that adults, like toddlers, are inclined to seek out emotional information from others when confronting unfamiliar situations. In one study, undergraduate students expecting to receive painful electric shocks specifically preferred to wait with other participants in a similar predicament rather than those allocated to a different, non-painful task. Participants apparently wanted to calibrate their emotional appraisals of what was about to happen in order to prepare themselves. But how does the interpersonal calibration process subsequently unfold?

One of Latané and Darley's (1968) famous experiments into social inhibition of emergency responses showed how mutual social comparison can affect people's orientations to an ambiguous emotional object, thus providing an early example of what would now be called social referencing (see Parkinson, Phiri, & Simons, 2012). The experiment focused specifically on how the presence of strangers affected speed of response in an apparent emergency situation. While participants filled out preliminary questionnaires, simulated smoke began to enter their waiting room through an air vent, suggesting that there was a fire elsewhere in the building. Some 75 per cent of individuals who were alone in the room made an attempt to report the incident within three and a half minutes. However, when participants waited with two other participants, only 38 per cent of the resulting three-person groups included a person who sought external help within the whole six minutes allotted.

Latané and Darley (1968) explained this effect in terms of pluralistic ignorance. They argued that participants were reluctant to show signs of panic in front of strangers and therefore affected an initially calm demeanour when the first traces of smoke appeared. An inadvertent consequence of concealing anxiety was to convey to each other that the situation was actually not that worrying after all. So, participants' apparent lack of concern signalled an unrealistically unthreatening appraisal of what was happening. In support of this account, participants were even less likely to report the incident when they waited with two experimental confederates who paid little attention to the fake smoke and affected a nonchalant attitude as the room filled with fumes.

The phenomenon of pluralistic ignorance suggests that social factors motivate emotion regulation (e.g. Kalokerinos, Tamir, & Kuppens, 2017), and the interpersonal and intragroup impact of this regulation reciprocally reinforces its operation, producing a mutually sustaining cycle. The dynamic social system reaches a stable outcome (collective inactivity) that does not depend on simple one-way interpersonal influence from any of the parties involved. However, Latané and Darley's data provide little direct evidence for the operation of these unfolding intragroup processes. From the findings alone, it is difficult to be sure whether participants explicitly directed emotional expressions to each other and engaged in inferences based on these expressions, or mutually calibrated their orientations by other means. Alternatively, some of the effects of co-presence may simply have reflected the reassurance derived from having other people around. More direct investigation of the dynamic attunement of attentional and orientation movements in similar settings is therefore needed to distinguish possible interpretations.

Some social appraisal studies have made initial attempts to clarify the mediation of interpersonal influence in situations where adults can interact directly with each other. Parkinson and Simons (2009) asked participants to report on their emotions and appraisals during social decision-making processes in their everyday lives using a diary-based method. Participants' perceptions of the other decision-maker's anxiety affected their own risk-related appraisals, suggesting that orientations to commonly faced options tended to become calibrated. However, emotion convergence was not fully mediated either by the target's appraisal inferences or by their explicit perception of the source's emotion, suggesting that more direct forms of mutual adjustment were involved. Because most of the data was collected only from one party to the decision and there was no possibility for direct observation, reciprocal processes could not easily be tracked.

Bruder, Dosmukhambetova, Nerb, and Manstead (2012) assessed whether visual contact with another participant affected emotional responses to movie clips intended to induce amusement, sadness, and fear. Pairs of friends or strangers either watched these clips separately or had visual access to the other participant, either directly in a co-present condition or via a real-time, silent video-feed of their facial activity. Participants tended to report similar emotional responses to those of their partner but only when that partner was a friend rather than a stranger and partners could see each other. There was no corresponding effect on self-reported appraisals, which did not mediate the interpersonal effects of emotion. These results suggest that participants with compatible perspectives reciprocally align their emotional orientations to mutually accessible objects in the environment. However, again, the results provide no evidence about ongoing dyadic dynamics. Further, the possibilities of interpersonal calibration were restricted by the fact that co-participants were passive viewers of the emotional stimuli and therefore unable to actively affect what was happening.

Parkinson and colleagues (2012) developed a methodology that increased online interactivity between participants and used a more practically relevant task as the object of common focus. Their adapted version of the social referencing procedure involved one adult participant (player) pumping up a simulated balloon on a computer screen in order to earn shared cash-related points, which were lost whenever a balloon unpredictably burst (the Balloon Analogue Risk Task, or BART, Lejuez et al., 2002). Thus, the target of emotional influence metaphorically approached the threat of a loss instead of a potentially dangerous visual cliff. Instead of a caregiver, the source of emotional influence was an adult friend (observer) whose facial reaction to the balloon inflating could be seen by the player across a two-way video link without an audio channel.

In order to manipulate the communication of emotion, observers were covertly instructed either to actively express anxiety as the balloon inflated or to suppress any expression of anxiety. The prediction was that players would calibrate their orientation to balloon inflation with the perceived emotional orientation of the observer, leading them to keep on pumping further when the observer's apparent anxiety was lower. This predicted effect on risk-taking was confirmed, but the effect was not mediated by either the observer's or the player's reported risk appraisals.

In a follow-up study, Parkinson, Shore, and Stephens (unpublished) assessed whether these effects were moderated by the player's knowledge that the observer was trying to suppress or express anxiety. The idea was that information about the observer's upregulation of anxiety should lead players to discount the appraisal implication of observers' emotion expressions if they believed that those expressions were upregulated, thus neutralizing any inferentially based social appraisal process. Although anxiety was greater across participants when the observer was instructed to express anxiety, the player's beliefs about regulation made no significant difference to this effect, suggesting again that interpersonal calibration was not achieved as a function of explicit inference.

A number of studies have investigated emotion convergence between co-present group members (e.g. Bartel & Saavedra, 2000; Totterdell, Kellett, Teuchmann, & Briner, 1998), taking us beyond more simple dyadic interactions. For example, Totterdell (2000) found that players on the same professional cricket team tended to share similar levels of happiness at different stages of a four-day match. The aggregated affective state of the team at each time point predicted individual players' affect. Affective similarity between players on each team could not be fully explained by commonly experienced hassles or performance during the match, suggesting that it depended on contact with other team members rather than convergent social-appraisal processes. Indeed, positive relations between team members' happiness levels were found only during periods of the match when they were fielding rather than batting. During fielding periods, all players have visual contact with each other (cf. Bruder et al., 2012), and they need to co-ordinate their activities in order to keep the opposing team's score low and get their batsmen out as soon as possible. By contrast, batting involves only two team members sharing the field at any one time.

The studies reviewed in this section all permitted contact between participants over an extended period while they commonly experienced emotionally relevant events. In each case, there is clear evidence that one person's emotion influenced someone else's emotion, appraisal, or orientation to what was happening more generally. However, none of the studies provides consistent support for the operation of explicit social appraisal processes such as reverse engineering. Whatever is mediating emotional convergence in these interactive situations seems to be operating at a less explicit level. Future studies need to track reciprocal processes of mutual influence using online dynamic measures (e.g. Butler & Randall, 2013) to clarify the operation of these kinds of emotion-related social influence. Some of the possible co-regulatory and interactive influences are set out in Figure 5.4.

5.5.3 Emotion contagion

When researchers fail to find evidence that emotional convergence depends on explicit forms of social appraisal, their usual recourse is to emotion contagion (e.g. Parkinson, 2011). The basic idea is that if exposure to common events or calibrated appraisals of these events cannot explain similarity between different people's emotions, then one person must be catching the emotion off the other person more directly. But how exactly might this happen?

Source/target   **Target/source**

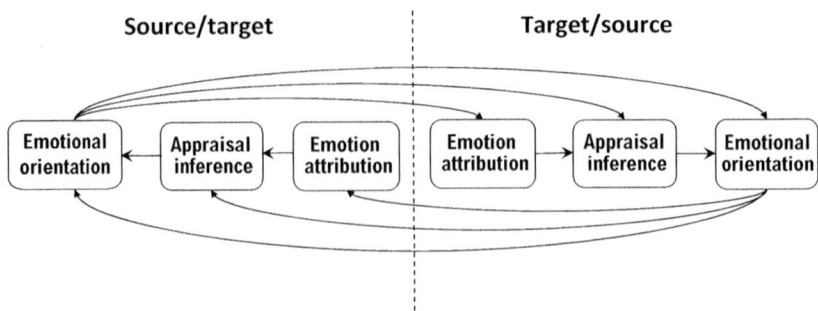

Figure 5.4 Possible processes of co-regulation and co-construction.

Note: This figure shows the possible influence processes operating between two people interacting with each other. Both parties to the exchange serve as both source and target of influence and all the influence paths set out in Figures 5.1 to 5.3 can thus operate in both directions, producing cycles of mutual influence.

Hatfield and colleagues (1994) distinguished a number of ways in which emotions might be contagious, including those requiring explicit inferential processes. However, most subsequent researchers have focused selectively on only one of their explanations, known as "primitive emotional contagion", perhaps because this sets out subprocesses most clearly. In primitive emotional contagion, targets automatically mimic source's facial expressions and bodily postures during interpersonal interaction. Internal signals from their mimicked movements then directly produce the subjective experience of a corresponding emotion.

There are a number of reasons for doubting the viability of primitive emotion contagion as an explanation for emotional influence (e.g. Parkinson, 2011). First, the acknowledged selectivity of mimicry (Chartrand & Bargh, 1999; Hatfield et al., 1994) already suggests that people's matching emotion communications tend to be specifically attuned to appropriate targets who are in-group members, allies, or otherwise share compatible perspectives or goals (Hess & Fischer, 2013). In other words, mimicry is not an automatic response to seeing any other person's nearby face or body under all circumstances. Second, reported facial and bodily feedback effects are neither strong nor consistent enough to produce full-blown matching emotional responses in targets. Third, the signals purportedly providing facial feedback are not universally associated with specific discrete emotions across all contexts in any case (e.g. Gendron, Crivelli, & Barrett, 2018; Parkinson, 2013), meaning that internal feedback would need to be supplemented by conceptual information to reveal distinctive emotional qualities. And the involvement of this conceptual information undermines the primitive contagion explanation.

However, dismissing a specific kind of emotion contagion does not rule out other kinds of emotion-calibration process operating at an automatic level. Indeed, the forms of reciprocal relation alignment described above might well be seen as contagious effects too. What distinguishes them from primitive emotion contagion is the fact that calibration does not operate at the level of specific movements (motor-matching) but instead also involves joint attention to emotion-relevant objects. Movements that manifest the orientations to those objects may well mutually adjust to one another over time in a kind of reciprocal entrainment process (e.g. McGrath & Kelly, 1986). No internal feedback process is then required to read off emotional significance that is already specified by the actor's mode of relation to what is happening. Urgently pushing against an obstacle to achieve physical progress already constitutes the experience conventionally labelled as English-language "anger" without any need to characterize the specifics of internal symptoms. As Frijda (2005) argued: "emotion experience is best characterised as a perception of a meaningful world that is filled with calls for action" (p. 474).

5.5.4 Directly interpersonal orientations

This chapter has focused specifically on interpersonal effects of emotions that are directed at objects and events to which both source and target have shared access. Assuming initial compatibility, the usual outcome is that their orientations to these objects and events converge. But what happens when the source's emotion is directed specifically at the target rather than at something or someone else? This can happen when the object of the source's emotion is a characteristic or quality of the target (e.g. love or hate of the target, contempt for the target), something that the target has done or not done that directly affects the source (e.g. anger or gratitude), or something that the source has done or not done that directly affects the target (e.g. guilt or disappointment). In all these cases, a central function of the emotion is to solicit particular interpersonal responses from the target. The process of emotional influence can thus produce complementary orientations of two or more people to one another, rather than calibrated orientations to a separate object. Needless to say, the processes underlying these forms of emotional influence may or may not involve explicit inference.

Exploring the range and operation of these processes would take us beyond the scope of the present chapter, but it is still worth noting that emotional influence not only leads to ASL about sources, objects, and the relations between them, but also about the more direct relationships between source and target. We acquire knowledge about what other people are like, and what they think of us on the basis of reverse engineering from these observed emotions, and we may arrive at new ways of getting on with other people or resisting their demands on us partly on the basis of other kinds of relation alignment.

5.6   Conclusions

Although social referencing provides a paradigmatic example of ASL, the processes whereby emotions produce changes in people's orientations to objects, events, and other people are not fully captured by the usual inferential interpretation of referencing effects. Research on adult emotional influence suggests that cuing, social attunement, and forms of reciprocal interpersonal adjustment may also play a role, but few of these mechanisms have been investigated directly.

Studies of caregiver–infant social interaction (e.g. Gergely & Király, Chapter 4, this volume; Kokkinaki, Vasdekis, Koufaki, & Trevarthen, 2017; Reddy, 2000) also suggest that active bidirectional forms of emotional influence operate at developmental stages preceding the onset of social referencing. Indeed, it seems likely that emotions achieve much of their power in referencing situations because toddlers have already learned how to use and respond to them at a more implicit level. It is only because toddlers have previous experience of their mother's object-oriented fear communications in more directly consequential circumstances that those communications provide such clear stop signals when facing the visual cliff. Even at an early age, interpersonally communicated emotions provide incentives and cues that help to drive and organize the infant's developing orientations and actions. My claim in this chapter is that many of these implicit co-constructed processes of reciprocal relation alignment continue to operate in triadic adult–adult–object transactions. Inferential reverse engineering and other forms of social appraisal are overlaid on to these processes and never entirely supersede them.

References

Adams, R. B., & Kleck, R. E. (2005). Effects of direct and averted gaze on the perception of facially communicated emotion. *Emotion, 5*, 3–11.

Bartel, C., & Saavedra, R. (2000). The collective construction of work group moods. *Administrative Science Quarterly, 45*, 197–231.

Bayliss, A. P., Frischen, A., Fenske, M. J., & Tipper, S. P. (2007). Affective evaluations of objects are influenced by observed gaze direction and emotion expression. *Cognition, 104*, 644–653.

Bruder, M., Dosmukhambetova, D., Nerb, J., & Manstead, A. S. R. (2012). Emotional signals in nonverbal interaction: Dyadic facilitation and convergence in expressions, appraisals, and feelings. *Cognition and Emotion, 26,* 480–502.

Buck, R., Savin, V. J., Miller, R. E., & Caul, W. F. (1972). Communication of affect through facial expressions in humans. *Journal of Personality and Social Psychology, 23,* 362–371.

Butler, E. A., & Randall, A. K. (2013). Emotional coregulation in close relationships. *Emotion Review, 5,* 202–210.

Campos, J. J., & Stenberg, C. (1981). Perception, appraisal, and emotion: The onset of social referencing. In M. E. Lamb & L. R. Sherrod (Eds.), *Infant social cognition: Empirical and theoretical considerations* (pp. 273–314). Hillsdale, NJ: Erlbaum.

Chartrand, T. L., & Bargh, J. A. (1999). The chameleon effect: The perception–behavior link and social interaction. *Journal of Personality and Social Psychology, 76,* 893–910.

Clément, F., & Dukes, D. (2017). Social appraisal and social referencing: Two components of affective social learning. *Emotion Review, 9,* 253–261.

de Melo, C. M., Carnevale, P. J., Read, S. J., & Gratch, J. (2014). Reading people's minds from emotion expressions in interdependent decision making. *Journal of Personality and Social Psychology, 106,* 73–88.

Elfenbein, H. A. (2007). Emotion in organizations: A review and theoretical integration. *Academy of Management Annals, 1,* 371–457.

Frijda, N. H. (1986). *The emotions.* Cambridge, UK: Cambridge University Press. (2005). Emotion experience. *Cognition and Emotion, 19,* 473–497.

Frijda, N. H., & Philipszoon, E. (1963). Dimensions of recognition of emotion. *Journal of Abnormal and Social Psychology, 66,* 45–51.

Gendron, M., Crivelli, C., & Barrett, L. F. (2018). Universality reconsidered: Diversity in meaning making about facial expressions. *Current Directions in Psychological Science, 27,* 211–219.

Hareli, S. (2014). Making sense of the social world and influencing it by using a naïve attribution theory of emotions. *Emotion Review, 6,* 336–343.

Hareli, S., & Hess, U. (2010). What emotional reactions can tell us about the nature of others: An appraisal perspective on person perception. *Cognition and Emotion, 24,* 128–140.

Hatfield, E., Cacioppo, J. T., & Rapson, R. L. (1994). *Emotional contagion.* New York, NY: Cambridge University Press.

Hess, U., & Fischer, A. (2013). Emotional mimicry as social regulation. *Personality and Social Psychology Review, 17,* 142–157.

Hess, U., & Hareli, S. (2018). On the malleability of the meaning of contexts: The influence of another person's emotion expressions on situation perception. *Cognition and Emotion, 32,* 185–191.

Kalokerinos, E. K., Tamir, M., & Kuppens, P. (2017). Instrumental motives in negative emotion regulation in daily life: Frequency, consistency, and predictors. *Emotion, 17,* 648–657.

Kokkinaki, T. S., Vasdekis, V. G. S., Koufaki, Z. E., & Trevarthen, C. B. (2017). Coordination of emotions in mother-infant dialogues. *Infant and Child Development, 26,* e1973.

Latané, B., & Darley, J. M. (1968). Group inhibition of bystander intervention in emergencies. *Journal of Personality and Social Psychology, 10,* 215–221.

Latané, B., & Wolf, S. (1981). The social impact of majorities and minorities. *Psychological Review, 88*, 438–453.

Leach, C. W., Spears, R., Branscombe, N. R., & Doosje, B. (2003). Malicious pleasure: Schadenfreude at the suffering of an outgroup. *Journal of Personality and Social Psychology, 84*, 932–943.

Lee, D. H., Susskind, J. M., & Anderson, A. K. (2013). Social transmission of the sensory benefits of eye widening in fear expression. *Psychological Science, 24*, 957–965.

Lejuez, C. W., Read, J. P., Kahler, C. W., Richards, J. B., Ramsey, S. E., Stuart, G. L., ... Brown, R. A. (2002). Evaluation of a behavioral measure of risk taking: The Balloon Analogue Risk Task (BART). *Journal of Experimental Psychology: Applied, 8*, 75–84.

Leventhal, H., & Scherer, K. R. (1987). The relationship of emotion and cognition: A functional approach to a semantic controversy. *Cognition and Emotion, 1*, 3–28.

Manstead, A. S. R., & Fischer, A. H. (2001). Social appraisal: The social world as object of and influence on appraisal processes. In K. R. Scherer, A. Schorr, & T. Johnstone (Eds.), *Appraisal processes in emotion: Theory, methods, research* (pp. 221–232). New York, NY: Oxford University Press.

McGrath J. E., & Kelly, J. R. (1986). *Time and human interaction: Toward a social psychology of time.* New York, NY: Guilford Press.

Mumenthaler, C., & Sander, D. (2012). Social appraisal influences recognition of emotions. *Journal of Personality and Social Psychology, 102*, 1118–1135.

(2015). Automatic integration of social information in emotion recognition. *Journal of Experimental Psychology: General, 144*, 392–399.

Parkinson, B. (1996). Emotions are social. *British Journal of Psychology, 87*, 663–683.

(2011). Interpersonal emotion transfer: Contagion and social appraisal. *Personality and Social Psychology Compass, 5*, 428–439.

(2013). Contextualizing facial activity. *Emotion Review, 5*, 97–103.

(2017). Comment: Respecifying emotional influence. *Emotion Review, 9*, 263–265.

Parkinson, B., & Manstead, A. S. R. (1993). Making sense of emotion in stories and social life. *Cognition and Emotion, 7*, 295–323.

Parkinson, B., Phiri, N., & Simons, G. (2012). Bursting with anxiety: Adult social referencing in an interpersonal Balloon Analogue Risk Task (BART). *Emotion, 12*, 817–826.

Parkinson, B., Shore, D., & Stephens, N. (unpublished). Expression regulation and perceived regulation and their interpersonal effects on risk behaviour in a dyadic Balloon Analogue Risk Task (BART).

Parkinson, B., & Simons, G. (2009). Affecting others: Social appraisal and emotion contagion in everyday decision-making. *Personality and Social Psychology Bulletin, 35*, 1071–1084.

(2012). Worry spreads: Interpersonal transfer of problem-related anxiety. *Cognition and Emotion, 26*, 462–479.

Petty, R. E., & Cacioppo, J. T. (1986). *Communication and persuasion: Central and peripheral routes to attitude change.* New York, NY: Springer-Verlag.

Reddy, V. (2000). Coyness in early infancy. *Developmental Science, 3*, 186–192.

Sander, D., Grandjean, D., Kaiser, S., Wehrle, T., & Scherer, K. R. (2007). Interaction effects of perceived gaze direction and dynamic facial expression: Evidence for appraisal theories of emotion. *European Journal of Cognitive Psychology, 19*, 470–480.

Schachter, S. (1959). *The psychology of affiliation*. Stanford, CA: Stanford University Press.

Scherer, K. R., Mortillaro, M., Rotondi, I., Sergi, I., & Trznadel, S. (2018). Appraisal-driven facial actions as building blocks for emotion inference. *Journal of Personality and Social Psychology, 114*, 358–379.

Smith, C. A., & Lazarus, R. S. (1993). Appraisal components, core relational themes, and the emotions. *Cognition and Emotion, 7*, 233–269.

Smith, C. A., & Scott, H. S. (1997). A componential approach to the meaning of facial expressions. In J. A. Russell & J.-M. Fernández-Dols (Eds.), *The psychology of facial expression* (pp. 229–254). New York, NY: Cambridge University Press.

Sorce, J. F., Emde, R. N., Campos, J., & Klinnert, M. D. (1985). Maternal emotional signaling: Its effect on the visual cliff behavior of 1-year-olds. *Developmental Psychology, 21*, 195–200.

Stern, D. N., Hofer, L., Haft, W., & Dore, J. (1985). Affect attunement: The sharing of feeling states between mother and infant by means of intermodal fluency. In T. N. Field & N. Fox (Eds.), *Social perception in infants* (pp. 249–268). Norwood, NJ: Ablex.

Totterdell, P. (2000). Catching moods and hitting runs: Mood linkage and subjective performance in professional sport teams. *Journal of Applied Psychology, 85*, 848–859.

Totterdell, P., Kellett, S., Teuchmann, K., & Briner, R. B. (1998). Evidence of mood linkage in work groups. *Journal of Personality and Social Psychology, 74*, 1504–1515.

van Doorn, E. A., van Kleef, G. A., & van der Pligt, J. (2015). Deriving meaning from others' emotions: Attribution, appraisal, and the use of emotions as social information. *Frontiers in Psychology, 6*, 1077.

van Kleef, G. A. (2009). How emotions regulate social life: The Emotions as Social Information (EASI) model. *Current Directions in Psychological Research, 18*, 184–188.

Walle, E. A., Reschke, P. J., Camras, L. A., & Campos, J. J. (2017). Infant differential behaviour responding to discrete emotions. *Emotion, 17*, 1078–1091.

Weiner, B., Russell, D., & Lerman, D. (1979). The cognition-emotion process in achievement-related contexts. *Journal of Personality and Social Psychology, 37*, 1211–1220.

CHAPTER 6

Socio-affective inferential mechanisms involved in emotion recognition

Christian Mumenthaler and David Sander

Emotional information conveyed by other people helps us understand social intentions, react to others, and evaluate the affective meaning of many events that we encounter in our environment (Bodenhausen & Todd, 2010; Lieberman, 2007; Manstead & Fischer, 2001). The concept of affective social learning (ASL; Clément & Dukes, 2017; Introduction, this volume) brings together different mechanisms through which emotional expressions of others can influence our acquisition of knowledge about the value of objects and situations in our environment. It is important to point out that the word "object" refers to both material things and individuals to whom a specified action or feeling is directed to, or expected from. In this chapter, we focus on social appraisal – one of the central mechanisms involved in ASL. In particular, we discuss the notion that, through a particular socio-affective inferential mechanism, social appraisal plays a significant role when the emotional expression of person A is used to learn about the value of the emotion expressed by person B.

The first section of this chapter provides a brief historical introduction to the relation between contextual information and emotion recognition in faces. Then, we focus on the construct of social appraisal and its manifestation in socio-affective inferential mechanisms involved in emotion recognition (Section 6.2). In the third section of this chapter, we will present empirical evidence supporting the automaticity of such socio-affective inferential mechanisms and discuss its implication for the theoretical framework of ASL proposed by Clément and Dukes (2017). Next, we discuss the idea that ambiguous situations may be particularly prone to social appraisal taking place (Section 6.4). Finally, we discuss how a social appraisal, underpinned by a socio-affective inferential mechanism can be integrated into the ASL framework.

6.1   Emotional faces in context

The idea that there are "basic" and universal facial expressions of emotions created by specific configurations of facial muscles (Ekman,

1972, 1993; Izard, 1971) has dominated research on emotion perception in faces since the second half of the twentieth century. According to this approach, the prototypical configuration of facial muscles contains information that is relevant to the recognition of basic facial expressions. A fundamental premise of this approach is that, for some emotions, all the information necessary for their recognition is expressed in the face. Therefore, prototypical basic expressions are signals that convey unambiguous emotional meanings.

The assumption that faces have all the required emotional information to be correctly associated with emotion categories had an important impact on emotion recognition research (see Aviezer, Hassin, Bentin, & Trope, 2008). Since then, emotion recognition has largely been studied as though immune to contextual information; emotional facial expressions were seen as a stable, predictable and accurate signal to convey emotion categories. The impact of this approach was not limited to the way generations of scientists think and test facial expressions of emotion during the last decades in psychology and cognitive neuroscience, but also spread over to popular culture in successful TV series such as *Lie To Me*, inspired explicitly by Ekman's research.

More recently, based on alternative theories and on a growing desire for more realistic experiments, researchers increasingly carried out their work on emotion recognition by embedding the face stimuli in richer contexts. In fact, studies investigating the influence of contextual information on emotion recognition in faces were already conducted at the beginning of the century (Landis, 1929) but had subsequently been heavily criticized because of the methodology used (Ekman, Friesen, & Ellsworth, 1972).

The most common and distinct source of context that influences emotion recognition in faces is the physical contextual information that accompanies someone's facial expressions. Information influencing face perception is very diversified and includes information conveyed by a producer's face, such as the gaze of the producer (e.g. Adams & Kleck, 2003, 2005; Cristinzio, N'Diaye, Seeck, Vuilleumier, & Sander, 2010; Sander, Grandjean, Kaiser, Wehrle, & Scherer, 2007), the information conveyed by the visual scene in which the face in embedded (e.g. Righart & de Gelder, 2008), or the body to which the face belongs (e.g. Aviezer, Bentin, Dudarev, & Hassin, 2011; Aviezer, Hassin, Bentin et al., 2008; Aviezer, Hassin, Ryan et al., 2008; Aviezer, Trope, & Todorov, 2012; de Gelder et al., 2006; de Gelder & van den Stock, 2012).

Social context plays an essential role in emotional interactions of everyday situations. In fact, because we often perceive people with other people surrounding them, the faces of others can frequently be used as contextual cues in social situations and provide crucial information. Back in 1956, Cline showed that when the drawings of two faces were presented together and orientated towards one another, observers' judgements were based on the whole social situation and not on the individual information provided by each face. Specifically, he showed that participants assigned a different meaning to the face depending on the emotional information of the other face that was paired with it. For example, participants perceived drawings of a smiling person as a more dominant, gloating, and taunting bully when paired with a depressed facial expression (glum) than when paired with a frowning facial expression (Cline, 1956; see Figure 6.1a). In a similar line of work, Russel and Fehr (1987) demonstrated that viewing an initial facial expression shifts the judgement of the following, target facial expression; for instance, a neutral target face was categorized as expressing sadness after the presentation of a happy face.

Interestingly, the effect of social contextual information on the recognition of emotional facial expressions appears to be influenced by the observer's culture. In fact, results have indicated that Japanese people tend to be more influenced by contextual information than Caucasians. This is based on an experiment when participants were presented with cartoons depicting a happy, sad, angry, or neutral person surrounded by other persons expressing either the same emotion as the central person or a different emotion. The Japanese participants actively incorporated the feelings of the background figures when they were asked to evaluate the central person's facial expressions (Masuda et al., 2008; see Figure 6.1b). Of course, such effects do not rule out the basic idea that facial expressions provide some critical information for emotion recognition (e.g. a facial expression involving the zygomaticus and orbicularis – muscles commonly involved in a facial expression of happiness – is unlikely to be recognized as disgust), but rather suggest that muscle configuration is not the only source of information that is used for emotion recognition from faces. Consider, for instance, the case of colour perception. While there is an obvious specific relation between wavelength variations and colour categories, various contextual effects have been shown in colour perception (see e.g. Olkkonen & Ekroll, 2016). Such contextual effects do not question the relationship between the concepts of "wavelength" and "colour", but interestingly provide evidence that we integrate several pieces of information when perceiving colours. With respect to emotion perception, the role of contextual information – in particular, social – is certainly much more important, but this does not mean that the context explains it all: it is likely to be an interaction effect that needs to be explained. Indeed, as discussed in the next section, accumulating evidence indicates that there is much more than the flexing of facial muscles that meets the eye when it comes to facial emotion recognition (for a review see Wieser, & Brosch, 2012).

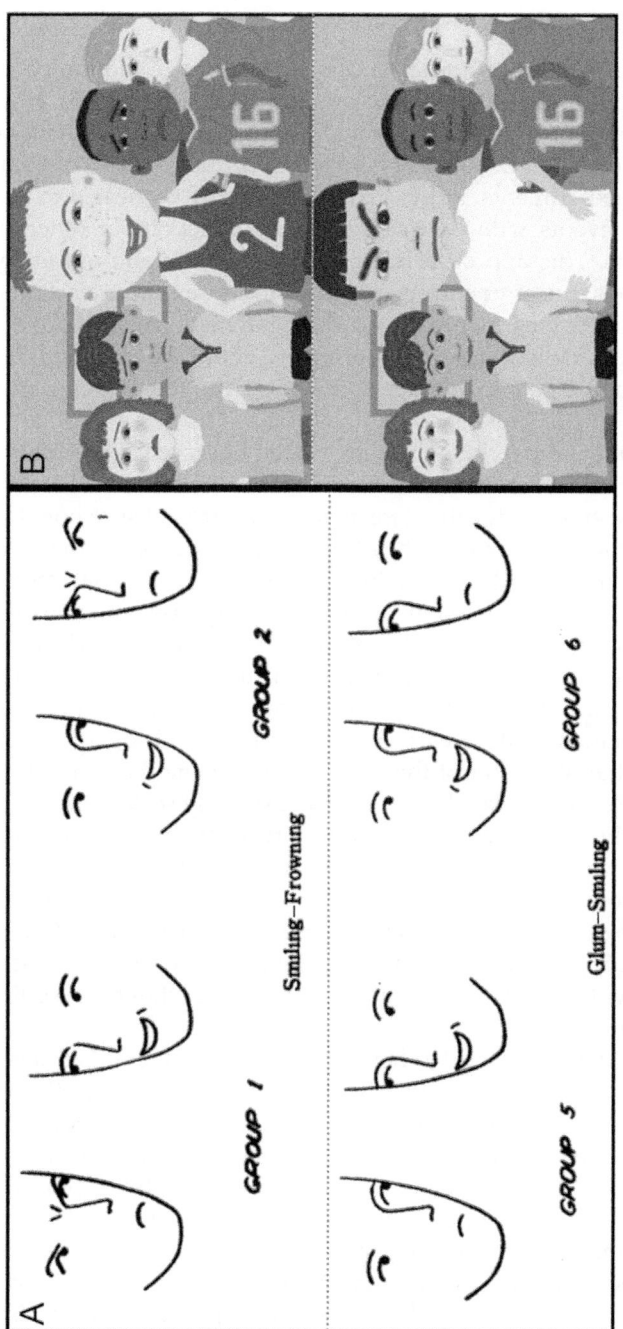

Figure 6.1 Stimuli used to investigate social contextual influences on emotion perception.
Note: (A) Example of stimuli used in Cline (1956). (B) Example of stimuli used in Masuda et al. (2008).

6.2   Socio-affective inferential mechanisms: a manifestation of a social appraisal process

The basic principles of appraisal theories recognize the importance of contextual information (Sander, Grandjean, & Scherer, 2005). However, appraisal processes have commonly been studied independently of the social context (see Clément & Dukes, Introduction, this volume). In laboratory experiments, individuals are typically requested to evaluate a series of events without considering the reactions of others to the same events. This approach is an efficient way to address many critical questions concerning the nature and structure of appraisal processes (e.g. the dimensions involved and their interactions; see Grandjean & Scherer, 2008). However, social information about the emotional reaction of others should be integrated at some point into the dynamic appraisal process.

Developmental psychologists have often observed how children use socio-affective information in their evaluation of a situation. In fact, when children are exposed to situations where they are not sure how to make sense of what is happening, they look around at others' faces to clarify things (Feinman, 1992). During this process, known as social referencing, children use facial expressions of others to appraise situations that are uncertain or ambiguous (e.g. Klinnert, Campos, Sorce, Emde, & Svejda, 1983). A clear example is observed when toddlers are exposed to the visual cliff paradigm. In this task, 12-month-old children have to decide to cross a simulated deep cliff (covered with clear Plexiglas) to get a toy located at the other end of this cliff while their mother provides facial feedback. Results revealed that toddlers explicitly seek additional information on how to proceed by looking toward their mothers. Therefore, if their mother, placed at the other side, was smiling, toddlers were more likely to cross the visual cliff toward an attractive toy, than when their mother showed a fearful or angry expression (Sorce, Emde, Campos, & Klinnert, 1985). Therefore, in this situation, the emotional expressions of others provided valuable information about the emotional significance of the situation.

In 2001, Manstead and Fischer incorporated and specified this social dimension into the theoretical framework of appraisal theories of emotion by introducing the concept of social appraisal. They proposed that "behaviors, thoughts or feelings of one or more other persons in the emotional situation are appraised in addition to the appraisal of the event per se" (Manstead & Fischer, 2001, p. 222). This proposal implies that the appraisal of an event made by an individual is influenced by the appraisal that other individuals make of the very same event (see Figure 6.2). This idea provides a possible explanation to the findings

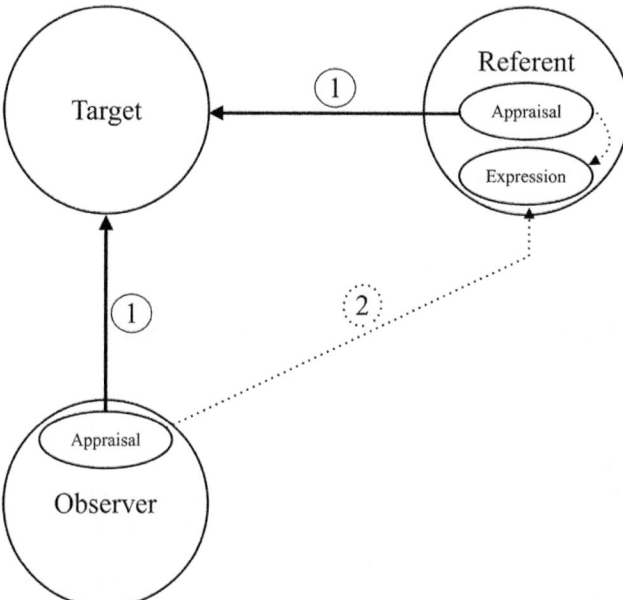

Figure 6.2 Two individuals (observer and referent) simultaneously facing a potentially emotion-eliciting situation (i.e.
target).

Note: The observer and referent appraise the situation
(path 1); when a social appraisal process takes place, the
expression of the referent indicating her/his ongoing appraisal
processes influences the ongoing appraisal process of the
observer (path 2). Therefore, the social appraisal path consists
of the integration of the referent's inferred appraisals into the
observer's appraisals (figure adapted from Bruder, Fischer, &
Manstead, 2014).

observed by developmental psychologists: Children include the information about a potential threat derived from the observed expressions (i.e.
their mother's expression) on their appraisal of an ambiguous situation
(i.e. the value of the visual cliff).

Previous studies investigating social appraisal mechanisms principally
focused on two facets of social appraisal. On the one hand, they studied
its role in the expression of emotions; that is, how people expressing their
emotions are influenced by the imagined social implications of those
expressions. For instance, Evers, Fisher, Mosquera, and Manstead (2005)
suggested that women were less likely than men to express their anger
because they were more likely to think that negative social consequences

would follow from doing so. In this specific case, participants were told that they would later meet the person who was the source of their anger. Therefore, social appraisal, when related to the imagined social implications of the participant's expression, was interpreted as influencing the actual expression of anger.

On the other hand, studies have also investigated the role social appraisal plays in the experience of an emotion. The relationship between social appraisal and emotional experience has been described as the way in which individuals evaluate an emotional event while being affected by the way in which others evaluate and feel about the same event (Fischer, Rotteveel, Evers, & Manstead, 2004). For example, these authors investigated the impact of others' emotional reactions on participants' self-reported emotion. Results showed that when others expressed anger, participants reported more intense anger, and when others expressed sadness, participants reported more intense sadness. The findings also showed that the extent of this emotional assimilation depended on one's interpersonal orientation (independent vs interdependent selves), and on the extent to which information about others' distinct emotional reaction was recognized and processed (see also Jakobs, Fischer, & Manstead, 1997).

Based on the assumption that facial expressions convey appraisal information (see de Melo, Carnevale, Read, & Gratch, 2014; Scherer, Mortillaro, Rotondi, Sergi, & Trznadel, 2018; Smith & Scott, 1997; van Reekum et al., 2004; Wehrle, Kaiser, Schmidt, & Scherer, 2000) an instance of social appraisal may correspond to the process of integrating the information from others' emotional expressions into one's own evaluation of a situation (see Bruder et al., 2014; Mumenthaler & Sander, 2012, 2015; Mumenthaler, Sander, & Manstead, 2018). Previous studies revealed that the appraisal of others, conveyed by their facial expressions, provides relevant information for the evaluation of a situation, influencing cognitive and emotional processes of the observer. For instance, van Doorn, Heerdink, and van Kleef (2012) showed that angry expressions made observers evaluate a situation as less cooperative than happy or sad expressions. Parkinson, Phiri, and Simons (2012) also revealed that others' expressions of anxiety lead participants to take fewer risks in a risk decision task (see also Parkinson & Simons, 2009).

Other lines of research have shown that emotional expressions of faces appearing in context might also be used to inform an affective evaluation directed to a person or an object. This evaluation could be interpreted as being part of a social appraisal process because participants integrate others' evaluations (reflected by their facial expression) in their evaluation of the event. For instance, concerning faces, Jones, DeBruine, Little, Burriss, and Feinberg (2007) showed that the attractiveness of a face was influenced by the emotional expression of a face looking at it. Female participants preferred a neutral male face when it had another woman smiling at it. For objects, Bayliss, Frischen, Fenske, and Tipper (2007) studied conjointly the effects of gaze direction and emotional facial expressions on the affective evaluation of neutral objects (e.g. a mug). Results indicated that objects looked at with a happy expression were liked more than objects looked at with an expression of disgust. However, object preference was influenced only when the gaze of the face was directed to the objects. Therefore, the mere presentation of a facial expression (happiness vs disgust) did not influence object preference. This indicates that an evaluative process can be inferred from the combined information provided by the facial expression and the gaze direction.

Based on the premise that the cognitive system typically infers causal relations between objects and living things (see Hassin, Bargh, & Uleman, 2002), we introduced the concept of a socio-affective inferential mechanism to refer to the situation where the apparent emotional reaction of a referent is directed at a particular person (i.e. target) also expressing an emotion, allowing the observer to infer a causal relationship between the emotions expressed by the referent and the target. In order to investigate the specificity of this effect, it is important to distinguish between the general impact on the observer of the emotion expressed by the referent and a more specific socio-affective inferential mechanism involving a social appraisal process (see Figure 6.3). In both cases, the observer processes socio-affective contextual information (i.e. the emotion expressed by the referent). However, in the socio-affective inferential mechanism, the apparent emotional reaction of the referent is directed at a particular person (i.e. target) allowing the observer to integrate the causal relation between the emotions expressed by both persons into his or her evaluation of the situation. This inferential mechanism relies on a social appraisal process, where the appraisal of the referent is integrated into the appraisal of the observer (see Figure 6.2).

Manipulating the social appraisal mechanism through the use of the combined information provided by the target (emotional facial expression) and the gaze direction of the referent (see Figure 6.3) provided the first evidence of such socio-affective inferential mechanisms in social appraisal process influencing emotion recognition (see Mumenthaler & Sander, 2012). In this study, we directly tested this proposal by asking participants to recognize dynamic facial expressions of emotion (fear, happiness, or anger) in a target face presented at the centre of a screen. Simultaneously a contextual face, which appeared in the periphery of the screen, either expressed an emotion (fear, happiness, anger) or didn't (neutral) and either looked at the target face or didn't (away). We

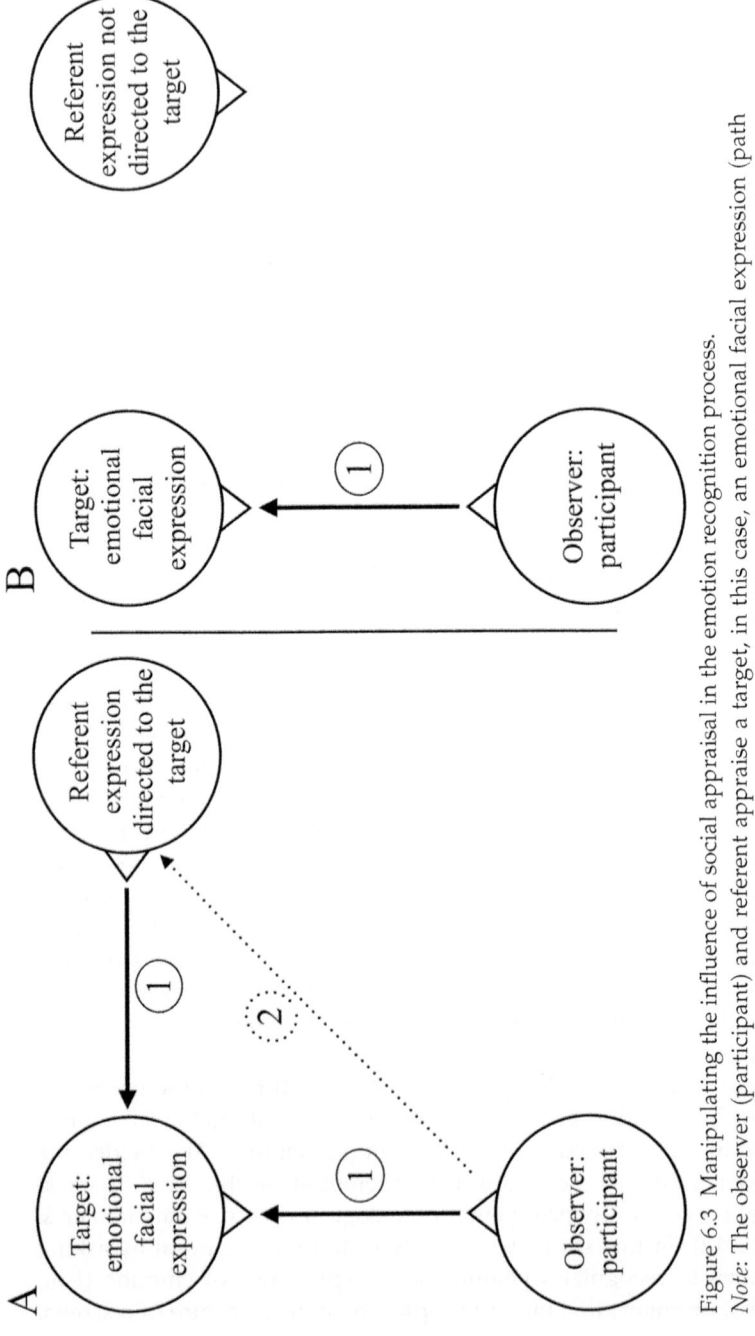

Figure 6.3 Manipulating the influence of social appraisal in the emotion recognition process.

Note: The observer (participant) and referent appraise a target, in this case, an emotional facial expression (path 1); in the social appraisal condition (A), the referent expression is directed toward the target stimulus (here, an emotional facial expression) and integrated into the ongoing appraisal process of the observer (path 2). In the mere context condition (B), the referent expression is not directed to the target (i.e. emotional stimulus). Therefore, the observer cannot infer an evaluative process of the emotional stimulus by the referent.

manipulated gaze direction to be able to distinguish between a mere contextual effect (gaze away from both the target face and the participant) and a specific social appraisal effect (gaze towards the target face; see Figure 6.4).

Results confirmed a social appraisal effect in emotion recognition, which differed from the mere effect of contextual information: whereas facial expressions were identical in both conditions, the direction of the gaze of the contextual face influenced emotion recognition. We believe that the social appraisal effect is based on a socio-affective inferential mechanism that is more specific than the one subserving the contextual effect. In terms of interpretation, given the paradigm used in this study, any modulation of the recognition of the emotion expressed by the target face could be both the result of affective priming and/or of an inferential process (in our case, social appraisal). For instance, the facilitation of anger recognition when a contextual face is angry could be the result of having processed the same emotional stimulus twice (i.e. affective priming). However, we reasoned that if the only process that explains the facilitation of anger recognition when a contextual face is angry is an affective priming process, then one would expect to observe a mere contextual effect but no effect of gaze direction on anger recognition. On the contrary, our findings revealed that both an affective priming effect (in the mere context condition) and a more inferential social appraisal effect (in the social appraisal condition) could facilitate emotion recognition in an additive way.

Results also revealed that the functional relation between the emotion pair of anger and fear is so powerful that the presence of an angry contextual face looking at the target face facilitates the recognition of fear expressed by this target face (see Mumenthaler & Sander, 2012). In other words, participants were more likely to correctly identify fear in the target face when the contextual face displayed anger, and this result occurred independently of which face expressed the emotion first. This temporal independence could be explained by what we referred to as a social-affective binding mechanism that gives priority to the functional causality between emotions over the temporal causality of stimulus presentations. Further studies should investigate this hypothesis by manipulating the limit of the stimulus onset asynchrony between the contextual and target emotion.

Recent evidence suggests that social appraisal mechanisms are not just limited to the powerful functional relation between the emotion pair of anger and fear, but also play a vital role in the recognition of social emotions. In fact, results revealed that when two avatars were engaged in social interaction, expression blends of shame and sadness were perceived as expressing more shame when the contextual face expressed disgust (Mumenthaler et al., 2018; see Figure 6.5). Our interpretation is that the functional relationship between the emotion of disgust and shame

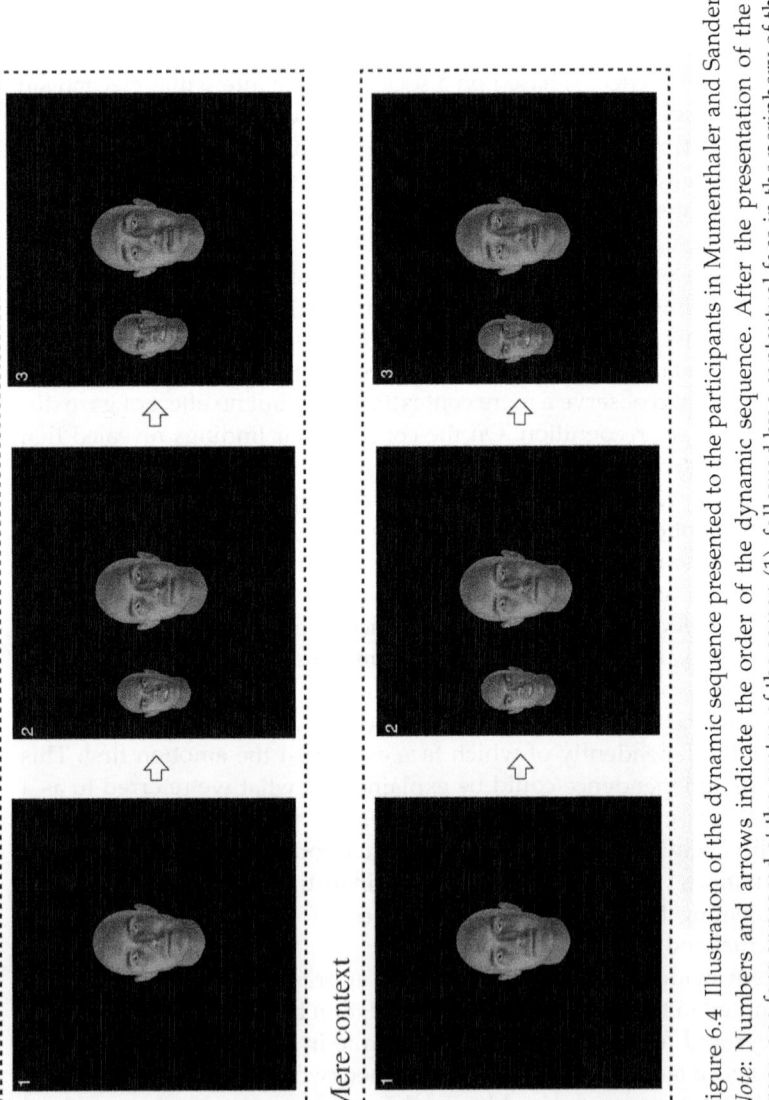

Figure 6.4 Illustration of the dynamic sequence presented to the participants in Mumenthaler and Sander (2012).

Note: Numbers and arrows indicate the order of the dynamic sequence. After the presentation of the fixation cross, one face appeared at the centre of the screen (1), followed by a contextual face in the periphery of the screen expressing an emotion with a gaze shift (2). In the social appraisal condition, the gaze shift was directed to the face at the centre of the screen, while in the mere context condition it was directed toward the outside of the screen. Following the gaze shift of the contextual face, the face in the centre of the screen expressed an emotion (3).

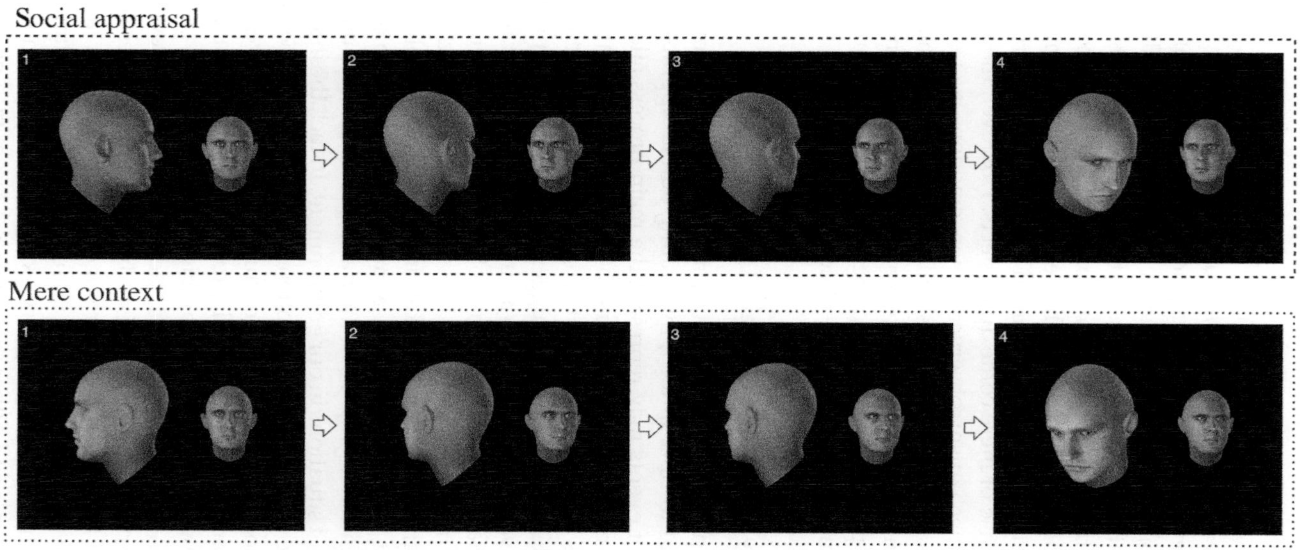

Social appraisal

Mere context

Figure 6.5 Illustration of the dynamic sequence presented to the participants in Mumenthaler et al. (2018).
Note: Numbers and arrows indicate the order of the dynamic sequence. After the presentation of the fixation cross, both faces appeared on the screen (1), followed by a shift of the head/gaze of both faces (2). In the social interaction condition, the faces looked at each other and shared a mutual gaze, while in the mere context condition they looked into opposite directions. Following the head/gaze shift, the contextual face expressed an emotion (3), and then the target face expressed an emotion (4). An animated sequence of the task is available at https://ieeexplore.ieee.org/document/8319988/media.

communicated to the participant that the target felt ashamed because of the referent's disgusted facial expression. In this case, the contextual disgust face conveyed a disapproving message of the person, increasing the perception of shame (see also Haidt, 2003).

These studies provide new evidence for understanding how social contextual information influences the perception and evaluation of emotional facial expressions. In fact, most studies focusing on the influence of contextual information on emotion recognition have investigated the congruency between the emotional information provided by the context and the face. Therefore, an increase in the recognition of the emotion expressed by the target face could be explained by priming or congruency effects, just as in the case of mere contextual effects. However, the socio-affective inferential mechanism observed when emotions were functionally related (i.e. anger–fear; disgust–shame pairs) revealed that the integration of social information in emotion recognition also depends on a complex inferential process that relies on social appraisal mechanisms, and not merely on priming or congruency effects.

6.3   Automaticity of the social appraisal

As discussed in the previous section, social appraisal mechanisms are proposed to be central to ASL. Indeed, integrating others' appraisals in our own evaluation of events may represent the main process allowing us to use emotional expressions of others to learn about the value of objects and situations in our environment. The dimension of intentionality proposed by Clément and Dukes suggests that a social appraisal mechanism is only involved when there is an intentional search for information by the potential learner (i.e. affective observation), or when both the potential learner and the "knower" have an intentional exchange (i.e. social referencing; see Clément & Dukes, Introduction, this volume). However, we suggest that a social appraisal mechanism may also occur when there is no intentional purpose in the transmission or reception of the value of objects and situations in our environment. In fact, the integration of socio-affective information in emotion processing, as presented, for instance, during social appraisal, may occur without the involvement of consciously deliberated or intentional processes, providing a clear functional advantage when dealing with ambiguous situations.

In experiments similar to the studies mentioned in the previous section, we asked participants to recognize dynamic facial expressions of emotion (blends of fear and surprise or anger and disgust) in a target face presented at the centre of a screen. Simultaneously, a subliminal contextual face appearing in the periphery expressed an emotion (fear, anger) or didn't (neutral) and either looked at the target face or didn't (away) (Mumenthaler & Sander, 2015; see Figure 6.6). Results showed

Social appraisal

Mere context

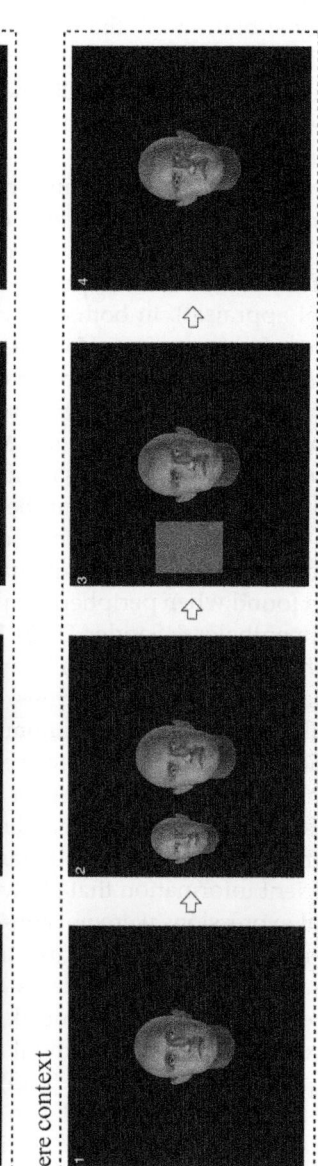

Figure 6.6 Illustration of the dynamic sequence presented to the participants in Mumenthaler and Sander (2015). Note: Numbers and arrows indicate the order of the dynamic sequence. After the presentation of the fixation cross, one face appeared at the centre of the screen (1), followed by a contextual face in the periphery of the screen expressing an emotion with a gaze shift (2). In the social appraisal condition, the gaze shift was directed to the face at the centre of the screen, while in the mere context condition it was directed toward the outside of the screen. Then, the contextual face was masked (3) and disappeared of the screen (4). To get the exact presentation times of the stimuli, please refer to the original paper. An animated version of the task is also available at http://dx.doi .org/10.1037/xge0000059.supp.

that the facial expression blends of fear and surprise were more often and more rapidly categorized as expressing fear when the subliminal contextual face expressed anger and gazed toward – rather than away from – the target face. Although the visual difference between the two angry faces was perceptually subtle – with the only difference being that the gaze direction was different between the two conditions – and with the angry face being visually masked, our results indicated that participants were still able to infer a functional relationship between the contextual angry face and the target fearful face.

As previously mentioned, to understand how social information influences the recognition of emotional facial expressions, we should make a distinction between the general affect expressed by others (mere contextual effect) and a more specific socio-affective inferential mechanism (social appraisal). In both cases, the observer processes socio-affective contextual information. However, in the socio-affective inferential mechanism, the apparent emotional reaction of others is directed at a particular person initiating a social appraisal process (see Figure 6.2). In previous experiments (see Mumenthaler & Sander, 2012), we had shown that both mechanisms impact emotion recognition when social contextual information can be consciously processed. However, the results also suggested that only socio-affective inferential mechanisms impact emotion recognition automatically. One reason that such effects have been found when peripheral expressions were available to consciousness (Mumenthaler & Sander, 2012), but not when they were subliminal (Mumenthaler & Sander, 2015), may be that only strongly disambiguating signals have an unconscious effect. Supporting this assumption, results also showed that this automatic effect does not generalize to the perception of all ambiguous facial expressions as the recognition of expression blends of anger and disgust was not influenced by a contextual face expressing anger. It seems that the functional relationship between a facial expression of anger and its targeted facial expression of fear provides sufficient information that allows for strong disambiguation when contextual expressions were not consciously available.

The existence of automatic socio-affective inferential mechanisms supports the proposal that cognitive systems can automatically integrate different sources of information (Mudrik, Faivre, & Koch, 2014) and perform complex causal inferences without the involvement of consciously deliberated processes (see Hassin, 2013). Such findings suggest that the dimension of automaticity should also be taken into consideration in the theoretical framework of ASL. For instance, the dimension of intentionality proposed by Clément and Dukes (2017) refers to the purpose involved in the transmission of values. On that dimension, emotional contagion is at one extreme (low in intentionality), followed by affective observation, social referencing, and natural pedagogy at the other extreme (high intentionality). However, we believe that these four components could also be sorted in terms of their automaticity. For instance, emotional contagion at the lower end on the dimension of intentionality is also, by definition, an automatic process, while natural pedagogy at the higher end of the intentionality dimension is not required to be automatic. Although extremes of the intentionality dimension are relatively easy to categorize regarding their automaticity, both components associated with social appraisal mechanisms (i.e. affective observation, social referencing) cannot be seen as purely automatic or entirely explicit because both of them can imply some level of automaticity. One proposition to include the automaticity dimension in the theoretical framework of ASL would be to investigate which of the features that characterize an automatic process are present in each one of these four components.

6.4   Ambiguity hypothesis

The notion that people are motivated to use social information to understand their environment is well accepted now in affective sciences. However, under which circumstances do we appraise others' emotions in order to understand our environment? The social comparison theory (Festinger, 1954) proposed that individuals have a need to evaluate their own opinions and beliefs by comparison with others. Trope (1986) proposed that when facing an ambiguous situation, the clarity of the contextual information also has an important impact on the identification of the situation. For instance, the effect of contextual information on emotion recognition should increase with the ambiguity of the facial expression and decrease with the ambiguity of the context (see Aviezer, Hassin, Bentin et al., 2008).

The assumption that the socio-affective inferential mechanisms involved in social appraisal processes are more likely to occur in uncertainty-inducing situations is congruent with results showing that contextual information modulates emotion recognition, especially when expressions convey ambiguous emotional information (for a review, see Barrett et al., 2011; Gendron, Mesquita & Barrett, 2013). In fact, using morphed facial expressions on a continuum between happy and fear, van den Stock, Righart, and de Gelder (2007) showed that the magnitude of the influence of the body expression depends on the ambiguity of the facial expression; the magnitude was greater when the facial expression was most ambiguous. Similarly, Aviezer, Hassin, Ryan et al. (2008) revealed that the magnitude of body contextual influence was strongly correlated with the degree of perceptual similarity between the target facial expression and the facial expression that was prototypically associated with the emotional context. Therefore, because of the high similarity that exists between the facial expression of disgust and anger, a disgust facial expression on an anger body would be more readily incorrectly perceived as expressing anger (Hassin, Aviezer, & Bentin, 2013).

The ambiguity of the situation plays a significant role in modulating the influence of social appraisal mechanisms. It makes sense to assume that people are more receptive to others' appraisals when they are uncertain about the emotional significance of an event (see Bruder et al., 2014). However, we do not imply that these mechanisms only occur in ambiguous situations, and previous studies have shown that socio-affective inferences involving social appraisal mechanisms also occur when no ambiguity is involved (see Mumenthaler & Sander, 2012). Nevertheless, it remains an open question whether other components of ASL that do not involve social appraisal mechanisms are particularly effective in ambiguous situations.

6.5   Conclusion and future perspectives

Social appraisal is a mechanism that was mainly proposed to take into account the fact that others' emotions can influence us when we appraise a given situation. In this conclusion, we would like to consider three ways where future research may investigate the role of social appraisal in ASL.

First, research is needed to elucidate the specific conditions under which we use the affective relationships that others entertain with specific objects or situations to shape our evaluation of these very same objects or situations. For instance, what are the temporal dynamics and boundaries that allow an optimal consideration of this affective relationship? Above, we discussed the fact that the functional affective relation between the emotion pair of anger and fear seems to be more powerful than the temporal causality between the two expressions (see Mumenthaler & Sander, 2012). In this case, a type of "social-affective binding mechanism" may influence our evaluative processes independently of some temporal boundaries. For instance, would our appraisal of an object be more positive if someone is smiling at the location of this object (versus at another location) *before* the object appears? A related research question concerns the level of processing needed to integrate the affective relationships that others entertain with specific objects or situations into our evaluation of these objects or situations. We mentioned earlier that there is some evidence that such integration may be automatic, but a better understanding of the conditions for automaticity to take place during social appraisal would bring important elements to the ASL framework. Another research question concerns the variables that determine the affective relationship either between the other individual and the appraised object (e.g. ownership) or between ourselves and the other individual (e.g. friendship). For instance, there are several ways in which how we trust the other individual may accentuate the social appraisal process such as how trustworthy the individual appears to be (Todorov, 2017) or how the specific expressions of emotion modulate trust (see Clément, Bernard, Grandjean, & Sander, 2013; Tang, Harris, Zou, & Xu, in press).

Second, and in connection with what we just discussed above, research may investigate the links between social appraisal and learning, with "learning about" being considered in the sense of "discovering" or "being informed that". Indeed, it seems to us that an important question corresponds to how one is using social appraisal to *discover* (i.e. learn about) the value of a particular event (e.g. object, situation, or relationship). Indeed, when we evaluate an event, we may for instance discover that this event is interesting because someone is appraising it as interesting, and therefore the emotion of interest is elicited in this person (or, for instance, that this event is dangerous because someone is appraising it as threatening and therefore the emotion of fear is elicited in this person). The way social appraisal would allow us to learn about the value of a specific event could be studied in connection with concern-relevance, and in particular for how events that are relevant for our concerns capture our emotional attention (see Pool, Brosch, Delplanque, & Sander, 2016). We think that a particularly useful research question would be to test how some events may *acquire* a certain relevance that is based on a social appraisal mechanism. As mentioned already above, research has focused on how social appraisal modulates the appraisal of a concern-relevant event (e.g. the recognition of emotional expressions in our work). However, another way to examine potential links between social appraisal and ASL would be to study potential direct effects of some social concerns (e.g. affiliation) on the way we appraise and learn about events. This may for instance be the case when a child learns about (i.e. discovers) the value of "interest" of an otherwise neutral object because the relationship with the other person is particularly concern-relevant (see Clément & Dukes, 2013).

Third, research may investigate the links between social appraisal and learning, with "learning" being considered as long-term memory-related processes (see Fischer, Chapter 7, this volume, for a detailed discussion of how we might learn from others' emotions). In other words: does social appraisal facilitate long-term learning of the value of specific events? Consistent with evidence that there is a bias of emotional attention towards relevant events (e.g. Pool et al., 2016), there is a large amount of evidence that both positively and negatively relevant events are also better encoded, consolidated, and recalled in episodic memory (LaBar & Cabeza, 2006). While the literature typically distinguishes between three systems involved in value learning (Pavlovian learning, instrumental learning, and goal-directed learning, see Daw & O'Doherty, 2014), to the best of our knowledge, research has not investigated how social appraisal may interact with these systems. Investigating the way emotions interact with these three systems is likely to lead to fascinating new results (see Moors, 2017), and there is work linking appraisal not only to goal-directed learning but also to Pavlovian learning (see Sennwald, Pool, & Sander, 2017). For instance, it has been suggested that the appraised relevance of stimuli may be the key determinant of facilitatory effects on Pavlovian learning (Stussi, Pourtois, & Sander, 2018).

Concerning social appraisal, a link can already be drawn with work on "vicarious" fear learning. Indeed, research on fear conditioning has shown that fear can be acquired indirectly through social observation (called "observational fear learning", see Olsson & Phelps, 2004) with no personal experience of the aversive event, and that such observational learning engages similar neural mechanisms as fear conditioning (Olsson, Nearing, & Phelps, 2007). This line of research suggests that, through observational fear learning, there can be some social transmissions of threats (Haaker, Golkar Selbing, & Olsson, 2017). Research may further consider the role of social appraisal in value learning through conditioning for other values than those that are threat-related, and may also study the influence of social appraisal on several learning mechanisms other than Pavlovian learning.

In conclusion, we see an important potential in integrating research on social appraisal in the framework of ASL (Clément and Dukes, Introduction, this volume). As reviewed in this chapter, evidence has accumulated indicating that social appraisal is indeed effective in shaping various processes (e.g. evaluation of events, emotion experience, and emotion recognition), and may do so at an automatic level, particularly in ambiguous situations. As also discussed in this concluding section, future research may focus on the boundary conditions under which social appraisal shapes the way we evaluate events, on how social appraisal allows us to discover the value of events that were not otherwise appraised as relevant, and on how social appraisal interacts with memory and learning systems facilitating Pavlovian learning, instrumental learning, and goal-directed learning. Given that appraisal is only one component of emotion, it would be particularly interesting to adopt a componential approach to emotion (see e.g. Sander, Grandjean, & Scherer, 2018) in order to study the effects of social appraisal, not only on the way we appraise events, but also to discover whether there are some specificities in the way social appraisal differentiates the other emotion components (expression, autonomic reaction, action tendencies, and feeling) when we engage in ASL.

References

Adams, R. B., Jr., & Kleck, R. E. (2003). Perceived gaze direction and the processing of facial displays of emotion. *Psychological Science, 14*, 644–647.

(2005). Effects of direct and averted gaze on the perception of facial communicated emotion. *Emotion, 5*, 3–11.

Aviezer, H., Bentin, S., Dudarev, V., & Hassin, R. R. (2011). The automaticity of emotional face–context integration. *Emotion, 11*, 1406–1414.

Aviezer, H., Hassin, R. R., Bentin, S., & Trope, Y. (2008). Putting facial expressions back in context. In N. Ambady & J. Skowronsky (Eds.), *First impressions* (pp. 255–286). New York, NY: Guilford.

Aviezer, H., Hassin, R., Ryan, J., Grady, C., Susskind, J., Anderson, A., … Bentin, S. (2008). Angry, disgusted, or afraid? Studies on the malleability of emotion perception. *Psychological Science, 19*, 724–732.

Aviezer, H., Trope, Y., & Todorov, A. (2012). Body cues, not facial expressions, discriminate between intense positive and negative emotions. *Science, 338*(6111), 1225–1229.

Bayliss, A. P., Frischen, A., Fenske, M. J., & Tipper, S. P. (2007). Affective evaluations of objects are influenced by observed gaze direction and emotional expression. *Cognition, 104*, 644–653.

Barrett, L. F., Mesquita, B., & Gendron, M. (2011). Context in emotion perception. *Current Directions in Psychological Science, 20*, 286–290.

Bodenhausen, G. V., & Todd, A. R. (2010). Social cognition. *Wiley Interdisciplinary Reviews: Cognitive Science, 1*(2), 160–171. doi:10.1002/wcs.28

Bruder, M., Fischer, A., & Manstead, A. S. R. (2014). Social appraisal as a cause of collective emotions. In C. von Scheve & M. Salmela (Eds.), *Collective emotions* (pp. 141–155). New York, NY: Oxford University Press.

Clément, F., Bernard, S., Grandjean, D., & Sander, D. (2013). Emotional expression and vocabulary learning in adults and children. *Cognition and Emotion, 27*(3), 539–548

Clément, F., & Dukes, D. (2013). The role of interest in the social transmission of values. *Frontiers in Psychology, 4*, 349.

(2017). Social appraisal and social referencing: Two components of affective social learning. *Emotion Review, 9*(3), 253–261.

Cristinzio, C., N'Diaye, K., Seeck, M., Vuilleumier, P., & Sander, D. (2010). Integration of gaze direction and facial expression in patients with unilateral amygdala damage. *Brain, 133*, 248–261.

Cline, M. G. (1956). The influence of social context on the perception of faces. *Journal of Personality, 25*(2), 142–157.

Daw, N. D., & O'Doherty, J. P. (2014). Multiple systems for value learning. In P. W. Glimcher & E. Fehr (Eds.), *Neuroeconomics* (2nd ed., pp. 393–410). New York, NY: Academic Press.

de Gelder, B., Meeren, H. K. M., Righart, R., Stock, J., van de Riet, W. A. C., & Tamietto, M. (2006). Beyond the face: Exploring rapid influences of context on face processing. *Progress in Brain Research, 155*, 37–48.

de Gelder, B., & van den Stock, J. (2012). Real faces, real emotions: Perceiving facial expressions in naturalistic contexts of voices, bodies and scenes. In A. J. Calder, G. Rhodes, J. V. Haxby, & M. H. Johnson (Eds.), *The handbook of face perception*. Oxford, UK: Oxford University Press.

de Melo, C. M., Carnevale, P. J., Read, S. J., & Gratch, J. (2014). Reading people's minds from emotion expressions in interdependent decision making. *Journal of Personality and Social Psychology, 106*(1), 73–88.

Ekman, P. (1972). Universals and cultural differences in facial expressions of emotion. In J. K. Cole (Ed.), *Nebraska symposium on motivation* (pp. 207–283). Lincoln, NE: University of Nebraska Press.

(1993). Facial expression of emotion. *American Psychologist, 48,* 384–392.

Ekman P., Freisen W. V., & Ellsworth P. (1972). *Emotion in the human face.* New York, NY: Pergamon Press.

Evers, C., Fischer, A., Mosquera, P., & Manstead, A. (2005). Anger and social appraisal: A "spicy" sex difference? *Emotion, 5,* 258–266.

Feinman, S. (1992). In the broad valley: An integrative look at social referencing. In S. Feinman (Ed.), *Social referencing and the social construction of reality in infancy* (pp. 15–54). New York, NY: Plenum Press.

Festinger, L. (1954). A theory of social comparison processes. *Human Relations, 7,* 117–140.

Fischer, A. H., Rotteveel, M., Evers, C., & Manstead, A. S. R. (2004). Emotional assimilation: How we are influenced by others' emotions. *Cahiers de Psychologie Cognitive/Current Psychology of Cognition, 22,* 223–245.

Gendron, M., Mesquita, B., & Barrett, L. F. (2013). Emotion perception: Putting the face in context. In D. Reisberg (Ed.), *Oxford handbook of cognitive psychology* (pp. 379–389). New York, NY: Oxford University Press.

Grandjean, D., & Scherer, K. R. (2008). Unpacking the cognitive architecture of emotion processes. *Emotion, 8,* 341–351. doi:10.1037/1528- 3542.8.3.341

Haaker, J., Golkar, A., Selbing, I., & Olsson, A (2017). Assessment of social transmission of threats in humans using observational fear conditioning. *Nature Protocols, 12*(7), 1378–1386.

Haidt, J. (2003). The moral emotions. In R. J. Davidson, K. R. Scherer, & H. H. Goldsmith (Eds.), *Handbook of affective sciences* (pp. 852–870). Oxford, UK: Oxford University Press.

Hassin, R. R. (2013). Yes it can: On the functional abilities of the human unconscious. *Perspectives on Psychological Science, 8,* 195–207.

Hassin, R. R., Aviezer, H., & Benton, S. (2013). Inherently ambiguous: Facial expressions of emotions, in context. *Emotion Review, 5,* 60–65.

Hassin, R. R., Bargh, J. A., & Uleman, J. S. (2002). Spontaneous causal inferences. *Journal of Experimental Social Psychology, 38,* 515–522.

Izard, C. E. (1971). *The face of emotion.* New York, NY: Appleton-Century-Crofts.

Jakobs, E., Fischer, A. H., & Manstead, A. S. R. (1997). Emotional experience as a function of social context: The role of the other. *Journal of Nonverbal Behavior, 21,* 103–130.

Jones, B. C., DeBruine, L. M., Little, A. C., Burriss, R. P., & Feinberg, D. R. (2007). Social transmission of face preferences among humans. *Proceedings of the Royal Society of London B: Biological Sciences, 274,* 899–903.

Klinnert, M. D., Campos, J. J., Sorce, J. F., Emde, R. N., & Svejda, M. (1983). Emotions as behavior regulators. In R. Plutchik & H. Kellerman (Eds.), *Emotions: Theory, research, and experience* (Vol. 2, pp. 57–86). New York, NY: Academic Press.

LaBar, K., & Cabeza, R. (2006). Cognitive neuroscience of emotional memory. *Nature Reviews Neuroscience, 7*(1), 54–64.

Landis, C. (1929). The interpretation of facial expression in emotion. *Journal of General Psychology, 2*(1), 59–72.

Lieberman, M. D. (2007). Social cognitive neuroscience: A review of core processes. *Annual Review of Psychology, 58*(1), 259–289.

Manstead, A. S. R., & Fischer, A. H. (2001). Social appraisal: The social world as object of and influence on appraisal processes. In K. R. Scherer, A. Schorr, & T. Johnstone (Eds.), *Appraisal processes in emotion: Theory, method, research* (pp. 221–232). New York, NY: Oxford University Press.

Masuda, T., Ellsworth, P. C., Mesquita, B., Leu, J., Tanida, S., & de Veerdonk, E. V. (2008). Placing the face in context: Cultural differences in the perception of facial emotion. *Journal of Personality and Social Psychology, 94*, 365–381.

Moors, A. (2017). Integration of two skeptical emotion theories: Dimensional appraisal theory and Russell's psychological construction theory. *Psychological Inquiry, 28*(1), 1–19.

Mudrik, L., Faivre, N., & Koch, C. (2014). Information integration without awareness. *Trends in Cognitive Sciences, 18*, 488–496.

Mumenthaler, C., & Sander, D. (2012). Social appraisal influences recognition of emotions. *Journal of Personality and Social Psychology, 102*, 1118–1135.

   (2015). Automatic integration of social information in emotion recognition. *Journal of Experimental Psychology: General, 144*, 392–399.

Mumenthaler, C., Sander, D., & Manstead, A. S. R. (2018). Emotion recognition in simulated social interactions. *IEEE Transactions on Affective Computing*. https://doi.org/10.1109/TAFFC.2018.2799593

Olkkonen, M., & Ekroll, V. (2016) Color constancy and contextual effects on color appearance. In J. Kremers, R. Baraas, & N. Marshall (Eds.), *Human color vision* (Springer Series in Vision Research, Vol. 5, pp. 221–232). Cham, Switzerland: Springer.

Olsson, A., Nearing, K. I., & Phelps, E. A. (2007). Learning fears by observing others: The neural systems of social fear transmission. *Social, Cognitive & Affective Neuroscience, 2*, 2–10.

Olsson, A., & Phelps, E. A. (2004). Learned fear of unseen faces after Pavlovian, observational and instructed fear. *Psychological Science, 15*, 822–828.

Parkinson, B., Phiri, N., & Simons, G. (2012). Bursting with anxiety: Adult social referencing in an interpersonal Balloon Analogue Risk Task (BART). *Emotion, 12*(4), 817–826. doi:10.1037/a0026434

Parkinson, B., & Simons, G. (2009). Worry spreads: Interpersonal transfer of problem-related anxiety. *Cognition & Emotion, 26*(3), 462–479.

Pool, E. R., Brosch, T., Delplanque, S., & Sander, D. (2016). Attentional bias for positive emotional stimuli: A meta-analytic investigation. *Psychological Bulletin, 142*, 79–106.

Righart, R., & de Gelder, B. (2008). Recognition of facial expressions is influenced by emotional scene gist. *Cognitive, Affective, & Behavioral Neuroscience, 8*, 264–272.

Russell, J. A., & Fehr, B. (1987). Relativity in the perception of emotion in facial expressions. *Journal of Experimental Psychology: General, 116*(3), 223–237.

Sander, D., Grandjean, D., Kaiser, S., Wehrle, T., & Scherer, K. R. (2007). Interaction effects of perceived gaze direction and dynamic facial expression: Evidence for appraisal theories of emotion. *European Journal of Cognitive Psychology, 19*, 470–480.

Sander, D., Grandjean, D., & Scherer, K. R. (2005). A systems approach to appraisal mechanisms in emotion. *Neural Networks*, *18*, 317–352.

(2018). An appraisal-driven componential approach to the emotional brain. *Emotion Review*, *10*(3), 219–231.

Scherer, K. R., Mortillaro, M., Rotondi, I., Sergi, I., & Trznadel, S. (2018). Appraisal-driven facial actions as building blocks for emotion inference. *Journal of Personality and Social Psychology*, *114*(3), 358–379.

Sennwald, V., Pool, E., & Sander, D. (2017). Considering the influence of the Pavlovian system on behavior: Appraisal and value representation. *Psychological Inquiry*, *28*(1), 52–55.

Smith, C. A., & Scott, H. S. (1997). A componential approach to the meaning of facial expressions. In J. A. Russell, & J. M. Fernández-Dols (Eds.), *The psychology of facial expression* (pp. 229–254). New York, NY: Cambridge University Press.

Sorce, J. F., Emde, R. N., Campos, J. J., & Klinnert, M. D. (1985). Maternal emotional signaling: Its effect on the visual cliff behavior of 1-year-olds. *Developmental Psychology*, *21*(1), 195.

Stussi, Y., Pourtois, G., & Sander, D. (2018). Enhanced Pavlovian aversive conditioning to positive emotional stimuli. *Journal of Experimental Psychology: General*, *147*, 905–923.

Tang, Y., Harris, P. L., Zou, H., & Xu, Q. (2019). The impact of emotional expressions on children's trust judgments. *Cognition and Emotion*, *33*(2), 318–331. doi: 10.1080/02699931.2018.1449735

Todorov, A. (2017). *Face value: The irresistible influence of first impressions.* Princeton, NJ and Oxford, UK: Princeton University Press.

Trope, Y. (1986). Identification and inferential processes in dispositional attribution. *Psychological Review*, *93*, 239–257.

van den Stock, J., Righart, R., & de Gelder, B. (2007). Whole body expressions influence recognition of facial expressions and emotional prosody. *Emotion*, *7*, 487–494.

van Doorn, E. A., Heerdink, M. W., & van Kleef, G. A. (2012). Emotion and the construal of social situations: Inferences of cooperation versus competition from expressions of anger, happiness, and disappointment. *Cognition & Emotion*, *26*(3), 442–461.

van Reekum, C., Johnstone, T., Banse, R., Etter, A., Wehrle, T., & Scherer, K. (2004). Psychophysiological responses to appraisal dimensions in a computer game. *Cognition & Emotion*, *18*, 663–688.

Wehrle, T., Kaiser, S., Schmidt, S., & Scherer, K. R. (2000). Studying the dynamics of emotional expression using synthesized facial muscle movements. *Journal of Personality and Social Psychology*, *78*, 105–119.

Wieser, M. J., & Brosch, T. (2012). Faces in context: a review and systematization of contextual influences on affective face processing. *Frontiers in Psychology*, *3*, 471.

CHAPTER 7

Learning from others' emotions

Agneta Fischer

By the time you read this chapter, you have probably learned that affective social learning (ASL) is not about learning maths, or learning to skate, but about learning what is important and meaningful, thus about the transmission of values in the broadest sense of the word. In today's society, values have become less and less determined by where one is born, who one's parents are and what they value, and increasingly more by one's own deliberate choices and one's social, emotional and cognitive abilities. In our current networked society, ASL is thus more important than ever, and this volume is therefore very timely.

The concept of ASL was introduced in a paper in *Emotion Review* (Clément & Dukes, 2017) on the role of others in appraising an emotional event, a phenomenon referred to as social appraisal (Bruder, Fischer, & Manstead, 2014; Manstead & Fischer, 2001, 2017) or social referencing (Klinnert, Campos, Sorce, Emde, & Svejda, 1983; Klinnert, Emde, Butterfield, & Campos, 1986). The basic idea is that others' emotional expressions can influence the way in which we value the world, or in other words, how we appraise emotional stimuli. ASL thus minimally implies three elements: a source expressing emotions, a target or learner observing the emotion and the object of the emotion expression (what the emotion is about). The source's emotional expression implies the signalling of a meaning about the object, such as 'this is threatening, disgusting, frustrating, painful, lovely, moving or amusing'. Whether the emotional expression thereby reflects a value about a specific object is not necessarily obvious, given the discussion about the definition of values. Rohan (2000), for example, refers to values as reflecting a more abstract system, rather than a specific evaluation or meaning of one object. Value systems can be organized at a personal level (self-schemata) or at a social (social value systems) or at a world-view level (Christian values), but in ASL they would become apparent through the specific expression of an emotion and can thus be regarded as an emotional evaluation of the object.

Prototypical evidence for ASL comes from research on social referencing and social appraisal, in which researchers have provided empirical support for the idea that others' facial expressions lead to different inferences of stimuli. For example, Mumenthaler and Sander (2012) showed that people are more likely to perceive a neutral face as fearful if another face shows anger towards this face. A more classic paradigm is the visual cliff, where babies who are faced with an anxious mother when approaching a 'visual cliff' seem to be re-appraising the cliff that initially did not seem scary (Bertenthal & Campos, 1984; Witherington, Campos, Anderson, Lejeune, & Seah, 2005), stop crawling, watch their mother's face and turn back. All though this has never been reported, to my knowledge, these children not only crawl back but also seem to have a change of emotion, from happy, or at least neutral, to anxious, which makes them turn around.

This could mean that others' emotional displays may not only affect the interpretation of the environment, but also their own emotions and related behaviours. This has been demonstrated in studies on emotional transfer (Parkinson, 2011; Parkinson & Simons, 2012). Parkinson, Phiri, and Simons (2012), for example, showed that the social appraisal of a source's anxiety increases the target's anxious expression as well. Social appraisals may thus influence one's emotions and/or emotion regulation. Another example is that the social appraisal of another's anger is more likely to lead to anger suppression (at least in women), if the target expects to meet the angry source than when she does not (Evers, Fischer, Rodriguez Mosquera, & Manstead, 2005). In other words, this research shows that others' visible emotions have an impact not only on how we appraise an external object, person or event, but also on how we appraise, label and regulate our own emotions and behaviours. Whether this change of emotion is the result or cause of a change in appraisal remains to be answered, but it is highly likely that this relation is bi-directional (see also Parkinson, 1997). In my view, the object of ASL is thus not only the transmissions of values about the world, but also values about our emotions and how to socially manage these emotions appropriately.

The question I want to focus on in this chapter is not on the fact that we *are* influenced by others' emotions, but on the conditions in which we actually learn from others' emotions and the processes underlying ASL. In other words, *how* we learn from others' emotions. The chapter will first discuss minimal requirements and then review different theoretical approaches to learning that may lead to a better conceptual understanding of the type of learning involved in ASL. I will finally relate this to the four components of ASL that are mentioned in the introductory chapter to this volume: emotional contagion, affective observation and social referencing (together social appraisal) and natural pedagogy.

7.1 Minimal requirements for ASL

ASL has two key elements that distinguish it from non-social and non-affective learning. The first is the *object* of ASL: ASL is about the transmission of values, not skills or non-social knowledge. This criterion does not necessarily distinguish ASL from other forms of social learning (e.g. observational learning or vicarious learning) or from conditioning, though it does raise the question whether the values can only be about the world and not about the target's own emotions. A second key criterion is *how* values are transmitted, namely by the perception of, or minimally, the awareness of, others' emotional reactions. This criterion is the most unique that distinguishes ASL from any other form of learning, and therefore I will focus on this second criterion.

There are three conditions that I think should be a minimal requirement for others' emotional reactions to have an initial impact on an individual (see also Clément & Dukes, Introduction, this volume). First, the source (displaying the emotion and from whom the target learns) needs to show some emotional appreciation. This may be with minimal cues, such as a short nod, or with full-blown emotions, like screaming to stay away from the stove. This does not necessarily need to be a deliberate attempt to teach the target (e.g. showing a fear face and instructing a child: 'watch out, this is a dangerous animal'). Emotional expressions or behaviours can have an effect without the explicit intentions of the source, because they operate as social signals, for example when the parent is afraid himself and shows fear when looking at the barking dog (Hareli & Hess, 2012; Hess & Fischer, 2014). The latter situation is typically the case in research on emotional contagion (Hatfield, Cacioppo, & Rapson, 1994; Hess & Blairy, 2001), or research using the social referencing paradigm. The stronger and more frequent the emotion expression, the larger the impact is assumed to be and the more the target learns an emotional response toward a certain object, person or event.

Second, the target pays attention to the source and is aware of the source's focus of attention and the relevance of the emotion expression for him or her. This can imply that the target and source are in the same location (physically or virtually). In addition, the target not only needs to be aware of the other's emotion, but also of the relation between the other's emotion and the object of the emotion display. Hence, it should be evident for the target *why* the source displays this emotion. This contingency relation is crucial for ASL to occur. For example, a child is not likely to learn from a parent's anxiety about the fact that he is riding his bicycle too quickly, because he is enjoying himself, does not pay attention and does not see any threat. In contrast, this may lead to a reversal role of target and source, with the target reassuring or encouraging the source not to be afraid.

Third, the source needs to put some trust in the source's judgement or evaluation of the world (Kret, Fischer, & de Dreu, 2015). Though the source and target need not know each other, for example, in the case of a flight attendant who shows fear when the plane is seriously bumping, ASL will generally be stronger if the source is an identification or attachment figure in whom the target has confidence. This is because we are more likely to trust the emotions of sources we trust, admire or identify with, rather than of persons we do not know.

7.2   When are we motivated to learn from others?

7.2.1   *Uncertainty and ambiguity*

Based on these minimal requirements, the next question is in which situations ASL will most likely occur, or in other words, what are the most likely contexts in which we are motivated to learn from others' emotions? In previous writings on social appraisal and social referencing, it has been suggested that the impact of others' emotions may be largest when the target is in a situation that is uncertain or ambiguous or in which he or she needs guidance on how to act. This is, for example, the case in research settings with babies who are innocently crawling towards a cliff, or with patients in a waiting room, anxious to know the doctor's conclusion about a physical test, or with the observation of faces presented without context. It is most likely that uncertain or ambiguous situations occur more often with children than with adults, but adults can also find themselves in situations where they are uncertain, anxious or ambivalent (see also Bruder et al., 2014; Parkinson et al., 2012). This may be due to the nature of the situation (sudden threat, novel situation or ambiguity about what to do) and its consequences for one's own behaviour. When one is uncertain about a situation, others' emotions are more likely to be guidance for one's own appraisal of the situation. This is nicely illustrated by research on the bystander effect (Darley & Latané, 1970; Latané & Darley, 1970). These studies have shown that when something unexpected happens that is not directly interpreted as an emergency situation (e.g. smoke coming from under a door), one is likely to take action if others do, and not, if, for example, others ignore the smoke. Similarly, when one is faced with a person in distress, the likelihood that one will help is reduced when there are passive bystanders in the critical situation. Importantly, the emotional information displayed by either the victims or the bystanders seems crucial, although this has never been directly examined. In a meta-analysis on the bystander effect (Fischer et al., 2011), the effect was shown to be reduced when the situation was urgent, or, in other words, when the emotional signals in the situation were clear.

In addition, the bystander effect increased when the emotional displays of the bystanders were neutral, suggesting that the situation was reappraised as less urgent. This evidence seems to suggest that the (neutral) emotional displays may have resulted in a change in appraisal of the situation.

The reason why uncertainty, anxiety or ambiguity may be the typical situations in which others' emotions are impactful, is because these are negative feelings that individuals want to suppress or avoid. This category of negative feelings is not only characterized by appraisals of negative valence, but more importantly by appraisals of uncertainty. Uncertainty, ambiguity or ambivalence have been shown to induce negative affect, which people try to solve in various ways (van Harreveld, Nohlen, & Schneider, 2015). In addition, uncertainty elicits social comparison processes, as demonstrated in Schachter's (1959) experiments showing that participants who were anxious at the prospect of being administered electric shocks expressed an overwhelming preference for waiting in the company of other persons rather than alone. When the level of threat was low, the majority of participants preferred to wait alone. One of the motives for wanting to be with others, is that under uncertainty, affiliation with others who share the same fate may provide the best way of evaluating the intensity, nature or appropriateness of one's emotional state (see also Mann, Feddes, Doosje, & Fischer, 2016; Rimé, 2007). This social comparison process was the explanation favoured by Schachter (1959). The motive to regulate appraisals of uncertainty may lead people to socially compare their own emotional responses to those of similar others (see also Festinger, 1954; Suls & Wheeler, 2012) and to seek for social information that can help them to reduce these negative and uncertain feelings. Others' emotional displays may thus be one important source of input that people search for in those situations, because it provides certainty about how others interpret a situation and thus reduces one's own uncertainty.

7.2.2   *Emotional situations*

But does ASL only occur in situations that evoke uncertainty and ambivalence, or can it also occur in emotional situations? Imagine a child is crying because he lost something valuable. Would the calm or upset reaction of a parent not teach the child how to evaluate the situation? In the latter case, the salience and nature of the others' emotion expression may make one re-evaluate the situation or make the child learn how to regulate his own feelings. An example can be found in similar situations as the visual cliff, for example when a child has to swim alone for the first time, or when she has to do an important test.

The social support that the child receives is not only valuable in that particular moment, but may also teach the child how to regulate strong emotions. This may be the case for anxiety, but also for sadness or anger. For example, a source's emotional display in response to a target's anger may also lead him to regulate this anger. An angry response may teach the child to suppress his anger, while an understanding or calm response may lead the child to think about this anger. Parents' reactions to children's behaviour in emotional situations also provide examples of how to deal with an emotional situation and hence set the norms of what an appropriate response is. We learn from others, either implicitly or explicitly ('be quiet', 'try to calm down') what the correct emotion in that situation is. Individual differences in emotion-regulation strategies (Gross & John, 2003; Gross, Richards, & John, 2006), such as differences in preferences to re-appraise or suppress one's emotions, for example, may be the result of how our parents deal with emotions. Indeed, there is abundant literature on the role of the family context in (dys)regulating one's emotions (e.g. Eisenberg, Cumberland, & Spinrad, 1998; Eisenberg & Valiente, 2004). For example, parents' negative or punitive responses in reaction to children's negative emotions are related to more escape or revenge-seeking strategies in reaction to anger-inducing situations (Eisenberg & Fabes, 1994). In addition, parental minimization of children's emotions is associated with avoidant emotion-regulation strategies, and parents' dismissive responses have been associated with increased anger displays by children. Parents' calm or neutral reactions towards their child's anger have been found to be associated with lower levels of expressed anger in other situations (Denham & Grout, 1993).

In sum, ASL does not only occur in situations where the target feels uncertain, either about themselves or about how to interpret the situation, but also in highly emotional situations. Indeed, systematic emotional reactions by parents to a child's display of emotions also provide the child with information on what is an appropriate emotional response in such a situation. The question is then whether others' (non-) emotional displays in reaction to an emotional reaction of a target, should be considered as a form of ASL. I would argue that it should. Such reactions not only teach an individual that their emotions are not encouraged or shared, but it also tells them something about how to appraise the object of the emotion. It could tell them how to deal with frustration, how to manage loss or that the expression of pride is not so appropriate in this context. These are social values, and in my view should be included as a form of ASL. Another question is whether neutral displays of others can be included in ASL. Again, I think it should. Neutral displays in an emotional situation can teach the child about the values of an object or a person, but only if the child reacts emotionally.

7.3 What type of learning is involved in ASL?

This leads us to another question that relates to the 'learning' aspect of ASL. It is important to distinguish between others' emotions having a temporary impact (van Kleef, 2009) and actually learning from others' emotions. In the latter case, the exposure to others' emotions and their subsequent influence is more likely to result in a permanent change in appraisal, emotions or behaviours if the exposure is not incidental, but recurring. An incidental emotional reaction by another can have an immediate short-term impact, for example, backing off when someone is angry with you or starting to cry when someone else is really sad. However, in order to qualify as learning, ASL should include a relatively permanent change (which, by the way, can also be unlearned again). This can be the consequence of multiple exposure to others' emotional reactions, though sometimes one exposure could be even sufficient if it is strong or unique enough to adjust one's future emotional reactions. For example, if parents tell their child he should be very aware of black children because they cannot be trusted, the encounter of a new black child in the classroom the following week is likely to have a more permanent effect on this child's perception of his new classmate. So multiple or significant exposures to others' emotions can lead to a more permanent association between a certain event or stimulus and another's emotional reaction, leading to an emotional response that is based on this emotional reaction.

Obviously, these and other examples raise the question of the processes underlying ASL: is ASL simply a question of observational learning, where we learn by seeing others' emotions? Is it then a specific form of imitation, as in emotional contagion (the first of the four stages in the Clément and Dukes model) or mimicry, where we are affected by merely watching others' emotions in certain situations? Or do we need more specific pairings between the target's behaviour and the source's emotion expressions, as in operant or evaluative conditioning? Or can ASL be regarded as a form of classical conditioning where unconditioned stimuli are coupled with positive or negative stimuli in order to create a conditioned response, as demonstrated in research on fear conditioning? In the following sections, we will compare the assumptions of ASL with three other forms of learning in order to gain more understanding of the processes underlying ASL: social learning, conditioning (classical and operant) and cognitive learning.

7.3.1 Social learning versus ASL

Social learning theory as developed by Bandura (Bandura, 1971) states that learning can occur without explicit instruction or tuition, but simply by watching others (see also Clément & Dukes, Introduction, this volume).

If ASL is indeed a form of social learning (SL), this would imply that the emotional expressions of others would be observed and imitated. Social learning, also referred to as vicarious or observational learning, does not need reward or punishment: the simple identification with a social model is sufficient to result in the learning of new social behaviours, customs or cultural practices. Identification here refers to the degree of similarity between the target and source, and the similarity can be imagined or real. Still, research does suggest that a rewarding (warm and nurturant) parent elicits more imitative behaviour than a cold and distant parent (Bandura, 1969), suggesting that emotional learning would also occur more in the case of sources with whom one holds warm relationships.

The learning of aggressive behaviour has been studied as one prominent example of social learning, exemplified by the classic Bobo doll experiments by Bandura and colleagues (Bandura, Ross, & Ross, 1961, 1963). In these experiments, children watched models being aggressive or passive towards a doll and found that children who were simply observing the aggressive model, also imitated the aggressive acts of the adult. In addition, children showed more aggression when the aggressive behaviour was rewarded versus punished, and the effect was present independent of whether the aggression was displayed by a live adult, a filmed adult or a cartoon figure. Since then, various research lines have provided support for observational learning, which has mainly been studied in children or adolescents.

One question concerns the role of emotion in observational learning. In the Bobo doll experiments, the imitated behaviour was emotional in nature (aggression), but this has never been explicitly debated as a crucial element, nor has it been tested against more neutral behaviours (e.g. eating with a knife and fork). According to social learning theories, any behaviour could be learned through observation and the only important requirement is some form of identification with the model. The explicit discussion of 'emotion' is sparse, but Bandura (1971) definitely assumes that emotions are part of observational learning: 'Similarly, emotional responses can be developed observationally by witnessing the affective reactions of others undergoing painful or pleasurable experiences. Fearful and defensive behavior [sic] can be extinguished vicariously by observing others engage in the feared activities without any adverse consequences' (Bandura, 1971, p. 2). This formulation may seem a conceptualization of ASL *avant-la-lettre*, but what are the similarities and differences between the two forms of learning?

ASL and SL are similar in assigning a crucial role to social models, but different in the role of the *emotion* display of the model. In ASL, this role is crucial because it helps the target in (re-)appraising the world or regulating one's own emotion. SL theory emphasizes the role of others as models or identification figures that children observe and imitate, but ASL is more specific and argues that learning primarily takes place because the others' emotions are the driving force in the learning process. One could argue that the main differences in the two theories are the motives that instigate the learning. In SL children learn through imitation because they identify with a model, and implicitly want to behave like their models. In ASL, on the other hand, children learn because they are in an uncertain emotional state, and they infer the 'normal', 'appropriate' or 'desired' emotional response from their parents' or peers' reactions. This may refer to an interpretation of a situation (e.g. a threat) or to their own emotional reaction, and its expression and regulation. Applying this, for example, to gender differences in emotional reactions, boys and girls are not only exposed to different parental and peer emotion displays (e.g. Brody & Hall, 2010; Fischer, 1993; Shields, 2013), but they may also receive different emotional reactions from others. Girls, for example, meet positive and reassuring reactions when they express female appropriate emotions, such as sadness, empathy or anxiety, whereas boys receive more negative, disappointing or contemptuous reactions when they cry or show fear (Brody, 2000).

A recent line of research that seems relevant in the discussion about observational learning of emotions is emotional contagion and mimicry. Emotional contagion has been defined as reacting with the same emotion as the one observed, or 'catching' another person's emotions (Hatfield et al., 1994). One route to emotional contagion is 'primitive emotional contagion', suggesting that when people perceive an emotion in others, they automatically mimic this emotion, and the bodily feedback derived from this mimicry also leads them to feel that emotion (Flack, 2006). Emotional mimicry is the imitation of the emotional expression of another person (Hess & Fischer, 2013) and both emotional mimicry and contagion result from observing others' emotions. In a review of research on emotional mimicry, Hess and Fischer (2013) concluded that there is robust evidence for the mimicry of smiles, but less for the mimicry of negative facial expressions. Often, studies have found mimicry of frowns, yet the nature of the paradigm in which mimicry has been studied, i.e. individuals watching photos with facial displays, does not lead to a clear conclusion of whether people mimicked, or simply were puzzled or concentrated. In addition, other negative emotion displays, such as fear or disgust, showed inconsistent evidence. What the research shows, however, is that mimicry is selective: we mimic more if the relationships with others are positive (among friends, or individuals one identifies with or feels connected to), and we also mimic more if the emotional signals that are displayed by the source are not antagonistic in nature. For example, we are less likely to mimic anger or disgust faces that are directed at us (e.g. signalling 'you are stupid' or 'you are smelly'), because it does not help to build an affiliative bond with others. In other words, research on emotional mimicry shows that people do imitate others, and probably catch others' emotions, even automatically, but the response is selective and does not occur if it is negative and directed at us.

7.3.2   Classical conditioning

Learning has been most frequently studied from a conditioning paradigm, based on the behaviourist theories of Pavlov, Watson, and Skinner. Pavlov's theory of classical conditioning states that an unconditional stimulus (UCS) elicits an unconditional response (UCR), but after repeated pairings between the old UCS and a new, conditional stimulus (CS), the UCR becomes a conditional response (CR). Fear conditioning is a well-known example of classical conditioning, where an aversive, unconditioned stimulus (an electric shock) elicits a UCR, in this case, a reflexive avoidance behaviour such as an eye-blink or eyelid closure. By repeatedly associating the UCS with the CS, such as a tone and a shock, this reflex behaviour is spontaneously elicited by the CS. Importantly, the CS and UCS must occur closely after each other, that is, be 'temporally contiguous', but the relation must also be contingent, such that the CS is always present when the UCS is, so that it has predictive value. A random association between CS and UCS does not lead to fear conditioning. Other research has shown that individuals not only learn a specific fear response but show a generalized fear reaction as well, as the withdrawal response is accompanied by reactions of the parasympathetic nervous system, showing changes in heart rate, respiration and GSR.

A famous example of fear conditioning is described by Watson and Rayner (1920), who examined whether it is possible to condition fear in a young child. Little Albert was 9 months old and showed no fear for live animals and various objects, but he was frightened when hearing a claw hammer strike a long steel bar behind his back. The researchers then aimed to condition him to fear a white rat. They showed Albert a white rat and banged the hammer on the steel bar behind his back, whenever Albert tried touching the white rat. After seven pairings of the rat and the bang, Albert started crying and withdrawing when he saw the rat, without any sound. Even worse, Albert also showed fear reactions to other objects with similar features as the rat: a rabbit, a dog and a sealskin coat, but he did not show fear response to wooden blocks or the hair of Watson' assistants (Harris, 1979). For Watson, fear was one of the basic human emotions that could be conditioned and transformed and transferred to many objects. The other two fundamental human emotions were rage and love (Watson & Morgan, 1917). Although this theory has not lasted, and his experiment has failed to replicate (Harris, 1979), fear conditioning has remained an important principle to explain pathological fear reactions, which can even be the result of one pairing of a highly traumatic event and another event, having nothing to do with the trauma, but still eliciting a fear response. The conditioning paradigm has also been used to study how fear can be successfully extinguished, which we now know is very difficult.

7.3.3   Indirect or social conditioning

Interestingly, whereas classical conditioning is based on first-hand experience, recent research on fear conditioning has suggested that emotions, such as pain (Vaughan & Lanzetta, 1980) and fear (Gerull & Rapee, 2002; Olsson & Phelps, 2004), can be conditioned by observing another person who is submitted to a conditioning paradigm. In this paradigm, participants watch a film in which another person is submitted to the same procedure as the participant expects to be submitted, and thus the (negative) facial expression of the other person serves as UCS. The participants are informed about the shock treatment in both the observation and test phase. The findings indicate that skin conductance rises after the conditioned stimulus (i.e. the fear face) and the shock. Olsson, Nearing, and Phelps (2007) further showed that the brain activity of participants in a social fear paradigm is similar to the brain activity in a normal fear-conditioning paradigm, where the amygdala in particular plays a crucial role.

Do the requirements of ASL fit the assumptions and evidence from the classical conditioning paradigm? Seeing adults react with fear towards certain objects (e.g. in the case of the visual cliff) can be considered as a fear-conditioning paradigm, because there is a systematic pairing between a certain object (US) and a negative reaction of a parent, leading to a conditioned response. One requirement for ASL is that the target is aware of the object of the source's emotional reaction and has a basic understanding that this object causes the emotion. Whether or not explicit awareness of the contingency relation is necessary for fear conditioning has been a source of debate, as some have proposed that there are distinct learning systems that operate independently of each other and are influenced by different factors. In order to gain insight in whether emotional awareness would be differentially required in different forms of learning, Olsson and Phelps (2004) compared Pavlovian, social and instructive learning, and additionally manipulated the explicit awareness of the reinforced conditioned (CS+), by masking the stimuli in one condition and presenting them unmasked in the other condition. This study, in which angry faces served as CS+, happy faces as CS– (unreinforced conditioned stimulus) and a neutral face as a mask, showed first of all that the conditioned response to the unmasked angry faces was significantly lower in all three learning groups than to the unmasked happy faces. Second, skin conductance level was also lower between the angry and happy faces in the masked condition, at least for the social learning, and marginally for the Pavlovian learning group. Thus, there need not be explicit awareness of the CS in order to learn fear, although the learning was much stronger in the unmasked conditions than in the masked conditions. In the case of the explicit instruction, this does seem to be necessary, based on this study, however. Learning a fear response by providing expectations and instructions only occurs if the CS can be seen.

The use of angry and happy faces as unconditioned stimuli also raises the question whether some classes of stimuli are more effective because they can be more easily paired with the to-be-conditioned emotional response. For example, snakes or spiders can be more easily conditioned with a fear response than chairs and bicycles. If this prepared learning (e.g. Öhman, Fredrikson, Hugdahl, & Rimmo, 1976) occurs for environmental stimuli, it can also be extended to social groups. Indeed Olsson, Ebert, Banaji, and Phelps (2005) argued that aversive learning can also be modelled in a sociocultural context. They designed a study where out-group members' black, neutral faces serve as the CS+ and in-group members' neutral faces as the CS–. During the fear acquisition phase, either the out-group or in-group faces were systematically paired with a mild electric shock; no shocks were given during the extinction phase. The results showed that the skin conductance response (difference between CSR to CS+ minus CS–) was higher for the CS+ stimuli (for both in-group and out-group faces), and thus participants learned a fear response towards black or white faces. More interesting, however, is that during the extinction phase, the conditioned skin conductance response towards the black faces was not fully extinguished, whereas it was for the white faces. This was a similar pattern to the first experiment where conditioned fear responses to snakes and spiders were not fully extinguished, whereas it was for butterflies and birds. This result suggests that some social categories are more easily associated with certain emotional responses, and that we may be biologically prepared to associate unfamiliar out-group faces with danger.

7.3.4   Evaluative conditioning

Evaluative conditioning is about changing likes and dislikes, which most theorists consider something that is learned rather than innate. It has been examined in an experimental paradigm in which people's preferences for neutral stimuli are paired with a positive or negative stimulus, resulting in a change of preference (see de Houwer, Thomas, & Baeyens, 2001, for a review). Many different types of stimuli have been used as conditioned stimuli, such as pictures, words, gustatory and haptic stimuli, as well as faces. Electric shocks have often been used as unconditioned stimuli, as in classical conditioning paradigms, but in the affective priming task, stimuli with mere positive or negative valence have been used. Evaluative conditioning has been considered a form of classical conditioning, although some important differences have been noted as well (de Houwer et al., 2001). For example, evaluative conditioning seems more resistant to extinction, contrary to classical conditioning (Baeyens, Crombez, van den Bergh, & Eelen, 1988), and the awareness of the relation between the CS and US seems more important than in classical conditioning.

In a meta-analysis with 214 studies, Hoffman and colleagues (Hofmann, de Houwer, Perugini, Baeyens, & Crombez, 2010) showed that evaluative conditioning is a robust phenomenon that occurs in a wide variety of circumstances. However, given the fact that the change in preferences does not always occur under all circumstances, Hoffman and colleagues (2010) evaluated various theoretical explanations of evaluative conditioning that especially differ in the role of higher-order processes. Whereas some accounts assume that EC is based on the automatic formation of associations in memory, namely the pairing of the UCS and CS, other accounts identify a role for more complex cognitive processes. The meta-analysis supports the idea that there is a role for higher-order mental processes because there are several important moderators of the effect. For example, evaluative conditioning effects are smaller in children than in adults, which suggests that it is not a mere automatic process but rather some form of consciously identifying the relation between the conditioned and unconditioned stimulus. This contingency awareness is also one of the largest moderators in the meta-analysis, and together with the effects of other moderators, suggest that the awareness of a link between conditioned and unconditioned stimulus increases the effect.

When applying the distinction between these two general theoretical models (association formation models versus higher-order cognitive models) on ASL, one could argue that ASL is based primarily on the latter models. This is related to the first requirement of ASL, namely that the target needs to perceive a connection between the emotion and the object of the emotion expression in the first place. Thus, when learning associations between others' emotional responses and an event, or one's own behaviour, the person should be aware of the association. ASL could thus be considered as a form of evaluative conditioning, with the presumption that the source's emotional expression is the positive or negative stimulus that is paired with one's own behaviour or preferences. Consistent anger, or consistent sadness towards what one does may lead to an increase of one's own anger or depressed reactions, simply because it is frequently paired.

7.3.5   Cognitive learning

In cognitive learning theories, it is assumed that knowledge and insight are the crucial elements in learning and that a mere behavioural change is not necessarily an indication of learning. More knowledge does not necessarily lead to a change of behaviour, what matters is whether the target has gained more insight. Jean Piaget is the pioneer of this approach and he argued that we build representations of the external world through two processes: assimilation and accommodation. Assimilation refers to the inclusion of new information into existing schemes, whereas accommodation requires a change of scheme because the new information does not fit the current scheme. ASL very likely entails cognitive learning, especially in the latter stages of the ASL scheme in which social referencing and natural pedagogy suggest that emotion expressions are used as powerful tools to teach children their perspectives on the world with the help of emotions.

7.4   ASL in the family

There are dramatic illustrations of ASL in the context of research on the origins of emotional psychopathology. Evidence of long-term effects of children's early experiences of maltreatment is abundant. Various studies have shown, for example, that children of depressed or anxious parents run a much higher risk of being diagnosed with depression or anxiety disorders (Beardslee, Gladstone, & O'Connor, 2011). This is partly due to biological predispositions and genetic influences, but also to being actually exposed to parents behaving in this way, as reflected in the fact that daily interactions between parents and children contribute to the intergenerational transmission of depression and anxiety (e.g. Murray et al., 2008). Indeed, parents' anxiety and depression have been shown to affect face-to-face interactions with their children, for example, because they show less positive affect, and thus smile less, or because they have less clear and more obscured emotional expressions (e.g. Nicol-Harper, Harvey, & Stein, 2007; Weinberg & Tronick, 1998).

In addition to the variety of factors that may be different when children are raised by anxious or depressed parents, the role of actual emotional expressions in interaction with their children seems important. For example, in a study on the role of parental anxiety on children's avoidant behaviour towards a stranger and a mechanical dinosaur, Aktar, Majdandžić, de Vente, and Bögels (2013) show that rather than the parent's level of anxiety state (obtained through a standardized interview protocol), it is the actual expression of fear during the interaction with the child that predicts the child's avoidant behaviour. Moreover, the interaction was only significant if the expressed parental fear was moderate to high (as scored from facial, vocal and verbal behaviour) and when the child's disposition to behavioural inhibition (fear, distress and avoidant responses averaged across different tasks) was also high. Thus, children must be receptive to the fear of their parents and the fear should be clearly expressed. These results suggest that fear can be learned by parents' actual emotional displays. In another study, Aktar, Majdandžić, de Vente, and Bögels (2014) showed that parents' expressed anxiety at 12 months (time 1), also had long term effects at 30 months (time 2). Children's avoidant behaviour towards a stranger and a robot was not predicted by parents' expressed anxiety at time 2, but only by their expressed anxiety at time 1.

We may conclude that parents' negative states of minds, whether based on anxiety or depression disorders or negative family circumstances, are likely to result in negative behaviour towards their children, such as rejection, or ignoring or expressing negative emotions, such as frustration, nervousness or anxiety. Although this type of ASL does not seem intentional, as the parents suffer from negative moods and thus do not deliberately transfer their negative moods on to others, this unintentional learning does illustrate the effects of continuous emotional reactions from caregivers. From the perspective of ASL, one would predict that children from parents who express negative emotions are also more likely to raise children with high negative emotionality, and that these children have similar tendencies to appraise certain objects or events negatively. In other words, these parents transfer negative values about important aspects of the (social) world. Such conditions thus fulfil the minimal requirements of ASL in my view: the source is an attachment figure, the children often find themselves in ambiguous or negative situations where they are looking for guidance and there is long-term exposure towards these parental emotions.

Although we have focused on the effects of parents' negative emotion expression, there is also much evidence for the effects of positive emotion expression and of the stimulation to talk about emotions (Zech & Rimé, 2005). Children who have learned to talk about their emotions, for example, as reflected in a larger emotion vocabulary, are also better at emotion recognition at a later age (Dunn, Brown, & Beardsall, 1991). In addition, emotion regulation is also learned in the family context from a young age onwards. Morris, Silk, Steinberg, Myers, and Robinson (2007) distinguish learning about emotion regulation in three ways: through observation, through parenting practices (learning about display rules) and through the emotional climate in the family (i.e. attachment relations, emotional quality of the marital relationship, parenting style). In their review, they suggest that parent's own emotion-regulation practices are likely to form the example of how children learn to regulate their emotions. In addition, the way parents react to their children's emotions also affects children's regulation strategies. For example, children who are punished for their emotion expression are more likely to learn ineffective emotion-regulation strategies (Eisenberg & Fabes, 1992) and are less emotionally and socially competent (Jones, Eisenberg, Fabes, & MacKinnon, 2002).

7.5   Conclusion: how we learn from others' emotions

In this chapter, I have tried to further clarify the types of processes involved in ASL, trying to answer the question of *how* we would learn from others. There are various types of learning that may be involved in ASL, and I think it is important to discuss which learning processes are involved when we learn from others' emotions. I would argue that ASL can involve direct as well as indirect or social conditioning, but also cognitive learning. What is crucial in my view is that individuals are aware of the contingency relation between the emotional expression and its object. The conditions under which individuals learn from the emotion expression is still to be determined, and I do not think the contexts should be restricted to ambiguous or uncertain situations. Although these types of situation have been shown to elicit the need for social information, there are also emotional situations that give rise to anger, fear or sadness where the emotional displays of others may teach us something about the world. This is why I believe that ASL should not only involve learning about the world, in terms of objects and events, but also about the self and one's relations with others. I would argue that the transmission of values can be about re-appraising the world, but also about re-appraising oneself, and one's own emotions.

In the Introduction to this volume, Clément and Dukes argue that ASL can be characterized by two dimensions: intentionality of the source and the extent to which there is social orientation involved. In the four stages of ASL that they identify (emotional contagion, affective observation and social referencing, natural pedagogics) there is an increasing intentionality as well as social orientation. It may well be that these different stages imply different types of learning, where the first stages involve more automatic learning and the latter stages more social cognitive learning. However, all learning is selective at all stages and the fact that it is often automatic does not mean that it cannot be selective. Children do not imitate or observe all parents under all circumstances, and not all of the parents' expressions have a long-term impact. So, the first question then is why a child would pay attention and take over their parents' emotional perspective on the world. I would argue when they are at loss, either because they do not know, or because they have strong undesirable emotions themselves. The second question is when the impact of an expression would be strong enough to generalize to future encounters with similar objects or events. Only then, has ASL taken place.

References

Aktar, E., Majdandžić, M., de Vente, W., & Bögels, S. M. (2013). The interplay between expressed parental anxiety and infant behavioural inhibition predicts infant avoidance in a social referencing paradigm. *Journal of Child Psychology and Psychiatry, 54*(2), 144–156.

Aktar, E., Majdandžić, M., de Vente, W., & Bögels, S. M. (2014). Parental social anxiety disorder prospectively predicts toddlers' fear/avoidance in a social referencing paradigm. *Journal of Child Psychology and Psychiatry, 55*(1), 77–87.

Baeyens, F., Crombez, G., van den Bergh, O., & Eelen, P. (1988). Once in contact always in contact: Evaluative conditioning is resistant to extinction. *Advances in Behaviour Research and Therapy, 10*(4), 179–199.

Bandura, A. (1969). *Principles of behavior modification.* Oxford, UK: Holt, Rinehart, & Winston.

(1971). *Social Learning Theory.* New York, NY: General Learning Press.

Bandura, A., Ross, D., & Ross, S. A. (1961). Transmission of aggression through imitation of aggressive models. *Journal of Abnormal and Social Psychology, 63*(3), 575–582.

(1963). Imitation of film-mediated aggressive models. *Journal of Abnormal and Social Psychology, 66*(1), 3.

Beardslee, W. R., Gladstone, T. R., & O'Connor, E. E. (2011). Transmission and prevention of mood disorders among children of affectively ill parents: A review. *Journal of the American Academy of Child & Adolescent Psychiatry, 50*(11), 1098–1109.

Bertenthal, B. I., & Campos, J. J. (1984). A reexamination of fear and its determinants on the visual cliff. *Psychophysiology, 21*(4), 413–417.

Brody, L. R. (2000). The socialization of gender differences in emotional expression: Display rules, infant temperament, and differentiation. In A. H. Fischer (Eds.), *Gender and emotion: Social psychological perspectives* (pp. 3–24). Cambridge, UK: Cambridge University Press.

Brody, L. R., & Hall, J. A. (2010). Gender, emotion, and socialization. In J. C. Chrisler & D. R. McCreary (Eds.), *Handbook of gender research in psychology* (pp. 429–459). New York, NY: Springer.

Bruder, M., Fischer, A., & Manstead, A. S. R. (2014). Social appraisal as a cause of collective emotions. In C. von Scheve & M. Salmela (Eds.), *Collective emotions* (pp. 141–155). Oxford, UK: Oxford University Press.

Clément, F., & Dukes, D. (2017). Social appraisal and social referencing: Two components of affective social learning. *Emotion Review, 9*(3), 253–261.

Darley, J. M., & Latane, B. (1970). Norms and normative behavior: Field studies of social interdependence. In J. Macaulay & L. Berkowitz (Eds.), *Altruism and helping behavior* (pp. 83–102). New York, NY: Academic Press.

de Houwer, J., Thomas, S., & Baeyens, F. (2001). Associative learning of likes and dislikes: A review of 25 years of research on human evaluative conditioning. *Psychological Bulletin, 127*(6), 853–869.

Denham, S. A., & Grout, L. (1993). Socialization of emotion: Pathway to preschoolers' emotional and social competence. *Journal of Nonverbal Behavior, 17*(3), 205–227.

Dunn, J., Brown, J., & Beardsall, L. (1991). Family talk about feeling states and children's later understanding of others' emotions. *Developmental Psychology, 27*(3), 448–455.

Eisenberg, N., Cumberland, A., & Spinrad, T. L. (1998). Parental socialization of emotion. *Psychological Inquiry, 9*(4), 241–273.

Eisenberg, N., & Fabes, R. A. (1992). Emotion, regulation, and the development of social competence. In M. S. Clark (Ed.), *Emotion and social behavior: Review of personality and social psychology* (pp. 119–150). Thousand Oaks, CA: Sage.

(1994). Mothers' reactions to children's negative emotions: Relations to children's temperament and anger behavior. *Merrill-Palmer Quarterly (1982–), 40*(1), 138–156.

Eisenberg, N., & Valiente, C. (2004). Elaborations on a theme: Beyond main effects in relations of parenting to children's coping and regulation. *Parenting: Science and Practice, 4*(4), 319–323.

Evers, C., Fischer, A. H., Rodriguez Mosquera, P. M., & Manstead, A. S. R. (2005). Anger and social appraisal: A 'spicy' sex difference? *Emotion, 5*(3), 258–266.

Festinger, L. (1954). A theory of social comparison processes. *Human Relations, 7*(2), 117–140.

Flack, W. (2006). Peripheral feedback effects of facial expressions, bodily postures, and vocal expressions on emotional feelings. *Cognition & Emotion, 20*(2), 177–195.

Fischer, A. H. (1993). Sex differences in emotionality: Fact or stereotype? *Feminism & Psychology, 3*(3), 303–318.

Fischer, P., Krueger, J. I., Greitemeyer, T., Vogrincic, C., Kastenmüller, A., Frey, D., … Kainbacher, M. (2011). The bystander-effect: A meta-analytic review on bystander intervention in dangerous and non-dangerous emergencies. *Psychological Bulletin, 137*(4), 517–537.

Gerull, F. C., & Rapee, R. M. (2002). Mother knows best: Effects of maternal modelling on the acquisition of fear and avoidance behaviour in toddlers. *Behaviour Research and Therapy, 40*(3), 279–287.

Gross, J. J., & John, O. P. (2003). Individual differences in two emotion regulation processes: Implications for affect, relationships, and well-being. *Journal of Personality and Social Psychology, 85*, 348–362.

Gross, J. J., Richards, J. M., & John, O. P. (2006). Emotion regulation in everyday life. *Regulation, 129*, 1–34.

Hareli, S., & Hess, U. (2012). The social signal value of emotions. *Cognition and Emotion, 26*(3), 385–389.

Harris, B. (1979). Whatever happened to little Albert? *American Psychologist, 34*(2), 151–160.

Hatfield, E., Cacioppo, J., & Rapson, R. (1994). Emotional contagion. *Current Directions in Psychological Science, 2*(3), 96–99.

Hess, U., & Blairy, S. (2001). Facial mimicry and emotional contagion to dynamic emotional facial expressions and their influence on decoding accuracy. *International Journal of Psychophysiology: Official Journal of the International Organization of Psychophysiology, 40*(2), 129–141.

Hess, U., & Fischer, A. (2013). Emotional mimicry as social regulation. *Personality and Social Psychology Review, 17*(2), 142–157.

(2014). Emotional mimicry: Why and when we mimic emotions. *Social and Personality Psychology Compass, 8,* 45–57.

Hofmann, W., de Houwer, J., Perugini, M., Baeyens, F., & Crombez, G. (2010). Evaluative conditioning in humans: a meta-analysis. *Psychological Bulletin, 136*(3), 390.

Jones, S., Eisenberg, N., Fabes, R. A., & MacKinnon, D. P. (2002). Parents' reactions to elementary school children's negative emotions: Relations to social and emotional functioning at school. *Merrill-Palmer Quarterly, 48*(2), 133–159.

Klinnert, M., Campos, J. J., Sorce, J. F., Emde, R. N., & Svejda, M. (1983). Emotions as behavior regulators: Social referencing in infancy. In R. Plutchik & H. Kellerman (Eds.), *Emotion: Theory, research, and experience* (pp. 57–86). London, UK: Academic Press.

Klinnert, M. D., Emde, R. N., Butterfield, P., & Campos, J. J. (1986). Social Referencing: The infant's use of emotional signals from a friendly adult with mother present. *Developmental Psychology, 22*(4), 427–432.

Kret, M. E., Fischer, A. H., & de Dreu, C. K. W. (2015). Pupil mimicry correlates with trust in in-group partners with dilating pupils. *Psychological Science, 26*(9), 1401–1410.

Latané, B., & Darley, J. M. (1970). *The unresponsive bystander: Why doesn't he help?* Upper Saddle River, NJ: Prentice Hall.

Mann, L., Feddes, A. R., Doosje, B., & Fischer, A. H. (2016). Withdraw or affiliate? The role of humiliation during initiation rituals. *Cognition and Emotion, 30*(1), 80–100.

Manstead, A. S. R., & Fischer, A. H. (2001). Social appraisal: The social world as object of and influence on appraisal processes. In K. R. Scherer, A. Schorr, & T. Johnstone (Eds.), *Appraisal processes in emotion: Theory, methods, research* (pp. 221–232). Oxford, UK: Oxford University Press.

(2017). Social referencing and social appraisal: Commentary on the Clément and Dukes (2016) and Walle et al. (2016) articles. *Emotion Review, 9*(3), 262–263.

Morris, A. S., Silk, J. S., Steinberg, L., Myers, S. S., & Robinson, L. R. (2007). The role of the family context in the development of emotion regulation. *Social Development, 16,* 261–288.

Mumenthaler, C., & Sander, D. (2012). Social appraisal influences recognition of emotions. *Journal of Personality and Social Psychology, 102*(6), 1118–1135.

Murray, L., de Rosnay, M., Pearson, J., Bergeron, C., Schofield, E., Royal-Lawson, M., & Cooper, P. J. (2008). Intergenerational transmission of social anxiety: The role of social referencing processes in infancy. *Child Development, 79,* 1049–1064.

Nicol-Harper, R., Harvey, A. G., & Stein, A. (2007). Interactions between mothers and infants: Impact of maternal anxiety. *Infant Behavior and Development, 30*(1), 161–167.

Öhman, A., Fredrikson, M., Hugdahl, K., & Rimmo, P. A. (1976). The premise of equipotentiality in human classical conditioning: Conditioned electrodermal responses to potentially phobic stimuli. *Journal of Experimental Psychology: General, 105*(4), 313–337.

Olsson, A., Ebert, J. P., Banaji, M. R., & Phelps, E. A. (2005). Psychology: The role of social groups in the persistence of learned fear. *Psychological Science*, 15(12), 822–828.

Olsson, A., Nearing, K. I., & Phelps, E. A. (2007). Learning fears by observing others: The neural systems of social fear transmission. *Social Cognitive and Affective Neuroscience*, 2(1), 3–11.

Olsson, A., & Phelps, E. A. (2004). Learned fear of 'unseen' faces after pavlovian, observational, and instructed fear. *Psychological Science*, 15(12), 822–828.

Parkinson, B. (1997). Untangling the appraisal-emotion connection. *Personality and Social Psychology Review*, 1(1), 62–79.

(2011). Interpersonal emotion transfer: Contagion and social appraisal. *Social and Personality Psychology Compass*, 5(7), 428–439.

Parkinson, B., Phiri, N., & Simons, G. (2012). Bursting with anxiety: Adult social referencing in an interpersonal Balloon Analogue Risk Task (BART). *Emotion*, 12(4), 817–826.

Parkinson, B., & Simons, G. (2012). Worry spreads: Interpersonal transfer of problem-related anxiety. *Cognition & Emotion*, 26(3), 462–479.

Rimé, B. (2007). The social sharing of emotion as an interface between individual and collective processes in the construction of emotional climates. *Journal of Social Issues*, 63(2), 307–322.

Rohan, M. J. (2000). A rose by any name? The values construct. *Personality and Social Psychology Review*, 4(3), 255–277.

Schachter, S. (1959). *The psychology of affiliation: Experimental studies of the sources of gregariousness.* Palo Alto, CA: Stanford University Press.

Shields, S. A. (2013). Gender and emotion. *Psychology of Women Quarterly*, 37(4), 423–435.

Suls, J., & Wheeler, L. (2012). Social comparison theory. In P. A. M. van Lange, A. W. Kruglanski & E. T. Higgings (Eds.), *Handbook of theories of social psychology: Volume 1* (pp. 460–483). London, UK: Sage.

van Harreveld, F., Nohlen, H. U., & Schneider, I. K. (2015). The ABC of ambivalence: Affective, behavioral, and cognitive consequences of attitudinal conflict. *Advances in Experimental Social Psychology*, 52, 285–324.

van Kleef, G. A. (2009). How emotions regulate social life: The emotions as social information (EASI) model. *Current Directions in Psychological Science*, 18, 184–188.

Vaughan, K. B., & Lanzetta, J. T. (1980). Vicarious instigation and conditioning of facial expressive and autonomic responses to a model's expressive display of pain. *Journal of Personality and Social Psychology*, 38(6), 909–923.

Watson, J. B., & Morgan, J. J. B. (1917). Emotional reactions and psychological experimentation. *American Journal of Psychology*, 28(2), 163–174.

Watson, J. B., & Rayner, R. (1920). Conditioned emotional reactions. *Journal of Experimental Psychology*, 3(1), 1.

Weinberg, M. K., & Tronick, E. Z. (1998). The impact of maternal psychiatric illness on infant development. *Journal of Clinical Psychiatry*, 59(2), 53061.

Witherington, D. C., Campos, J. J., Anderson, D. I., Lejeune, L., & Seah, E. (2005). Avoidance of heights on the visual cliff in newly walking infants. *Infancy*, 7(3), 285–298.

Zech, E., & Rimé, B. (2005). Is talking about an emotional experience helpful? Effects on emotional recovery and perceived benefits. *Clinical Psychology and Psychotherapy*, 12(4), 270–287.

PART IV

Applications of affective social learning

CHAPTER 8

Chastening the future

What we learn from others' regret

Antony Manstead, Magdalena Rychlowska and
Job van der Schalk

When people are asked to name emotions, regret is one of the most frequently named (second only to love, in Shimanoff's 1984 study). According to the definition offered by Zeelenberg and Pieters (2007, p. 3),

> Regret is the emotion that we experience when realizing or imagining that our current situation would have been better, if only we had decided differently. It is a backward-looking emotion signalling an unfavourable evaluation of a decision. It is an unpleasant feeling, coupled with a clear sense of self-blame concerning its causes and strong wishes to undo the current situation.

This captures the essential attributes of regret: It is a counterfactual emotion, involving feelings of personal responsibility and arising from the thought that we would now be better off if we had chosen differently. As such, regret conceptually overlaps with the emotion of guilt: while the latter is experienced predominantly in situations of interpersonal harm, regret is observed in the contexts of both intrapersonal *and* interpersonal harm (Zeelenberg & Breugelmans, 2008).

It has been argued that regret is a useless emotion, implying that it serves no function. For example, the New Zealand author Katherine Mansfield (1920) wrote that "Regret is an appalling waste of energy; you can't build on it; it's only good for wallowing in." Such negative views of regret presumably stem from the fact that we cannot undo what has happened in the past, much though we might like to do so. Ruminating about our actions or failure to act, and wishing that we had behaved differently, is therefore wasted energy. An opposing view of regret is reflected in a quotation attributed to another author, James Ellis (as quoted in Douglas, 1917), "Regrets over the past should chasten the future", the idea being that decisions we regret will feed forward to condition the way in which we make future decisions. We can learn lessons from our past mistakes, and the discomfort of the regret we experience as we reflect on these mistakes is a hedonic marker that we carry forward into our future decision-making. When confronted with a similar set of circumstances, we consciously or unconsciously take account of the past mistake and decide to act differently.

In this chapter, we will adopt a perspective consistent with this second view, arguing that regret is not only useful to the individual who experiences regret, but – to the extent that the regret is overtly expressed – also useful to human observers. Most research on regret (like most research on emotion in general) is focused on the *intrapersonal origins* or *intrapersonal consequences* of this emotion. The present chapter, by contrast, focuses on the *interpersonal* and *intergroup consequences* of seeing someone else regret the decision they have made. Such expressions of regret tell us something about the aversive consequences of a decision made by another person and influence our own behaviour when confronted with a similar situation. This "lesson" that we learn by witnessing another person's regret can also be extended to relations between groups. If we see that members of an out-group regret the way in which they have acted in favour of their own group and at the expense of our group, does this help to reduce tension or to restore trust between the two groups?

We believe that the experiments described below provide good evidence for the operation of affective social learning (ASL). As Dukes and Clément explain in the introductory chapter of this volume, ASL is an umbrella term that includes processes that range from *emotional contagion* to *natural pedagogy*. The phenomena examined in the studies described in the present chapter fall in the mid-range of these processes, and can be seen as examples of *affective observation* or *social referencing*, depending on the extent to which the exemplar (or "knower", in Dukes and Clément's terms) engages in *deliberate* emotion signalling. This is an issue we will return to at the end of the chapter.

8.1   Regret in decision-making

In everyday life we make hundreds of decisions, ranging from relatively routine decisions like how early to get out of bed, what to eat for breakfast, how to travel to our place of work or study and how to spend our leisure time, to more consequential decisions like where to live, whether to buy consumer good A or B, whether to go out on a date with someone and which career to pursue. Post-decisional regret is common, because it is rarely the case that the chosen alternative is all good and the rejected one all bad. Indeed, this insight forms one of the cornerstones of cognitive dissonance theory (Festinger, 1957). The discomfort we experience when we are aware of the fact that the rejected alternative might have been better than the chosen one is known as a state of "cognitive dissonance". According to cognitive dissonance theory people are motivated to reduce this negative state, for example, by seeking additional justifications for our initial choice. But this is not always possible, and the remaining discomfort is what we might more colloquially call regret, because it precisely conforms to Zeelenberg and Pieters' (2007) definition: it is an emotional state we experience when we believe that we would be better off now if we had decided differently. Given the ubiquity of decision-making, there is plenty of scope for experiencing regret and, indeed, this emotion is very common (Shimanoff, 1984).

The fact that regret is felt so frequently raises interesting questions about its influence on behaviour. A line of research on anticipated regret, stimulated by theorizing in economics (Bell, 1982; Loomes & Sugden, 1982) as well as by Janis and Mann's (1977) influential book on the psychology of decision-making, has advocated that the anticipation of how much regret you would experience if you were to act in a certain way has an influence on the decisions you take. People may not spontaneously anticipate this regret, however; in one of the earliest psychological studies of anticipated regret, Richard, van der Pligt, and de Vries (1996) showed that instructing participants to focus on their anticipated feelings made future regret salient and influenced subsequent behaviour. When undergraduate students were asked to predict how much regret they would experience if they were to engage in unprotected sex, and were then asked five months later to report on their condom use, they reported greater use than their control condition counterparts, who had not been asked to anticipate regret.

This and similar studies led researchers to examine whether anticipated feelings of regret could explain additional variance in intentions and behaviour, over and above other known factors that predict behaviour according to the theory of planned behaviour (TPB; Ajzen, 1985). Sandberg and Conner (2008) reported a meta-analysis of this work and concluded that anticipated regret added significantly to the prediction of both intentions and behaviour, beyond the variance that can be explained by TPB factors. This illustrates the function that regret has as an anticipated emotion that influences future behaviour.

The more general idea that anticipated emotion is influential in shaping behaviour has been proposed by Baumeister, Vohs, DeWall, and Zhang (2007). On their account, a decision taken at a particular time leads to an outcome that (for example) you regret. This emotional experience implies that you reflect on your decision and how you could have decided differently. The next time you make a similar decision, an automatically activated "affective residue" of regret alerts you to the possibility of a negative outcome. This increases the likelihood of you making a different decision at a later time.

In sum, a substantial body of research links intrapersonal regret to decision-making. However, observed regret also matters. A neuroimaging study by Canessa, Motterlini, Alemanno, Perani, and Cappa (2011) provided support for this claim by examining economic decisions and patterns of brain activity during a gambling task. When participants were exposed to regret-inducing outcomes – i.e. losing money as a result of a risky decision, or not gaining money as a result of a non-risky decision for which they were personally responsible – they tended to change their decisions in the subsequent rounds of the task. Specifically, less desirable outcomes associated with non-risky decisions increased risk-seeking and negative outcomes resulting from risky decisions decreased risk-seeking. More interestingly, however, these effects were observed not only when participants themselves experienced the regret-inducing outcomes, but also when such outcomes applied to another individual playing in the nearby room. These behavioural changes in reaction to both first- and third-person experience were accompanied by overlapping activations in the brain regions associated with risk processing. This experiment suggests that observing another individual confronting the undesirable effects of his/her actions can exert a powerful social influence, comparable to the personal experience of regret, and can be seen as an example of affective observation. In the current chapter, we take this argument a step further by proposing that people who observe others' expressions of regret infer why this feeling is experienced, which then influences their own actions.

8.2   Social appraisal

People's emotions are not simply the direct result of events that happen to them, or the result of their own choices and actions. Instead, emotions depend on the way individuals evaluate or appraise events, their choices or actions. What is a daunting obstacle in the eyes of one person may strike another as an exciting challenge. However, how we appraise an event depends not only on our own evaluations of what is at stake and how well we can cope: The way we appraise and respond emotionally to events is also influenced by the feelings of other people who are exposed to the same situation. We call this "social appraisal" (Bruder, Fischer, & Manstead, 2014; Manstead & Fischer, 2001). To the extent that the event in question is ambiguous, and to the extent that we interpret the emotional reactions of others as genuine, we are likely to be influenced by their emotional expressions.

There is no shortage of evidence that we make use of others' emotional expressions to help us to disambiguate situations and events. In their classic research on bystander intervention in emergencies, Latané and Darley (1968) showed that when naïve participants were exposed to a potentially dangerous situation (i.e. smoke entering the room they were in) while in the company of two confederates who were instructed to act as if nothing out of the ordinary was happening, the participants were slower to take action. Despite the possible risk to their own safety, the participants' interpretation of the situation was influenced by the apparent calmness of the two confederates. In equally classic research on social referencing, Sorce, Emde, Campos, and Klinnert (1985) showed that 12-month-olds who had to decide whether or not to cross a "visual cliff" (i.e. a solid tabletop surface that changed to a transparent one, thereby creating an apparent drop at the edge of the "cliff") were strongly influenced by the facial expression of their mother, who was standing beyond the "deep" side of the cliff. These infants were making use of their caregivers' emotion expressions to help them to decide whether or not it was safe to proceed. In a diary study of naturalistic decisions, Parkinson and Simons (2009) found that the amount of excitement and anxiety that participants reported in reaction to everyday decisions impacting their own and other people's lives was affected by the perceived anxiety and excitement of another person who was present during decision-making. As a final example, Mumenthaler and Sander (2012; see also Chapter 6, this volume) have shown that the way we interpret ambiguous facial expressions in a target face can be influenced by the presence of another, contextual face. For example, a fear–surprise blend is more likely to be interpreted as fear in the presence of a contextual face that is expressing anger – but only if the contextual face is looking at the target face.

Some of the studies just mentioned also provide evidence about the process mediating these social appraisal effects. According to social appraisal theory, perceivers infer the evaluations (or appraisals) underlying the observed expression and these inferred appraisals are integrated with perceivers' own assessment of the event in question. Consistent with this reasoning, Parkinson and Simons (2009) found that, in the process of joint decision-making, the effect of another person's anxiety on someone's own anxiety was partially mediated by the appraisals of the importance of the decision and of the perceived risk involved in each option. There is also good evidence for the notion that perceivers can deduce appraisals from other people's facial expressions, a process that has been labelled "reverse appraisal". For example, Hareli and Hess (2010) showed that people were able to make inferences about a person's character from his/ her emotional expressions. Someone who reacted to blame by becoming angry was judged to be more aggressive and self-confident but also less warm and gentle than someone who reacted by expressing sadness. Importantly, such inferences were mediated by participants' ratings of how the target person appraised the situation (for example, in terms of unpleasantness and goal conduciveness). More directly relevant to the research described below, de Melo, Carnevale, Read, and Gratch (2014) showed that, in the context of a Prisoner's Dilemma game, emotion displays affected participants' beliefs about others' appraisals. These beliefs, in turn, influenced participants' expectations of other people's intentions in the game, and thereby shaped how participants played the game. For example, they were more likely to cooperate with a counterpart who expressed joy after mutual cooperation and regret after exploiting the participant than with a counterpart who expressed regret following mutual cooperation and joy after exploiting the participant. These effects were mediated by appraisals that were also systematically influenced by facial expressions. Smiling meant that the counterpart found the outcome goal-conducive, whereas regret meant the counterpart found the outcome goal-obstructive and blamed himself for it.

8.3   Regret and interpersonal decisions

An initial step in our own research programme was to establish whether exposure to another person's expression of regret about a decision would influence the behaviour of an observer. In Studies 1A and 1B reported by van der Schalk, Kuppens, Bruder, and Manstead (2015), participants played an online version of the Ultimatum Game (UG; Güth, Schmittberger, & Schwarze, 1982). In the two-person version of this game, the "allocator" decides how to divide a sum of money between self and other by making an offer to the "receiver". The latter can either accept the offer, in which case both players receive the division that was proposed, or reject it, in which case neither player receives anything. The resource for which the allocator and the receiver played was £100, represented by 50 "tokens" of £2 each. The number of tokens that allocators were willing to share with receivers served as our measure of fair behaviour. It was explained that we would randomly select two pairs of participants who would be paid in accordance with how they had played the game.

To examine how others' emotions affected players' allocations, we exposed them to either a written transcript (study 1A) or a video recording (study 1B) in which they read, or saw and heard, the thoughts and feelings of someone described as a "previous participant in this experiment". This person (the "exemplar") wrote or said that s/he had considered dividing the 50 tokens in different ways: 45(self):5(other), 25:25, or something in between these two options. To vary exemplar behaviour, the decision taken was either a 25:25 split (fair behaviour) or a 45:5 split (unfair behaviour). It was also stated that this offer was accepted. To manipulate emotion, the exemplar said that he or she felt "good", "proud", and "pleased" about the decision (pride condition); or "bad", "sorry", and "regretful" about the decision (regret condition). In the control emotion condition, there was no mention of emotions in the thought transcript or video. After being exposed to the exemplar emotion, the participant was asked to rate how much *pride* or *regret* they would experience if they were to act in the same way as the exemplar, before making an offer in their own round of the Ultimatum Game. What we expected to find was

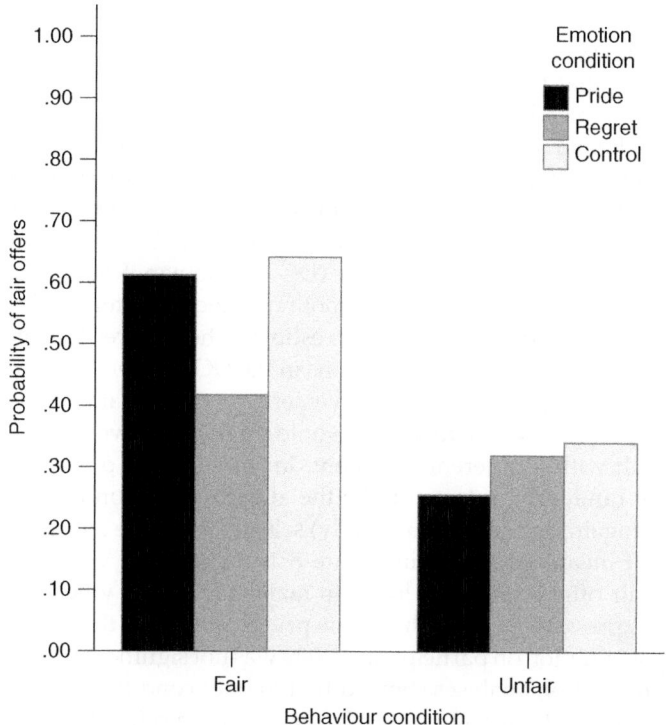

Figure 8.1 Predicted probabilities of fair offers as a function of exemplar behaviour and exemplar emotion (from van der Schalk et al. (2015), adapted with permission).

an interaction between exemplar behaviour and exemplar emotion, such that participants would be more likely to make a fair offer if they had been exposed to an exemplar who was proud – rather than regretful – about being fair, or regretful – rather than proud – about being unfair.

To increase the reliability of the findings, we pooled the data from the two studies into one analysis, controlling for study. The pattern of means is shown in Figure 8.1, which shows that participants were indeed more likely to make a fair offer if they had been exposed to an exemplar who was proud, rather than regretful, about being fair. Furthermore, mediation analysis showed that in the fair behaviour condition, the effect of exemplar regret on participants' offers was fully mediated by an increase in anticipated regret and a reduction in anticipated pride. In summary, these findings provide support for our argument that we learn about the psychological implications of making allocation decisions from observing the regret or pride expressed by another person who has taken the same decision. However, exemplar emotion did not have an effect on players' offers in the unfair condition. Given that very few participants (1.5 per cent) in the unfair condition made offers lower than or equal to 45:5, it may be the case that this behaviour struck participants as extremely unfair and overshadowed the influence of exemplar emotion.

To establish whether a less extreme degree of exemplar unfairness would elicit different effects we conducted a further study with a design very similar to that used in the two previous studies, but with unfair exemplar behaviour that was less extreme (35:15, unfair vs 25:25, fair). In addition, the study used the Dictator Game (DG; Kahneman, Knetsch, & Thaler, 1986). In the DG, the responder cannot reject the allocator's offer, meaning that the allocator does not have to estimate the chances that an offer might be rejected. This makes allocations in the DG a purer measure of fairness. To increase participants' involvement, we also changed the procedure such that they knew that they would be playing two rounds of the game, each with a different opponent. In round 1, the opponent was (apparently randomly) selected to be the allocator; in round 2, the participant was (again, apparently randomly) selected to be the allocator.

The pattern of means is shown in Figure 8.2. Participants who had received an unfair offer were more likely to make a fair offer when the exemplar had expressed regret rather than pride. Although the direct effect of exemplar emotion on participants' offers was not significant in the fair condition, mediation analyses showed that in both conditions, there were significant indirect effects of exemplar emotions on offers through anticipated regret and anticipated pride. In other words, participants who had been exposed to an unfair exemplar who expressed regret – as opposed to pride – were more likely to anticipate regret and less likely to anticipate pride if they were to act the same way, and these anticipated emotions affected the likelihood of participants making a fair allocation. There were corresponding (but, of course, mirror-image) indirect effects in the fair condition. Again, this suggests that we learn from the regret expressed by others. When they are seen to regret a decision, we expect to feel the same way if we were to make the same decision and this makes us more likely to behave differently when faced with a similar choice.

Recalling the earlier discussion of social appraisal, it is worth pointing out that in the studies just described, the exemplar's appraisal of the decision he or she had just made was relatively easy to infer, because in expressing regret or pride the exemplar also made it clear why he or she felt that way. For example, in the unfair/regret condition, the exemplar said (or wrote, depending on the study concerned), "I feel bad about how I played the game. I feel sorry that I chose to make some additional profit and was not fair. I regret my decision." Thus, the appraisal underlying the regret was one that focused on selfishness and unfairness. The same two appraisals were mentioned in the other four conditions, the only changes being what the exemplar was sorry or pleased about (making or

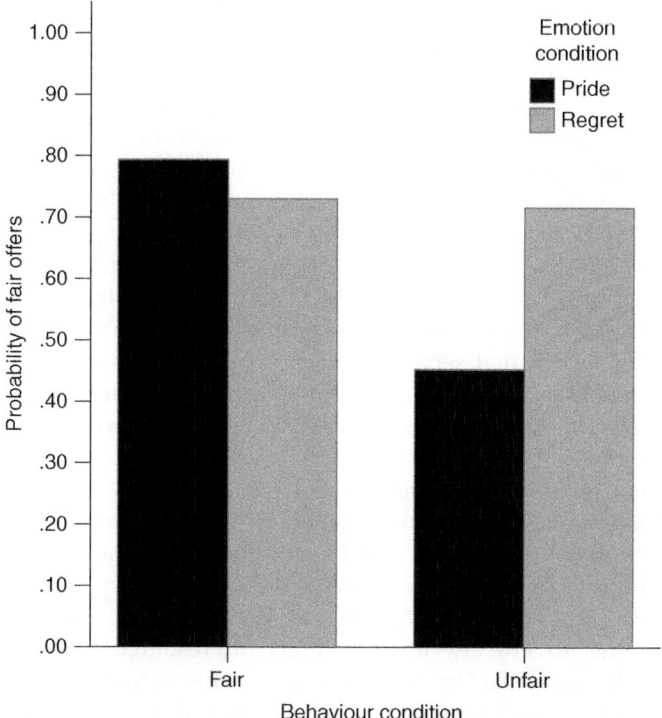

Figure 8.2 Predicted probabilities of fair offers as a function
of exemplar behaviour and exemplar emotion (study 2) (from
van der Schalk et al., 2015, adapted with permission).

not making a profit and being or not being fair). As a consequence, the
participants did not really have to infer the exemplar's appraisals from his
or her emotional expressions. In sum, the evidence from the two studies
shows that expressions of emotion accompanied by verbal messages
communicating appraisals have an impact on how the perceiver expects
to feel in a similar set of circumstances, as well as on the perceiver's
behaviour. In the experiments described below, emotions experienced by
the other person were conveyed simply by facial expressions, without
any accompanying verbal statements.

8.4   Regret and intergroup decisions

In subsequent studies we examined whether observed emotions could
influence decisions in the context of intergroup relations. It is well
established that groups are more competitive with each other than
individuals are (e.g. Balliet & van Lange, 2013; Insko, Schopler, Hoyle,

Dardis, & Graetz, 1990; Wildschut, Pinter, Vevea, Insko, & Schopler, 2003), and that intergroup relations are characterized by greater mutual suspicion and distrust than are interpersonal or within-group relations (e.g. Brewer, 1999). As Brewer (1999, p. 442) puts it, "the very factors that make in-group attachment and allegiance important to individuals also provide a fertile ground for antagonism and distrust of those outside the ingroup boundaries". Nowhere is this more apparent than when comparing the effects of intergroup apologies – which are largely ineffective (see Wohl, Hornsey, & Philpot, 2011) – with interpersonal apologies, which are generally effective (e.g. McCullough, Worthington, & Rachal, 1997). It follows that expressions of regret by out-group members in the wake of behaviour that serves the interest of their own group at the expense of the observers' in-group might be less influential than are similar expressions of regret made by individuals who have behaved in a self-serving manner.

In a first set of studies, we (Rychlowska, van der Schalk, Gratch, Breitinger, & Manstead, 2019) examined whether regret expressed by a representative of one of two groups could restore trust after their group had behaved unfairly. To do this, we made use of an intergroup version of the trust game (Berg, Dickhaut, & McCabe, 1995). In this game, one player (hereafter the "trustor") decides how much of a resource to send to the other player (hereafter the "trustee"). Any resource sent to the trustee is tripled. The trustee then has to decide how much of his/her resources to send back to the trustor. From the trustor's perspective, sending more resource is risky because the trustee could decide to return little or even none of the resource. However, sending more offers a way to increase resources for both parties – provided the trust is reciprocated – because of the tripling.

In study 1 of this series, participants belonged to a four-person group that ostensibly played two rounds of the trust game with a remote group, working in a different room. The two groups appeared to be connected by audio and video links. In fact, the remote group's actions were prerecorded. Unknown to participants, their own group included a confederate who had been instructed and trained to behave in different ways, depending on the experimental condition. The computer program that controlled the experiment selected, apparently at random, the confederate to participate in the first round, and the other participants were asked to stand behind her computer screen to see how the game would be played. Before leaving the room, the experimenter started the video connection with the other group, such that participants could see the outgroup, complete with its representative seated in front of a computer and the other three members standing behind her.

The on-screen instructions explained that the confederate's task was to send to the other group a proportion of the ten-lottery-ticket endowment that each group had been given at the start of the round. When the confederate was asked to decide how many tickets she would like to pass to the other team, she always sent seven tickets, a trusting move. This allocation was automatically tripled to twenty-one tickets for the out-group. Participants were then informed that the out-group representative would discuss with other members of her team how many tickets to send back. Participants then saw a video of the representative turning toward her group, before learning that the out-group had decided to return either fourteen tickets (fair condition) or no tickets (unfair condition). The final video showed the out-group representative displaying a positive (smile) or a negative (regret) facial expression. The latter involved lip pressing and downward head movements. Participants were then asked to play the second round of the game seated at individual computers, playing with an anonymous member of the out-group and knowing that any tickets they gained would be pooled with those gained by other in-group members. The key dependent variable was the number of tickets that participants in the four conditions decided to send to the out-group. We expected a main effect of out-group behaviour, such that fewer tickets would be sent to out-groups that had been unfair in round one, but also that this effect would be moderated by the out-group representative's emotional expression, such that more tickets would be sent in the unfair/regret condition than in the unfair/happiness condition. Within the unfair condition there was the predicted difference in tickets sent as a function of emotion expressed, with more tickets being sent to out-groups that had expressed regret rather than happiness. A similar, albeit weaker, effect was found in a follow-up study in which the emotion expressed by the out-group was manipulated not by facial expressions, but by means of ratings on a set of pictogram scales that conveyed the valence and arousal of the out-group's feelings about the decision they had made.

In a third study we used a new set of videotaped expressions and included a control condition as well as a measure of perceived willingness to change the decision – an appraisal that should be related to expressions of regret. Given that in the two previous studies emotion did not affect participants' decisions in the fair conditions, we focused on the effects of emotion following unfair behaviour. In a within-subjects design, participants saw a representative of the out-group displaying happiness, regret and a neutral facial expression, ostensibly in relation to the outcome of the round. After seeing each expression, participants imagined that they were playing a second round of the same game with another member of the out-group team and indicated the number of lottery tickets that they would send to this other person. Participants who saw the regret expression reported that they would send more tickets than participants who saw the neutral expression, who in turn did not differ from those who saw the happy expression. This suggests that the differences observed in the two previous studies reflect the impact of expressions of regret, rather than an effect of expressions of happiness. Furthermore, participants' perceptions of the extent to which the out-group representative would like to change her decision were also affected by the facial expression she displayed, such that the regret expression elicited higher scores than did the neutral and the happy expressions.

These studies examining the effects of emotion expressions in the context of intergroup relations show that expressions of emotion that are purely non-verbal in nature can influence the subsequent behaviour of members of another group. They also show that the emotions of one out-group member influence behaviour towards other members of the same out-group. Thus, from the perspective of ASL, the inferences that observers of out-group emotional expressions draw from an expression of regret attenuate the impact of unfair out-group behaviour posing a threat to intergroup cooperation. The observers "learn" that the out-group is not entirely happy with this behaviour and that it might well decide to behave differently (and therefore more cooperatively) on a subsequent occasion.

8.5   In-group expressions of negative emotion

A final empirical example of how lessons can be learned from others' emotional expressions comes from another line of work in which we (Shore, Rychlowska, van der Schalk, Parkinson, & Manstead, 2018) examined the impact of guilt expressed by an in-group member about not reciprocating a trusting move made by the out-group in a trust game. Before describing the study further, it is worth considering the relation between regret and guilt. As signalled at the start of this chapter, these two emotions are similar in that they arise from events in which the self is appraised as responsible for producing negative outcomes.

Berndsen, van der Pligt, Doosje, and Manstead (2004) argued that the most important difference between these two emotions is whether people are responsible for negative outcomes for themselves (in which case they experience regret) or for others (in which case they experience guilt). However, a series of three studies by Zeelenberg and Breugelmans (2008), revealed that regret is elicited by undesirable outcomes for both the self (intrapersonal) and for another person (interpersonal). More recent research by Wagner, Handke, Dörfel, and Walter (2012) has provided further evidence of the similarities between guilt and interpersonal regret. Comparing conditions in which decisions had intrapersonal or interpersonal consequences, these authors concluded:

> Obviously, while there can be regret without substantial guilt (as shown in the intrapersonal condition), it may be impossible to

experience guilt without regret in interpersonal conditions, and the high correlation between the two emotions suggests that they do not only co-occur in these contexts, but indeed strongly overlap conceptually. In other words, guilt and interpersonal regret may describe essentially the same core emotion. (p. 9)

Thinking back to the definition of regret offered by Zeelenberg and Pieters (2007), this claim seems entirely logical. According to their analysis, regret is an emotion that we experience when we reflect on a decision and believe that things would have been better if we had decided differently. If the outcome of the regretted decision is that harm was caused to another person, it would also be a basis for guilt. In other words, it seems likely that – to the extent that harm caused to another person resulted from a decision that one took more or less freely – many episodes of guilt will also be tinged with regret about not having arrived at a different decision. I may feel regret about the decision I took and guilty about the harm that the decision caused you.

Returning to the study by Shore et al. (2018), an out-group representative decided to send seven lottery tickets out of her group's endowment of ten tickets to the in-group, with the result that the in-group now had thirty-one tickets (twenty-one new tickets plus its ten-ticket endowment). However, this trusting move was rebuffed by the in-group when an in-group representative decided to return no tickets to the out-group. We were able to achieve this outcome by ensuring that the in-group member who was apparently randomly chosen to be the group's representative in this first round was always a confederate.

Following this breach of trust, the representative acted in one of three pre-determined ways, to create three emotion expression conditions. The program running the experiment asked the representative how guilty and happy she felt about the number of tickets returned to the other group. She answered this question using a standardized script. In the guilt condition she sighed, looked down, and said, "Now I don't feel so good about it", before selecting *very much* for the guilt rating and *a little* for the happiness rating. In the happiness condition, she laughed, nodded her head, and said, "I feel pretty good about it", before choosing *very much* for the happiness rating, and *a little* for the guilt rating. In the control condition, the representative was not asked about how she felt and did not express any emotion.

In round two of the game, each in-group member played in the role of trustee with an anonymous out-group trustor. Now the trustor sent four tickets out of an endowment of ten, meaning that the trustee now had twelve new tickets. Our key dependent variable was how many of these tickets the trustee decided to return to the trustor. Figure 8.3 shows the mean number of tickets returned to the out-group trustee in each of the

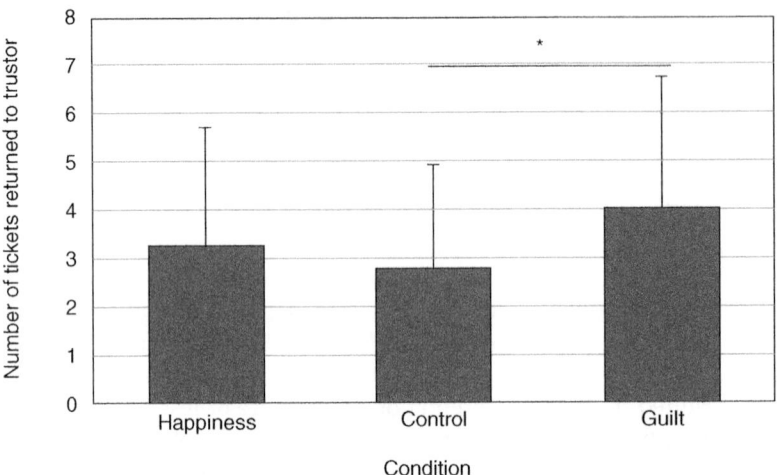

Figure 8.3 Number of tickets returned to trustor in the trust game as a function of emotion expression of in-group representative following breach of trust (from Shore et al., 2018, adapted with permission).

Note: Error bars represent standard deviations. The asterisk indicates significance at $p < .05$.

three conditions. It is evident that participants who had been exposed to a fellow in-group member who expressed guilt about her failure to reciprocate trust returned more tickets to another anonymous out-group member than did counterparts in the no expression control condition. There was no significant difference in tickets returned between the guilt and happiness or happiness and control conditions.

Further analysis showed that the expression of guilt by the in-group representative had the effect of increasing the amount of guilt felt by participants, and that this increased guilt mediated the effect of the guilty expression on number of tickets sent. In the way that would be predicted by social appraisal theory, seeing another person express guilt about a decision led others who were implicitly involved in that decision to experience greater guilt, and this greater guilt seems to have led them to be more generous in the number of tickets they returned to another out-group trustor.

8.6   Conclusions

We believe that the experiments described above provide evidence for the operation of ASL. As argued in the introduction to this chapter, the phenomena examined in these studies fall in the "mid-range" of the family of processes referred to under the umbrella of ASL, and can be seen as examples of affective observation or social referencing, depending on the extent to which the exemplar is seen as engaging in *deliberate* emotion signalling. In the experimental settings used in the present studies, where emotional expressions were intentionally varied, there is of course a real sense in which the emotional signal was ostensive, or deliberate, and could therefore be regarded as closer to social referencing. However, for the expression to be credible, its deliberate nature should not have been apparent to naïve participants. Indeed, if participants had been aware that the emotions expressed were intentional, rather than spon-taneous, it is possible that they would have discounted them. A recent study by Shore and Parkinson (2017) supports this prediction by showing that perceiving expressions of guilt as strategic undermined the trust-repairing effects of this emotion. In a more naturalistic setting, however, the emotional expressions would typically be made spontaneously and interpreted as honest signals. As a consequence, the process would be closer to affective observation. In describing this process, Dukes and Clément argue that, "when entering a group, individuals are prone to detect, simply by observing others' affective reactions, what is socially relevant and what is not" (Introduction, this volume). This, we suggest, is very close to the process underlying the effects found in the experiments reported in the present chapter.

Participants in these and similar studies can frame the game they are playing in cooperative or competitive terms. Indeed, this is the very point of mixed-motive games: They pit collective interest against self- (or group-) interest, or concern for the welfare of the other against concern for the welfare of the self. It is well established that framing such games in terms of cooperation (e.g. "the Community Game") results in more cooperative behaviour than does framing them in terms of competition (e.g. "the Stock Market Game;" Ellingsen, Johannesson, Mollerstrom, & Munkhammar, 2012). A theoretical framework that can account for such framing effects (and indeed many other phenomena) in experimental games is the "appropriateness framework" proposed by Weber, Kopelman, and Messick (2004). These authors argue that "The definition of the situation is the heart of the appropriateness framework. Is this a cooperative situation or a competitive situation? ... The definition of the situation informs the person about the norms, expectations, rules, learned behaviours, skills, and possible strategies that are relevant. It should be, therefore, the prox-imal mediator of behavioural choice" (p. 285). Our contention is that the effects of emotional expression in the experiments described in the pre-sent chapter are due to shifts in the perceived appropriateness of certain behaviours. By expressing regret or guilt, an individual or group member is in effect signalling that a competitive norm is not as applicable to the current context as his or her recent decision may have implied, and that a cooperative norm would be more applicable. In this way, participants in our studies learn about the appropriateness of behaviour by observing others' emotional expressions. When we see others expressing regret or guilt about a decision they took, this does indeed "chasten the future", in the sense that we draw different inferences from their decision-making than we would if these people had expressed happiness or pride and that these inferences moderate our own decisions as a result.

References

Ajzen, I. (1985). From intentions to actions: A theory of planned behaviour. In J. Kuhl & J. Beckmann (Eds.), *Action control: From cognition to behaviour* (pp. 11–39). Berlin, Germany: Springer-Verlag.

Balliet, D., & van Lange, P. A. M. (2013). Trust, conflict, and cooperation: A meta-analysis. *Psychological Bulletin, 139,* 1090–1112.

Baumeister, R. F., Vohs, K. D., DeWall, C. N., & Zhang, L. (2007). How emotion shapes behavior: Feedback, anticipation, and reflection, rather than direct causation. *Personality and Social Psychology Review, 11,* 167–203.

Bell, D. E. (1982). Regret in decision making under uncertainty. *Operations Research, 30,* 961–981.

Berg, J., Dickhaut, J., & McCabe, K. (1995). Trust, reciprocity, and social history. *Games and Economic Behavior, 10,* 122–142.

Berndsen, M., van der Pligt, J., Doosje, B., & Manstead, A. S. R. (2004). Guilt and regret: The determining role of interpersonal and intrapersonal harm. *Cognition and Emotion, 18,* 55–70.

Brewer, M. B. (1999). The psychology of prejudice: Ingroup love or outgroup hate? *Journal of Social Issues, 55,* 429–444.

Bruder, M., Fischer, A. H., & Manstead, A. S. R. (2014). Social appraisal as a cause of collective emotions. In C. von Scheve & M. Salmela (Eds.), *Collective emotions* (pp. 141–155). New York, NY: Oxford University Press.

Canessa, N., Motterlini, M., Alemanno, F., Perani, D., & Cappa, S. (2011). Learning from other people's experience: A neuroimaging study of decisional interactive-learning. *Neuroimage, 55*(1), 353–362.

de Melo, C. M., Carnevale, P. J., Read, S. J., & Gratch, J. (2014). Reading people's minds from emotion expressions in interdependent decision making. *Journal of Personality and Social Psychology, 106,* 73–88.

Douglas, C. N. (Ed.) (1917). *Forty thousand quotations: Prose and poetical.* New York, NY: Halcyon House.

Ellingsen, T., Johannesson, M., Mollerstrom, J., & Munkhammar, S. (2012). Social framing effects: Preferences or beliefs? *Games and Economic Behavior, 76,* 117–130.

Festinger, L. (1957). *A theory of cognitive dissonance.* Stanford, CA: Stanford University Press.

Güth, W., Schmittberger, R., & Schwarze, B. (1982). An experimental analysis of ultimatum bargaining. *Journal of Economic Behavior & Organization, 3,* 367–388.

Hareli, S., & Hess, U. (2010). What emotional reactions can tell us about the nature of others: An appraisal perspective on person perception. *Cognition and Emotion, 24*, 128–140.

Insko, C., Schopler, J., Hoyle, R., Dardis, G., & Graetz, K. A. (1990). Individual-group discontinuity as a function of fear and greed. *Journal of Personality and Social Psychology, 58*(1), 68–79.

Janis, I. L., & Mann, L. (1977). *Decision making: A psychological analysis of conflict, choice and commitment.* New York, NY: The Free Press.

Kahneman, D., Knetsch, J. L., & Thaler, R. H. (1986). Fairness and the assumptions of economics. *Journal of Business, 59*, S285–S300.

Latané, B., & Darley, J. M. (1968). Group inhibition of bystander intervention in emergencies. *Journal of Personality and Social Psychology, 10*, 215–221.

Loomes, G., & Sugden, R. (1982). Regret theory: An alternative theory of rational choice under uncertainty. *Economic Journal, 92*, 805–825.

Mansfield, K. (1920). Je ne parle pas français. In *Bliss and other stories* (pp. 71–115). Plymouth, UK: Mayflower Press.

Manstead, A. S. R., & Fischer, A. H. (2001). Social appraisal: The social world as object of and influence on appraisal processes. In K. Scherer, A. Schorr, & T. Johnstone (Eds.), *Appraisal processes in emotion: Theory, methods, research* (pp. 221–232). Oxford, UK: Oxford University Press.

McCullough, M. E., Worthington, E. L., & Rachal, K. C. (1997). Interpersonal forgiving in close relationships. *Journal of Personality and Social Psychology, 73*(2), 321–336.

Mumenthaler, C., & Sander, D. (2012). Social appraisal influences recognition of emotions. *Journal of Personality and Social Psychology, 102*, 1118–1135.

Parkinson, D., & Simons, G. (2009). Affecting others: Social appraisal and emotion contagion in everyday decision making. *Personality and Social Psychology Bulletin, 35*, 1071–1084.

Richard, R., van der Pligt, J., & de Vries, N. (1996). Anticipated regret and time perspective: Changing sexual risk-taking behavior. *Journal of Behavioral Decision Making, 9*, 185–199.

Rychlowska, M., van der Schalk, J., Gratch, J., Breitinger, E., & Manstead, A. S. R. (2019). Beyond actions: Reparatory effects of regret in intergroup trust games. *Journal of Experimental Social Psychology, 82*, 74–84. http://dx.doi.org/10.1016/j.jesp.2019.01.006

Sandberg, T., & Conner, M. (2008). Anticipated regret as an additional predictor in the theory of planned behaviour: A meta-analysis. *British Journal of Social Psychology, 47*(4), 589–606.

Shimanoff, S. B. (1984). Commonly named emotions in everyday conversations. *Perceptual and Motor Skills, 58*, 514.

Shore, D., & Parkinson, B. (2017). Interpersonal effects of strategic and spontaneous guilt communication in trust games. *Cognition and Emotion, 32*(6), 1382–1390. doi:10.1080/02699931.2017.1395728

Shore, D., Rychlowska, M., van der Schalk, J., Parkinson, B., & Manstead, A. S. R. (2018). Intergroup emotional exchange: Ingroup guilt and outgroup anger increase resource allocation in trust games. *Emotion, 19*(4), 605–616. doi: 10.1037/emo0000463

Sorce, J. F., Emde, R. N., Campos, J., & Klinnert, M. D. (1985). Maternal emotional signaling: Its effect on the visual cliff behavior of 1-year-olds. *Developmental Psychology, 21,* 195–200.

van der Schalk, J., Kuppens, T., Bruder, M., & Manstead, A. S. R. (2015). The social power of regret: The effect of social appraisal and anticipated emotions on fair and unfair allocations in resource dilemmas. *Journal of Experimental Psychology: General, 144,* 151–157.

Wagner, U., Handke, L., Dörfel, D., & Walter, H. (2012). An experimental decision-making paradigm to distinguish guilt and regret and their self-regulating function via loss averse choice behavior. *Frontiers in Psychology, 3*(431). doi: 10.3389/fpsyg.2012.00431

Weber, J. M., Kopelman, S., & Messick, D. M., (2004). A conceptual review of decision making in social dilemmas: Applying a logic of appropriateness. *Personality and Social Psychology Review, 8,* 281–307.

Wildschut, T., Pinter, B., Vevea, J. L., Insko, C. A., & Schopler, J. (2003). Beyond the group mind: A quantitative review of the interindividual-intergroup discontinuity effect. *Psychological Bulletin, 129,* 698–722.

Wohl, M. J., Hornsey, M. J., & Philpot, C. R. (2011). A critical review of public apologies: Aims, pitfalls, and effectiveness. *Social Issues and Policy Review, 5*(1), 70–100.

Zeelenberg, M., & Breugelmans, S. M. (2008). The role of interpersonal harm in distinguishing regret from guilt. *Emotion, 8,* 589–596.

Zeelenberg, M., & Pieters, R. (2007). A theory of regret regulation 1.0. *Journal of Consumer Psychology, 17,* 3–18.

CHAPTER 9

Insights from culture and emotion research for affective social learning

Emotional enculturation and acculturation

Jozefien De Leersnyder

Culture, emotion and affective social learning (ASL) scaffold one another. Culture – i.e. a group's shared system of meanings and practices that reflect what is 'good', 'normal' and 'valuable' and, of course, what is 'bad', 'abnormal' and 'worthless' – would hardly exist without the ASL processes that allow for the transfer of evaluations from one person to another. Emotions (often implicitly) reflect our evaluations and are, therefore, not only vehicles of ASL, but also the 'most experience-near carriers of culture' (Markus & Kitayama, 1994, p. 100). Finally, without a cultural meaning system and thus some consensus about what is good, normal and valuable, ASL would be non-relevant; in that case, evaluations of the world would be either hyper-diverse or random, rendering it unnecessary to learn them.

In the current chapter, I aim to gain more insight into ASL – i.e. the processes that 'allow people to learn what is valuable in their specific socio-cultural environment' (see Clément & Dukes, Introduction, this volume) – by revisiting the literature on culture and emotion. As I will outline below (Section 9.1), emotions reflect our evaluations of the world. When people then experience *similar* patterns of emotions across daily situations, we may infer that they share their evaluations of the world. Therefore, we can consider the processes that instigate emotional similarity between individuals and their sociocultural group as processes of ASL.

Capitalizing on this idea, I will review the literature on how both children (Section 9.2) and immigrant minorities (Section 9.3) come to 'fit in emotionally' with their sociocultural context and thus learn to evaluate the world in culturally appropriate ways. In line with the framework outlined in the introductory chapter of this book, I will structure the section on emotional *en*culturation in children by distinguishing between ASL processes that are rather implicit and automatic (Section 9.2.1)

The preparation of this chapter was funded by a post-doctoral grant from the Flemish Research Council (FWO) with the number 12L7816N.

versus those that are more explicit and deliberate (Section 9.2.2). Furthermore, and to gain as much as possible from the emerging literature on emotional *acculturation* in immigrant minorities, I will describe the nature of this phenomenon (Section 9.3.1) before focusing on its underlying processes that may reflect ASL (Section 9.3.2). In closing this chapter (Section 9.4), I will reflect on ASL from the currently available insights from culture and emotion research, as well as formulate ways in which future research may advance our understanding of ASL.

9.1   Culture, emotions and cultural fit in emotions

Before focusing on the ASL processes that instigate people's emotional fit with culture, I wish to outline how I understand culture, emotion and the phenomenon of 'emotional fit'. Only then, may we come to grasp why children and other newcomers to a society are socialized to experience the culturally appropriate emotions and why the processes of emotional enculturation and acculturation are in fact processes of ASL.

9.1.1   Culture

Whenever people live together in groups, they readily develop a 'culture' – that is, a socially transmitted system of meanings and practices that is shared among group members and that helps them navigate their daily, social and spiritual lives. A cultural group's system of *meanings* is made up by the values, ideas, attitudes, representations, prototypes, stereotypes, etc. that reflect what is good, normal and valuable. It constitutes the backdrop against which people perceive and evaluate the world – as reflected in thoughts, feelings and behaviours – as well as shaping their cultural practices. These *practices* include cultural products (e.g. advertisements, children's books), typical ways of engaging in interpersonal interactions and institutions (Markus & Hamedani, 2007). In turn, these practices are affording, encouraging and rewarding thoughts, feelings and behaviours that are in line with the cultural meaning system, while limiting, discouraging and punishing those that are not.

Some well-studied examples of cultural differences in meanings and practices are the so-called 'cultural models of self and relating' that reflect what it means to be a 'good person' and to have 'good relationships' with others (e.g. Markus & Kitayama, 1991; Vignoles et al., 2016). Two prototypes – those of *independence* and *interdependence* – have been used throughout the literature as a heuristic to illustrate how cultural contexts may differ from one another. In the current chapter, I'll also rely on this dichotomy, not with the intent of neglecting the wide intra- and intercultural variance, but as one way to describe 'culture' and hence to better understand variation in people's evaluations of the world.

The independent model of self and relating that is prevalent in Western European and North American middle-class contexts (Markus & Kitayama, 1991; Stephens, Markus, & Phillips, 2014) defines a good person as independent, in control, successful and unique (Kim & Markus, 1999; Rothbaum, Pott, Azuma, Miyake, & Weisz, 2000; Triandis, 1995). Good relationships are those in which each partner remains autonomous, self-reliant and high in self-esteem (Heine, 2003; Hochschild, 1995) – something people (unconsciously) achieve by focusing on both their own and their interaction partners' positive and unique characteristics, such as through complimenting and rewarding each other for every level of achievement (d'Andrade, 1984). In contrast, the interdependent model, which is most prevalent in East Asian, Mediterranean and working-class contexts (Güngör, Karasawa, Boiger, Dinçer, & Mesquita, 2014; Markus & Kitayama, 1991; Stephens et al., 2014) defines a good person as interdependent, adjusting herself to the situation and as maintaining relational harmony (Heine, 2003; Kim & Markus, 1999; Lebra, 1992). Good relationships are those in which partners are mutually dependent, interconnected and that adjust to each other's expectations – something that can be achieved through emphasizing either closeness or saving 'face' (Boiger, Güngör, Karasawa, & Mesquita, 2014; Güngör et al., 2014; Kitayama, Markus, Matsumoto, & Norasakkunkit, 1997). Both stem from an awareness of both one's own shortcomings and the other's needs, which can be practised through, for instance, extensive politeness rules and moments of (collective) self-reflection (i.e. *hansei*; Lewis, 1995).

As can be inferred from the above, culture is both 'in the heads' of individuals and 'in the worlds' that they create for one another (Adams & Markus, 2004). This implies that regardless of tremendous individual variation in people's endorsement of a culture's meanings, everybody engages – to a certain extent – in its practices and associated reward structures. Moreover, it implies that although each individual navigates at the intersection of multiple sociocultural contexts (e.g. country, social class, religion, gender), it remains relevant to compare people in different sociocultural contexts, since 'powerful contexts' – like the national one – importantly shape the institutions, products and practices people engage in. Finally, it implies that, since people (un)willingly engage in these cultural worlds and are subjected to its reward structures, they may all benefit from 'fitting in'.

In the current chapter, I focus on people's *emotional* fit with culture, because emotions reflect our evaluations of the world. As such, the processes that instigate cultural fit in emotions can be considered processes of ASL. However, to fully understand this reasoning, I'll first outline what I mean when I use the term 'emotions' and then describe what we know on cultural fit of emotions.

9.1.2   *Emotions*

Emotions are not merely subjective feelings; they are, above all, stances in our social world (see also Mesquita, 2010; Mesquita, Vissers, & De Leersnyder, 2015; Solomon, 2004). Indeed, experiencing an emotion implies giving a particular meaning to the world and preparing yourself for appropriate action (e.g. Frijda, 1986). For instance, when you are angry, you do not accept how others treat you, you feel entitled to get more than you got and hold others responsible for that negative outcome. By communicating your anger, whether through slamming a door or clenching your teeth, you aim to gain control, influence the other person and correct his or her behaviour (Frijda, 2007; Frijda, Kuipers, & Schure, 1989; Stein, Trabasso, & Liwag, 1993). In contrast, when you are ashamed, you think you have failed in the eyes of others, have fallen short of certain social norms and hold yourself responsible. By communicating your shame, either through blushing, apologizing, stumbling or hiding, you seek to signal your awareness of the transgression and, as such, aim to restore your social relationships (e.g. Keltner & Buswell, 1997). Thus, since emotions imply meaning and social action, they are 'not an inner phenomenon so much as a way of being-in-the-world' Solomon, 1984, p. 250).[1]

Since the most valued stances of being-in-the-world and relating to others differ across cultural contexts, we may expect systematic cultural variation in how people experience situations. Indeed, when European American and Japanese participants recounted offensive situations from their own daily life, they systematically reported different appraisals and action tendencies (Mesquita et al., 2006). For example, only 0–5 per cent of European American participants, but 40–56 per cent of Japanese participants reported to have taken the perspective of a third person and sympathized with the offender, respectively. These different appraisals

---

[1] However, saying that particular emotions imply particular meanings and action tendencies, is not to say that *all* instances of an emotion category, such as 'anger' or 'shame' imply the exact same meanings and action tendencies. They don't, and variety within the *population* of 'anger' or 'shame' categories is the norm rather than the exception (e.g. Barrett, 2017; Boiger et al., 2018; Kuppens, van Mechelen, Smits, de Boeck, & Ceulemans, 2007). In addition, this is not to say that meanings and action tendencies represent an 'essence' or 'core' of the emotion that is somehow hard-wired. Rather, it is to say that people who live together and interact share (and thus agree upon) concepts of emotions such as 'anger' and 'shame' that include one or all of the above-mentioned components, implying that different groups of people may differ slightly in the content of their emotion concepts (Boiger et al., 2018). Finally, saying that emotions are 'out there in the world' does not deny they are associated with physical changes and thus embodied states. Instead, it is saying that people readily apply certain emotion concepts to (perceptions of other people's) physical sensations in such a way that the concepts provide the best fit given previous experiences by ourselves or others in our group (see also Barrett, 2017). Hence, emotions can be conceived of as embodied and culturally agreed-upon ways to communicate meaning and intentions to act.

can be understood from the cultures' models of self and relating: a European American independent model likely encourages a first-person perspective that helps to protect self-esteem, whereas a Japanese interdependent model encourages a third-person perspective that helps to maintain social harmony (Cohen & Gunz, 2002; Grossmann, Ellsworth, & Hong, 2012; Heine, 2003). People's emotional experience thus reflected the culturally valued stances in the situation.

Extrapolating from this offensive type of situation to the myriad of situations that characterize daily life, we may expect that those emotions that are in line with a culture's model of self and relating are experienced more frequently and intensely than emotions that are not (e.g. Mesquita, 2003; Tsai, Knutson, & Fung, 2006). Indeed, instances of anger and pride that highlight separateness from others, uniqueness and personal autonomy, tend to be more prevalent in independent than in interdependent contexts, whereas the opposite is true for instances of shame and closeness that highlight one's awareness of shortcomings and/or one's concern for maintaining harmony and being connected (Boiger, Mesquita, Uchida, & Feldman Barrett, 2013; Kitayama, Mesquita, & Karasawa, 2006; Tsai, Miao, Seppala, Fung, & Yeung, 2007). There are thus systematic cultural differences in the frequencies and intensities with which people experience emotions, implying that different cultural contexts are characterized by different 'typical' patterns of emotion.

This latter observation suggests that people who engage in the *same* cultural context experience more *similar* patterns of emotion – and thus evaluations of the world – than people who do not. At the same time, it raises the following questions: (i) To what extent do individuals 'fit in' emotionally with their culture? (ii) Is this fit beneficial? And, if so, (iii) *how* are individuals' emotions socialized to fit in with their culture (i.e. ASL).

9.1.3 Emotional fit with culture

The phenomenon of emotional fit with culture can be inferred from the observation that the most prevalent types of emotions in a cultural context match its prevalent cultural model (e.g. Kitayama et al., 2006; Tsai et al., 2006). In addition, fit can be quantified as the profile correlation between an individual's pattern of emotional experiences (i.e. intensities) in a particular situation and a sociocultural group's *typical* or average pattern of emotion in that type of situation (see De Leersnyder, Mesquita, & Kim, 2011, for the full procedure). Employing this latter method among monocultural samples of European Americans, Koreans, Belgians and Turks, we recently provided further evidence for the phenomenon of emotional fit with culture (De Leersnyder, 2014; De Leersnyder, Kim, & Mesquita, 2018). Specifically, we asked the participants to report their experiences in 2–4 different types of emotional situations from their own daily life and calculated each individual's fit with the corresponding typical emotional patterns of both their *own* cultural group and *another* cultural group. We found that whereas European Americans fitted significantly better with the typical European American than the Korean patterns, the opposite was true for Koreans. Similarly, whereas Belgians fitted better with the typical Belgian than the Turkish patterns of emotion, the opposite was true for Turks. Thus, across all four groups, people's patterns of emotion were more similar to the typical patterns of their own cultural group than that of the other group.

In a series of follow-up studies, we explored the potential benefits of emotional fit with culture by linking participants' levels of emotional fit with their own culture to both their relational and psychological well-being. We found that relational well-being – i.e. being satisfied with one's social relationships and social support – was positively associated with emotional fit in relatedness-promoting situations and that this was true across the European American, Korean and Belgian samples (De Leersnyder, Mesquita, Kim, Eom, & Choi, 2014). Furthermore, we found that psychological well-being – i.e. being satisfied with oneself and showing no symptoms of depression – was positively associated with emotional fit in those culture-specific situations that optimally allow people to embody their cultural model of self and relating (De Leersnyder, Kim, & Mesquita, 2015). For instance, whereas European Americans' psychological well-being was higher to the extent they fitted with autonomy-promoting situations at work, Koreans' well-being was higher to the extent they fitted with relatedness-promoting situations at home. These findings are in line with earlier research showing that people's subjective well-being is higher, and depression is lower, when people experience more of the emotions that match their cultural model of self and relating (Kitayama et al., 2006; Tsai et al., 2006). Together, these studies suggest that it is beneficial to experience the culturally appropriate emotions and hence, to make meaning and intend to act in the culturally shared way.

To date, not much is known about the exact mechanisms that link emotional fit with culture to well-being. However, studies on emotional similarity in dyads and small groups provide several clues for potential underlying mechanisms. One such mechanism is that of *social inclusion*. When people experience similar emotions, they signal to share (cultural) evaluations, which instigates a 'shared reality' that not only validates people's interpretation of the situation (Fulmer et al., 2010; Hardin & Higgins, 1996), but also strengthens social bonds (Fischer & Manstead, 2008; Hatfield, Cacioppo, & Rapson, 1994). When people fail to experience and communicate emotions that are expected by others, however, they are readily perceived as morally inferior and are sanctioned as a consequence (Szczurek, Monin, & Gross, 2012). A second potential mechanism is that of *stress*. It has been shown that when dyads experience similar emotions before engaging in a stressful task, they experience less stress during that challenging task (Townsend, Kim, & Mesquita, 2013). Yet, when people fail to be culturally concordant (in cognitive domains), they tend to experience more stress (Dressler, Balieiro, Ribeiro, & Dos Santos, 2007). Hence, both stress and social exclusion may account for the above reported positive associations between emotional fit with culture and well-being.

In sum, people tend to not only fit emotionally with their culture, but also benefit from doing so. Therefore, it may be important for children and other newcomers to a particular sociocultural context to learn how to experience – and hence evaluate – the world in culturally appropriate ways. Stated like this, it becomes apparent that emotion socialization processes like emotional enculturation and acculturation that increase people's emotional fit with culture, are in fact processes of ASL.

9.2   The enculturation of emotions: how children learn to experience the world in culturally appropriate ways

Just like parents and caregivers regulate their child's experiences of hunger, thirst and need for affection, they actively co-regulate her affective experiences. And, just like other parental practices, this co-regulation of affect is guided by culturally shared beliefs, such as the prevalent models of self and relating and the associated beliefs about emotions. Below, I describe some of the processes through which parents and caregivers socialize their children to become 'culturally emotionally competent' (Friedlmeier, Corapci, & Cole, 2011; Friedlmeier & Trommsdorff, 2002). In line with the ASL framework, I will distinguish between more implicit strategies of emotional enculturation in which either parents or children are not aware they are either teaching or learning how to evaluate and experience the world (Section 9.2.1) and more explicit ones (Section 9.2.2). The distinction is not always that sharp, but may be worthwhile maintaining as it helps to distinguish between ASL processes based on descriptive versus prescriptive feeling norms, and resonates with distinctions made in the emotion regulation literature (e.g. Gross & Thompson, 2007; Gyurak, Gross, & Etkin, 2011).

9.2.1   *Implicit processes of emotion enculturation*

As discussed in the Introduction to this volume, children may come to experience the world in a culturally valued way through both the processes of emotional contagion and affective observation. In the case of contagion, it is argued that young children are susceptible to the affective states of others and pick these up through either conscious or unconscious imitation (e.g. Geangu, Benga, Stahl, & Striano, 2010, but see Ruffman, Lorimer, & Scarf, 2017 for alternative accounts on infants' 'emotional contagion'). In the case of affective observation, the idea is that when socializers experience and express particular emotions in particular situations, children pick up on this information and incorporate it into their (future) emotional functioning (e.g. Denham, Bassett, & Wyatt, 2007). Indeed, children tend to experience and express emotional patterns that are similar to those of their caregivers (Halberstadt, Fox, & Jones, 1993; see also Valiente et al., 2004). Specifically, children from parents who experience and express more positive emotions tend to express more positive affect themselves (Isley, O'Neil, Clatfelter, & Parke, 1999) and children from angry and tense mothers tend to be more angry themselves (Denham, 1998; Garner & Estep, 2001; Isley et al., 1999; Newland & Crnic, 2011; Smith & Walden, 1999). If caregivers across different cultural contexts, then, experience and express different patterns of emotion, their children may come to incorporate these culture-specific patterns through either contagion or affective observation. However, to my knowledge, there are no studies directly testing this hypothesis.

In addition to these obvious processes of ASL, the literature on emotional enculturation suggests several other ways in which children's affect aligns with cultural meaning systems. One very implicit process is parental co-regulation through differential strategies of being sensitive to children's needs (see also De Leersnyder, Boiger, & Mesquita, 2013). *Proactive* strategies imply the constant monitoring of the child's surroundings in order to intervene before he experiences full-blown negative affect; *reactive* strategies allow negative situations to happen and restrict interventions to when it appears to adults that the child is distressed (Trommsdorff & Rothbaum, 2008). As such, proactive strategies convey the connotation that high arousal negative emotions are less/not accepted, whereas reactive strategies convey that these emotions are OK. In line with the idea that high-arousal negative emotions may both ascertain one's own needs and disrupt social harmony, research has documented that proactive strategies are more prevalent in interdependent contexts (Japan, Cameroon, Kenya), whereas reactive strategies are more prevalent in independent cultural contexts (Germany, United States; Keller, Yovsi, & Voelker, 2002; LeVine, 2004; Morelli & Rothbaum, 2007; Trommsdorff & Friedlmeier, 2006 as cited in Trommsdorff & Rothbaum, 2008). As such, infants come to align their negative emotional experiences with culture through parents' regulatory strategies.

A similar process of emotion enculturation has been observed in the realm of positive emotions. Specifically, studies show that (typically proactive and interdependent) Kenyan Gusii mothers tend to turn away from their baby when it gets positively excited in the hope that by ignoring it, the child will calm down (LeVine, 2004). This is in sharp contrast to (typically reactive and independent) European American mothers who actively aim to amplify and prolong their child's positive expressions of emotion (LeVine, 2004). In this way, children of European American parents may come to value high-arousal positive states, whereas children of Gusii parents come to value low-arousal affective states above high-arousal ones. Through parental practices of allowing and amplifying versus preventing and ignoring negative/positive affect, children may thus come to align their emotional experiences – and hence, their evaluations of the world – with their cultural context.

When children grow older, the parental shaping of affect through affirming versus downplaying certain affective states becomes more elaborate. When it is clear that children experience a particular affect in reaction to a particular event, caregivers may reward children for emotional experiences they consider appropriate and punish or correct them if this is not the case. As such, caregivers provide a form of feedback – which we could consider an unsolicited form of social appraisal – that teaches children how to evaluate the world. For instance, parents in Germany versus Japan and India react very differently to their toddlers' distress after they experience a mishap (Trommsdorff, 2006; Trommsdorff & Friedlmeier, 1993, 2010). Specifically, German mothers tend to focus on their babies' distress, thereby affirming that mishaps provide good reasons to experience and express negative emotions. Yet, Japanese and Indian mothers tend to ignore their babies' negative emotions, thereby challenging their babies' interpretation of a mishap as distressful. Again, these differences can be understood from the different self-views endorsed in Germany versus India and Japan. In an independent model of self, mishaps and failing may harm self-esteem and are, therefore good reasons for distress. Yet, in an interdependent model of self, personal mishaps may be more accepted since they do not threaten social relationships and, instead, provide opportunities for further self-improvement. By ignoring versus paying attention to their children's distress in this situation, parents and caregivers thus challenge rather than validate their children's appraisal of the situation and teach them the culturally appropriate meaning of the situation.

Relatedly, studies by Cole and colleagues among the Tamang and Brahman cultural groups in Nepal illustrate how parents and caregivers socialize their children's general stance in the world (instead of their reactions to single events) through affirming or challenging emotional reactions (Cole, Bruschi, & Tamang, 2002; Cole, Tamang, & Shrestha, 2006). Although both ethnic groups share core cultural values of interdependence, Tamang Buddhists value egalitarianism, humbleness, compassion and social harmony more than the high-caste Brahman Hindus, who emphasize ethnic pride, social dominance and self-control. In line with these values, Tamang adults consider anger as interfering with egalitarianism and compassion but appreciate shame because it implies awareness of one's actions through the eyes of others. In contrast, Brahman adults believe anger should be restrained in its expression but accepted as experience since it signals dominance, and consider shame as inappropriate since it signals personal weakness and threatens one's pride in being Brahman (Cole et al., 2002). Accordingly, a natural observation study among 91 households in 14 Nepali villages (Cole et al., 2006) documented that whereas Tamang caregivers responded to their 3–5-year-old's anger by rebuking it (e.g. thorough scolding, hitting or teasing the child), Brahman caregivers validated this emotion by interacting with the angry child in a positive way (e.g. teaching, nurturing). In contrast, Tamang caregivers responded with reasoning and nurturing to shameful children, whereas Brahman caregivers largely ignored them, thereby challenging the child's appraisal and communicating that shame is undesirable. By providing these unsolicited social appraisals that validate versus challenge children's appraisals of the situation and/or reward versus punish a child's experience, Tamang and Brahman parents socialize their children to evaluate the world from a perspective of social harmony and egalitarianism versus one of social dominance and personal restraint, respectively.

9.2.2   Explicit processes of emotion enculturation

As soon as children acquire language, the implicit emotion enculturation strategies are complemented by more explicit ones, such as those in which parents and caregivers reminisce about emotional events or read storybooks with emotional content to their children (e.g. Ross & Wang, 2010). Indeed, by selecting particular events to reminisce about with their children, parents explicitly communicate which events are considered worth elaborating upon. In line with the cultural models of independence and interdependence, it has been found that whereas European American middle-class mothers tend to engage their children in discussions about either personal or non-social events, Chinese mothers tend to discuss social events in which other people were involved (Wang, 2007). In addition, by adopting a particular conversational style or highlighting certain aspects of the situation, parents may guide their child's evaluations of the events they reminisce about. Specifically, it has been found that European American mothers tend to use a highly elaborative conversational style that highlights the child's own role in the emotional event (Wang, 2007). In contrast, Chinese mothers were found to elaborate much less on the child's own experience of the event, but emphasized the perspective of others as well as elaborated on the expected appropriate social behaviour. In this way, European American mothers encouraged their children to adopt a first-person perspective that evaluates the world in terms of personal autonomy and independence, whereas Chinese mothers encouraged their children to adopt a third-person perspective that evaluates events in light of social harmony, norms, roles and interdependence.

These parental practices of highlighting culturally important aspects of events not only encourage certain evaluations of the world (see above), but also provide children with the opportunity to (re-)experience the culturally valued emotions and create opportunities for caregivers to explain which emotions/evaluations *should* have been experienced/ made. For instance, when children recall events by emphasizing their own actions, achievements or needs, they get opportunities to (re-)experience autonomy-promoting emotions such as pride or anger, especially since caregivers can then easily praise the child (for positive events) or encourage her to be 'tough' and stand up for herself (in negative events; Miller, Wiley, Fung, & Liang, 1997). Likewise, when children recall events by emphasizing other people's expectations or perspectives, they get opportunities to (re-)experience relatedness-promoting emotions such as feeling close and ashamed, especially since caregivers can then easily highlight the child's embeddedness in relationships and/or point out the child's flaws (Fung, 1999). Hence, caregivers' conversations about emotional events may importantly shape (and 'correct') the ways in which children perceive and evaluate the world.

Another, and perhaps the most explicit strategy to enculturate children's emotions, is to expose them to cultural products such as storybooks that explicitly teach which emotions should be experienced in which types of situations. To my knowledge, no studies to date have documented culture-specific situation-emotion *patterns* in storybooks. Yet, the existing studies do document the overall frequencies with which different *types* of emotion occur in the stories. For example, Tsai and her colleagues found that the best-selling children's books in North America typically portray their main characters with excited smiles, whereas those in Taiwan typically portray them with calm smiles (Tsai, Louie, Chen, & Uchida, 2007; study 2). Similarly, yet within the negative domain and comparing the United States to Belgium, Boiger and colleagues found systematic differences in the prevalence of anger and shame (Boiger, de Deyne, & Mesquita, 2013; study 2). Although both the United States and Belgium can be characterized as independent cultural contexts, the US variant of independence focuses more on competition, achievement and mastery whereas the Belgian variant focuses more on universalism, harmony and equality (Schwartz & Ros, 1995). In line with these different foci, anger episodes that signal an individual's concern for achievement and mastery were more frequent in American than in Belgian storybooks (see Vander Wege et al., 2014 for a US–Turkey–Romania comparison). In contrast, shame episodes that point to an individual's failure and need to restore social harmony were completely absent from American storybooks but were portrayed in 26 per cent of the Belgian ones (where they actually tended to follow the anger episodes as if the angry character later 'regretted' their actions and felt shame). As such, storybooks may teach children which emotions, and accordingly, which evaluations of the world, are appropriate in their cultural context.

In sum, parents, caregivers and children engage in a myriad of processes that align children's emotional experiences – and, therefore, their evaluations of the world – with what is 'good' and 'normal' in their cultural context. These processes range from very implicit ones such as contagion, affective observation and parental sensitivity, over (attentional) reinforcement learning and (unsolicited) social (re-)appraisal, to very explicit processes of teaching the 'right' emotions through reminiscing or telling stories. In all these ways, children not only develop (culture-specific) emotion concepts (see also Barrett, 2017) and learn how to apply them, but they also learn to take a culturally valued stance in the world from which to evaluate events, objects and other people.

9.3   The acculturation of emotions: how immigrant minorities come to fit in emotionally

Children are not the only newcomers to sociocultural contexts – the same fate is experienced by immigrant minorities who have been raised and enculturated in a different context. There is an extensive literature on immigrant minorities' *acculturation* – i.e. the changes in their original cultural patterns due to contact with a new cultural context (Sam & Berry, 2010). However, most of this literature focuses on immigrant minorities' attitudes *about* the new (or heritage) culture, their *motivations* to become/stay part of them and the extent to which they *identify* with them. Consequently, this literature has long ignored potential changes in other psychological processes such as self-concept and emotion, which are – as I have explained above (Section 9.1) – closely intertwined with cultural meanings and practices. Taking these insights seriously, my colleagues and I advocate a cultural psychological view on acculturation (De Leersnyder, 2014; Mesquita, De Leersnyder, & Jasini, 2018) in which not only attitudes and identities, but *all* psychological processes may be subject to changes due to contact with another culture. Specifically, my research focuses on the phenomenon and underlying mechanisms of *emotional acculturation* – i.e. the changes in minorities' patterns of emotional experience due to contact with another culture – that may thus reflect changes in how they make meaning of everyday situations. Below, I will describe the nature of this phenomenon (Section 9.3.1) as well as the processes that may account for it (Section 9.3.2), since these can be considered processes of ASL.

9.3.1   The nature of emotional acculturation

If people's patterns of emotion are contingent upon the cultural meanings and practices in which they engage (see Section 9.1.3), we may expect that (i) recent immigrant minorities experience a mismatch between their own emotional patterns and those that are typical for the (culturally different) majority group, and that (ii) with increased engagement in the majority meanings and practices, minorities may come to 'fit in' emotionally. To test these expectations, we asked Korean Americans (De Leersnyder et al., 2011, study 1), Turkish Belgians (De Leersnyder et al., 2011, study 2) and minority youth in Belgium (N > 3,000; Jasini, De Leersnyder, Phalet, & Mesquita, 2018), to describe and rate recent emotional situations from their own daily life. In the lab, we then calculated each individual's emotional fit with their respective majority culture by correlating each individual's emotional pattern to the majority culture's typical pattern of emotion in the corresponding type of situation (see Section 9.1.3 for the full method). Confirming our expectations, first-generation minorities had significantly lower fit to the majority culture's typical emotional patterns than majority members themselves, and this fit increased with each later gener-ation (i.e. second, third), such that there was no difference anymore between the fit of majorities and those third-generation minorities (De Leersnyder et al., 2011; Jasini, De Leersnyder, Phalet et al., 2018; see Consedine, Chentsova-Dutton, & Krivoshekova, 2014 for a conceptual replication of these findings in a large sample of minority women in the United States).

Furthermore, and also as expected, we found that minorities' emo-tional fit with the typical majority patterns was higher to the extent they had spent more years in the majority culture, had migrated at a younger age, reported to have more daily social contacts with majority members (De Leersnyder et al., 2011; Jasini, De Leersnyder, Phalet et al., 2018) and had more friendship ties with majority members, as apparent from socio-metric friendship data in the minorities' classes at school (Jasini, De Leersnyder, Phalet et al., 2018). However, unexpectedly yet interestingly, we found that minorities' attitudes towards adopting the values and cus-toms of the new culture – that is, the traditional indices for acculturation (e.g. Ryder, Alden, & Paulhaus, 2000) – were unrelated to their levels of emotional fit with the majority. This suggests that minorities' (explicitly measured) willingness to be part of the majority culture is unrelated to their (implicitly measured) cultural affiliation in terms of emotional fit – minorities' emotional change, and thus change in how they evaluate the world, was only predicted by their actual exposure to, and social interactions with the majority culture.

Follow-up studies, however, suggest that minorities' acquisition of the majority's ways of evaluating and experiencing the world, does not replace their heritage way of experiencing the world. Instead, both meaning systems may come to co-exist, such that minorities can switch between the two depending on their context of interaction – a phenomenon that can be understood as 'cultural frame switching' and that mirrors findings in the domains of cognition (Hong, Morris, Chiu, & Benet-Martínez, 2000), personality (Ramírez-Esparza, Gosling, Benet-Martínez, Potter, & Pennebaker, 2006), and self-construal (Verkuyten & Pouliasi, 2006). Specifically, in these studies, we calculated Korean Americans' and Turkish Belgians' emotional fit with both their respective majority groups and their respective heritage cultural groups, i.e. Turks in Turkey and Koreans in Korea (De Leersnyder et al., 2018). When we then compared minorities' fit with the typical majority versus heritage emotional patterns across home/family versus work/school contexts (De Leersnyder et al., 2018), we obtained the first evidence of cultural frame switching in emotions: In situations that had taken place in work/school contexts (i.e. in majority settings), minorities fitted better with the typical majority emotional patterns than their heritage patterns, whereas the opposite was true for situations that had taken place in home/family contexts (and that represent their heritage culture; see also Perunovic, Heller, & Rafaeli, 2007). Further evidence came from a social interaction experiment with Turkish Belgians showing that the same event was accompanied by different emotional expressions depending on whether it occurred in a Belgian majority versus Turkish heritage cultural setting (De Leersnyder & Mesquita, 2018). Thus, minorities' acquisition of new emotional patterns does not necessarily replace the old ones; both evaluative systems may come to co-exist and different contexts of interaction may activate the corresponding system.

In sum, it appears that when people have sustained contact with another culture, their emotional patterns – and thus the way in which they make meaning of everyday situations – come to change, such that when they navigate the new cultural environment, their emotional responses increasingly fit those that are typical for and rewarded by the new cultural context. Yet, *how* do immigrant minorities come to experience these new emotional patterns? And thus, what processes of ASL instigate this emotional fit?

9.3.2   *The processes underlying emotional acculturation*

Parallel to the literature on children's emotional enculturation, a myriad of processes operates in conjunction to align minorities' emotions with their new majority culture's system of meanings and practices. These processes again range from very implicit to explicit ones. Given that empirical evidence is still lacking, I will rely on the broader cultural psychological literature to outline how and why these processes may account for emotional acculturation.

Perhaps the most implicit way in which minorities' (and majorities') emotions get aligned with cultural meanings and practices is through engaging in daily life. In fact, it has been shown that the most frequent interactions and situations in a cultural context afford culturally valued experiences. This principle was illustrated in a cross-cultural study by Kitayama and colleagues (Kitayama et al., 1997), which first sampled daily situations from both European Americans and Japanese, and then presented these in the form of vignettes to novel samples of these cultural groups. Across both European Americans and Japanese, it was found that European American daily situations encouraged self-enhancement, which facilitates autonomy promoting experiences such as pride, whereas Japanese daily situations afforded self-criticism, which facilitates relatedness promoting experiences such as shame. A similar method was used by Boiger and colleagues (Boiger, Mesquita et al., 2013, study 1), except that situations were limited to those that typically elicit anger (e.g. Grandma saying you are fat, a friend is late for a meeting) versus shame (e.g. no money at the checkout, your mother saying you disappointed her at your graduation) and that Americans and Japanese not only rated the intensity of their feelings, but also the frequency with which these situations occurred. The analyses revealed that the more situations were perceived as affording anger, the more they were perceived as frequent by Americans and the less they were rated as frequent by Japanese. In contrast, the more situations were perceived as affording shame, the more they were perceived as frequent by Japanese, and the less they were perceived as frequent by European Americans (see Boiger et al., 2014 for a replication contrasting Japanese and Turkish cultural contexts). Thus, since everyday life offers *more* opportunities to experience the culturally condoned emotions than to experience the culturally condemned ones, immigrant minorities may come to experience different emotional patterns upon engaging in a new cultural context.

Further evidence for this idea comes from an experiment by Savani and colleagues (Savani, Morris, Naidu, Kumar, & Berlia, 2011, study 5), which exposed Indian and European American students to previously sampled interpersonal influence situations (in which a friend proposes to (not) do something) from both India and the United States.

Previous studies (Savani et al., 2011, study 1–4) had shown that whereas these American situations contained more self-serving motives from the 'friend' and afforded more influence/less accommodation from participants, the Indian situations included more other-serving motives that would benefit the relationship and hence afforded more accommodation from participants. Furthermore, these previous studies had shown that whereas the typical US response was to try to influence the situation, the typical Indian response was to accommodate the friend. Yet, the experiment demonstrated that after the participants had been exposed to 100 situations from both cultures, their response styles converged. This finding suggests that the structural conditions of the situations afforded different sets of appraisals (encouraging influence versus accommodation) and that with enough exposure to the situations of another culture, one's 'default' way of appraising the world may shift. Thus, by actively engaging in daily life in a new cultural context, immigrant minorities may come to experience more of the majority culture's normative emotions because they more frequently encounter majority types of situations that encourage the typical majority ways to evaluate the world.

Other implicit – yet unstudied – ways through which minorities may come to shift their evaluations of the world is through observing majority members' emotional reactions. These instances can occur when the minority is either a bystander to the situation or is its subject and majorities are present. The former process implies affective observation and would suggest that with more exposure to the new cultural context, immigrant minorities have more opportunities to observe the situation-emotion patterns that are typical for the majority cultural group. These situation-emotion patterns may inform them about the meanings that majorities typically ascribe to situations. The latter process involves social referencing as majorities may provide the emoting minority member with clues about how (not) to experience the situation. Thus, similar to the ways in which parents affirm/challenge their children's appraisals, majority members may affirm/challenge the emotional responses of minority members. In both cases, minorities are confronted with the meanings that majority members ascribe to situations – meanings they may consciously or unconsciously draw upon when experiencing similar situations in the future.

A more explicit process instigating ASL is the process of *grounding* – i.e. the exchange and negotiation of information to make our meanings intelligible to one another and, as such, expand our common ground (Kashima, Klein, & Clark, 2010). This collaborative act tends to emerge in the context of a joint activity in which people are committed to work towards a shared goal and is omnipresent throughout our lives. In its most simple form, grounding consists of two phases: (i) a speaker utters a statement that represents some information/knowledge/meaning and

(ii) the listener accepts this meaning and signals understanding. Before uttering anything though, the speaker estimates the extent to which she shares information/knowledge/meanings with the listener – i.e. the initial common ground – in order to decide how much she needs to explain. Once the listener has accepted the utterance and the speaker is aware of that, their common ground has been expanded (Clark & Brennan, 1991). Yet, when the listener cannot accept the utterance because there is either a lack of information or it does not fit his current meaning system, a series of exchanges may occur in which the interaction partners negotiate the utterance and associated meanings until they can expand their common ground (Clark & Brennan, 1991). Once this 'contextualized common ground' between particular interaction partners – e.g. a shared opinion about out-group members – gets generalized to interactions with others and thus becomes shared within a group – e.g. in the form of a stereotype – it can be considered as 'generalized common ground' (Kashima et al., 2010) and part of the culturally shared meaning system.

Although grounding can be applied to any topic and occurs both in monocultural and intercultural interactions, this process may be particularly important in instigating immigrant minorities' emotional fit with the majority for (at least) two reasons: (i) it allows minority and majority members to negotiate the meanings of situations directly, and (ii) it allows the negotiation of the (subtle) meanings of emotions themselves. To instigate emotional fit through grounding minority and majority members have to talk about emotional episodes with one another. Yet, since grounding can be applied to any topic and is so omnipresent in our lives, it may also play an important role in the negotiation and exchange of non-emotional meanings, which may, in themselves, constitute the backdrop against which future situations are evaluated and (emotionally) experienced.

Taken together, there is some evidence suggesting that immigrant minorities come to fit in with the patterns of emotions that are typical within their new cultural environment, but no direct evidence as yet about *how* they exactly do so. Nevertheless, studies on how daily situations prompt evaluations of the world and on how grounding shapes people's meaning systems, suggest that these may be important processes of ASL that align minorities' emotions, and hence their evaluations, within their new cultural context.

9.4   New insights into ASL: conclusions and future directions

Now that I have revisited the literature on culture and emotion with an eye for ASL, I will take a step back and reflect on what they can actually teach us about the nature of ASL and how future research based on these insights may provide a deeper and more nuanced understanding of it.

9.4.1   *Further connecting different literatures*

I started this chapter by arguing that culture, emotion and ASL scaffold one another. It is only by grace of the existence of a cultural meaning system that parents and caregivers can engage in socialization practices to teach their children what is 'good' and 'normal' in their community. And it is by grace of these ASL processes that children (and immigrant minorities) become competent members of their community who 'naturally' experience – and thus evaluate – the world in culturally appropriate ways. Of course, there may be idiosyncratic cases in which, for example, 'children learn from their troubled parent that bananas are dangerous' (Dukes & Clément, 2018, personal communication), but in general, parents' socialization practices are informed by the cultural meaning systems they endorse themselves and are geared towards raising 'competent' members of the sociocultural community (Greenfield, Keller, Fuligni, & Maynard, 2003). Therefore, culture provides the 'content' of ASL, implying it should be integral to its study.

In addition, since emotions are gateways to capturing how people evaluate the world, but nevertheless 'feel' so natural, unique and personal, they are often the (implicit) carriers of meaning. People are aware neither of the extent to which they fit in emotionally with their culture, nor of the myriad of structural, interpersonal and intrapersonal processes that instigate this fit (see also De Leersnyder et al., 2013; Mesquita, De Leersnyder, & Albert, 2014). Hence, emotions are an important 'vehicle' for ASL, implying that the cultural shaping of emotion may be one fruitful route to study it.

Realizing how culture, emotion and ASL are intertwined, provides a starting point to connect different literatures to one another. First, the field of ASL could provide a bridge between the literatures on child enculturation and developmental cultural psychology on the one hand, and the mainstream literature on emotion socialization on the other hand. To date, culture is largely absent from empirical studies and reviews on emotion socialization in children (e.g. Denham et al., 2007, but see Friedlmeier et al., 2011; Halberstadt & Lozada, 2011; Trommsdorff & Heikamp, 2013). This leads to the danger that the WEIRD (Western, Educated, Industrialized, Rich, Democratic; Henrich, Heine, & Norenzayan, 2010) perspective on emotion socialization is portrayed as reflecting 'human' socialization. For instance, particular socialization strategies (e.g. ignoring) or the experience of particular emotions (e.g. shame and sadness) are considered potentially harmful for children because they have turned out that way in WEIRD contexts (e.g. Denham et al., 2007), while they may be useful in conveying meanings and fostering valued self-views in non/less WEIRD cultural contexts (see e.g. Fung, 1999; Koopmann-Holm & Tsai, 2014). Integrating both fields may bear a more nuanced conceptualization of emotion socialization in which children are encouraged/discouraged to experience their culture's valued/unvalued emotions – a conceptualization that may be fundamental to the study of ASL.

Second, the field of ASL may benefit from connecting to the broader literature on cultural dynamics (e.g. Kashima, 2008, 2016) that is concerned with all the processes that afford either cultural stability or cultural change. Processes that have been studied to date include grounding (Kashima et al., 2010), observational learning, imitation, etc. (e.g. Caldwell & Millen, 2009) and enable us, just like ASL, to understand the 'micro-genesis' of culture – i.e. how macro-level cultural meaning systems are instigated, maintained and changed through micro-level interactions (McIntyre, Lyons, Clark, & Kashima, 2003). Putting ASL in this framework raises the question about the extent to which both parental practices and children's resistance not only maintain but also change the macro-level cultural meanings and practices. It puts the agency back into ASL, acknowledging that people are not merely passive recipients and 'reproductors' of the cultural meaning system but also that they can actively change it in a bottom-up way.

9.4.2 Broadening the framework

Another insight stemming from this review of the literature on culture and emotion is that the current ASL framework could be expanded in at least three different ways. First, and as I hope to have shown, many more processes qualify as processes of ASL than emotion contagion, observational learning, social referencing and natural pedagogy. In the realm of rather implicit ASL, reinforcement learning or 'conditioning' is an important route through which both children and immigrant minorities come to experience and evaluate the world in the appropriate way. In both interpersonal interactions and the broader society, reinforcement structures are omnipresent, ranging from interaction partners' verbal and non-verbal signs of approval versus disapproval (Szczurek et al., 2012), over the initiation and maintenance of friendships (Jasini, De Leersnyder, Kende et al., 2018), to obtaining the best outcomes in negotiations (van Kleef, 2016). And, since approval may translate into experiences of social validation and shared reality (Higgins, 2016), whereas disapproval may instigate social isolation (Szczurek et al., 2012) and stress (Dressler, 2012), reinforcement is very effective in encouraging people to fit in. In the realm of rather explicit processes, cultural products (e.g. children's books) and grounding or the (deliberate) negotiation of meanings may be other everyday routes through which people engage in ASL.

Second, the literatures that were reviewed here call for an extension of the ASL framework beyond the dyadic relationship. Culture is not only situated 'in the head' but also 'in the world'. Therefore, people learn meaning systems through engaging in a culture's practices, everyday situations and cultural products. For instance, storybooks are important tools for socializing emotions in children, while advertisements, self-help-books and religious texts may do the same job for adults (Kim & Markus, 1999; Morling & Lamoreaux, 2008; Tsai, Miao, & Seppala, 2007). Everyday situations, in turn, encourage people to appraise and experience the world in particular ways. The structures of children's environment, like a school system that rewards every minor achievement via praise and smiley-stickers, encourages certain experiences over others. And the slightly different majority situations and structures in immigrant minorities' daily lives encourage a slightly different evaluation of the world than before. Hence, the dyadic processes of ASL work in tandem with those embedded in the structural factors of our sociocultural environments.

Third, the above-reviewed findings on emotional acculturation speak to the nature of both meaning systems and the ASL processes that scaffold them. In line with a dynamic constructionists view on emotion (e.g. Barrett, 2017; see also footnote 1), the existence of emotional acculturation suggests that emotions/evaluations are not hard-wired in the brain, but contingent on the cultural meanings and practices we engage in and that there is plasticity in one's emotional/evaluative life beyond initial socialization. And, in line with a dynamic constructionists view on culture (e.g. Hong et al., 2000), the evidence on emotional frame switching suggests that meaning systems are rather fluid networks of (implicit) knowledge that are triggered by cues in one's environment and that people can acquire multiple meaning systems at a time. Conceptualizing the nature of ASL in this way extends its relevance to adult psychological functioning and expands its scope to studying the interplay between multiple evaluative systems when they are acquired simultaneously (in bicultural children) or sequentially (in immigrant adults).

9.4.3   Limitations and future directions

Finally, I wish to point out that my current analysis of ASL through the lens of culture and emotion research is still a simplified presentation of what may be actually going on. Throughout the chapter, I (deliberately) overlooked several factors important to ASL. By pointing them out here, I hope to inspire future research to incorporate them.

First, many ASL processes described in this chapter pertain to the socialization of meaning and evaluation via the socialization of emotion, in which 'emotions' often not only take the role of 'objects of socialization' (i.e. to learn appropriate emotions), but also the role of 'tools for socialization'. Indeed, in many ASL processes – such as contagion, affective observation, social referencing, teaching through storybooks and reinforcement learning – emotions function as the *tools* to teach children and immigrant minorities how to evaluate and experience the world. This presupposes that the cultural novices have at least *some* knowledge of these emotion concepts; otherwise they cannot infer the meanings these are intended to convey. This raises a 'chicken and egg problem', begging to delve into the feedback loops between learning the meaning *of* emotions and learning meaning *through* emotions. Given the very few studies that speak of this feedback loop (e.g. Röttger-Rössler, Scheidecker, Funk, & Holodynski, 2015) and to not complicate matters even further, I have deliberately overlooked this issue in the current chapter. Yet, a full understanding of ASL requires an understanding of this loop.

Second, while talking about emotional enculturation and acculturation, I have spoken about ASL as if it would only affect cultural novices like children and immigrant minorities. This is a huge oversimplification since our rapidly changing multicultural worlds render ASL relevant for cultural majority members as well. Through changes in the available cultural products (e.g. imported movies, books, etc.), the structures of social interaction (e.g. through novel ways of communicating), and being exposed to novel cultural meaning systems (e.g. by engaging with cultural minorities), it is likely that majority members also undergo shifts in how they evaluate the world. Of course, power dynamics may render changes in majorities' meaning systems to be slower (and perhaps more diffuse) than changes observed in immigrant minorities and children, for whom (not) fitting in bears more consequences. Nevertheless, extending the study of ASL to include majority members is important since it acknowledges the complexities of cultural dynamics and does justice to potential minority influence (e.g. Moscovici & Naffrechoux, 1969).

A final, yet very important oversimplification is that, so far, I neglected all personal and contextual factors that may shape the effectiveness and perhaps even the course of ASL. For instance, contexts may vary in their emphasis on fitting in and thus in the extent to which they expect their cultural group members to share a cultural meaning system. One of the concepts that comes closest to operationalizing this idea, is the cultural dimension of tightness–looseness (Gelfand et al., 2011), with tight contexts being characterized by many more rules, roles, obligations and pressures to fit in than loose contexts. Therefore, we may expect to observe either more numerous or more elaborate attempts for ASL in tighter than looser contexts. Likewise, both macro-level (i.e. societal) and meso-level contexts like schools, workplaces and communities, vary in the extent to which they expect minorities to assimilate to the majority, which may shape the speed and course of processes of ASL. If minorities feel pressure to fit in and are rewarded for doing so, ASL may only matter for minorities and be quite effective; when diversity climates are more welcoming, however, ASL may become a matter of both minorities and majorities. In this latter case, grounding may be a particularly important ASL process because it does not assume a 'novice learner' and an 'expert knower' (like many other ASL processes such as natural pedagogy), but allows both interaction partners to be 'expert knowers' who can come to learn novel meanings about the world. Complicating matters even further, both the aforementioned diversity climates and a culture's ideas about hierarchy may co-shape power differences that define who should learn the 'right' meanings from whom and whose interpretations and evaluations can be trusted – enter the dimension of 'epistemic trust', outlined in the Introduction to this volume, and completely overlooked here.

If anything, ASL is likely to be much more complex than assumed until now. Approaching it from the domain of culture and emotion has been fruitful in (i) shedding light on the nature of ASL, (ii) extending its scope from children to immigrant minorities and even adult majorities and (iii) extending the number of processes that qualify as processes of learning to evaluate the world. Challenges for future research include to (i) further integrate ASL with other literatures like the ones on cultural (developmental) psychology and cultural dynamics and (ii) empirically study some of the complexities and contextual factors that may shape both the speed and course of ASL. In doing so, the field of ASL may go beyond offering an umbrella for studies and insights scattered across different domains and disciplines to become a mature and multi-disciplinary approach that stimulates novel research to increase our understanding of meaning-making in context.

References

Adams, G., & Markus, H. R. (2004). Toward a conception of culture suitable for a social psychology of culture. In M. Schaller & C. S. Crandall (Eds.), *The psychological foundations of culture* (pp. 335–360). Mahwah, NJ: Lawrence Erlbaum.

Barrett, L. F. (2017). *How emotions are made: The secret life of the brain*. Boston, MA: Houghton Mifflin Harcourt.

Boiger, M., Ceulemans, E., De Leersnyder, J., Uchida, Y., Norasakkunkit, V., & Mesquita, B. (2018). Beyond essentialism: Cultural differences in emotions revisited. *Emotion, 18*(8), 1142–1162.

Boiger, M., de Deyne, S., & Mesquita, B. (2013). Emotions in 'the world': Cultural practices, products, and meanings of anger and shame in two individualist cultures. *Frontiers in Psychology, 4*(December), 1–14.

Boiger, M., Güngör, D., Karasawa, M., & Mesquita, B. (2014). Defending honour, keeping face: Interpersonal affordances of anger and shame in Turkey and Japan. *Cognition and Emotion, 28*(7), 1255–1269.

Boiger, M., Mesquita, B., Uchida, Y., & Barrett, L. F. (2013). Condoned or condemned: The situational affordance of anger and shame in the United States and Japan. *Personality and Social Psychology Bulletin, 39*(4), 540–553.

Caldwell, C. A, & Millen, A. E. (2009). Social learning mechanisms and cumulative cultural evolution. *Psychological Science, 20*(12), 1478–1483.

Clark, H. H., & Brennan, S. E. (1991). Grounding in communication. In L. B. Resnick, J. M. Levine, & S. D. Teasley (Eds.), *Perspectives on socially shared cognition* (pp. 127–149). Washington, DC: APA Books.

Cohen, D., & Gunz, A. (2002). As seen by the other …: Perspectives on the self in the memories and emotional perceptions of Easterners and Westerners. *Psychological Science, 13*(1), 55–59.

Cole, P. M., Bruschi, C. J., & Tamang, B. L. (2002). Cultural differences in children's emotional reactions to difficult situations. *Child Development, 73*(3), 983–996.

Cole, P. M., Tamang, B. L., & Shrestha, S. (2006). Cultural variations in the socialization of young children's anger and shame. *Child Development, 77*(5), 1237–1251.

Consedine, N. S., Chentsova-Dutton, Y. E., & Krivoshekova, Y. S. (2014). Emotional acculturation predicts better somatic health: Experiential and expressive acculturation among immigrant women from four ethnic groups. *Journal of Social and Clinical Psychology, 33*(10), 867–889.

d'Andrade, R. (1984). Cultural meaning systems. In R. A. Shweder & R. A. LeVine, (Eds.), *Culture theory: Essays on mind, self and emotion* (pp. 88–119). Cambridge, UK: Cambridge University Press.

De Leersnyder, J. (2014). *Emotional acculturation.* Leuven, Belgium: University of Leuven.

De Leersnyder, J., Boiger, M., & Mesquita, B. (2013). Cultural regulation of emotion: Individual, relational, and structural sources. *Frontiers in Psychology, 4*(February), 1–11.

De Leersnyder, J., Kim, H., & Mesquita, B. (2015). Feeling right is feeling good: Psychological well-being and emotional fit with culture in autonomy- versus relatedness-promoting situations. *Frontiers in Psychology, 6*(May), 1–12.

  (in review). My emotions belong here and there: Extending the phenomenon of emotional acculturation to heritage cultural contexts.

De Leersnyder, J., & Mesquita, B. (in review). Emotional frame switching in biculturals: How salient cultural concerns may shape emotion.

De Leersnyder, J., Mesquita, B., & Kim, H. S. (2011). Where do my emotions belong? A study of immigrants' emotional acculturation. *Personality and Social Psychology Bulletin, 37*(4), 451–463.

De Leersnyder, J., Mesquita, B., Kim, H., Eom, K., & Choi, H. (2014). Emotional fit with culture: A predictor of individual differences in relational well-being. *Emotion, 14*(2), 241–245.

Denham, S. A. (1998). *Emotional development in young children.* New York, NY: Guilford Press.

Denham, S. A., Bassett, H. H., & Wyatt, T. (2007). The socialization of emotional competence. In J. E. Grusec & P. D. Hastings (Eds.), *Handbook of socialization: Theory and research* (pp. 614–637). New York, NY: Guilford Press.

Dressler, W. W. (2012). Cultural consonance: Linking culture, the individual and health. *Preventive Medicine, 55*(5) 390–393.

Dressler, W. W., Balieiro, M. C., Ribeiro, R. P., & Dos Santos, J. E. (2007). Cultural consonance and psychological distress: Examining the associations in multiple cultural domains. *Culture, Medicine and Psychiatry, 31*(2), 195–224.

Fischer, A. H., & Manstead, A. S. R. (2008). Social functions of emotion. In M. Lewis, J. M. Haviland-Jones, & L. F. Barrett (Eds.), *Handbook of emotion* (3rd ed., pp. 456–468). New York, NY: Guilford Press.

Friedlmeier, W., Corapci, F., & Cole, P. M. (2011). Emotion socialization in cross-cultural perspective. *Social and Personality Psychology Compass, 5*(7), 410–427.

Friedlmeier, W., & Trommsdorff, G. (2002). Emotional kompetenz im kultural vergleich [Emotional competence in cross-cultural comparison]. In M. von Salisch (Ed.), *Emotionale kompetenz entwickelen: Grundlagen in kindheit und jugend* (pp. 229–262). Stuttgart, Germany: Kohlhammer.

Frijda, N. H. (1986). *The emotions.* Cambridge, UK: Cambridge University Press. (2007). *The laws of emotions.* New York, NY: Lawrence Erlbaum.

Frijda, N. H., Kuipers, & Schure, T. (1989). Relations among emotion, appraisal, and emotional action readiness. *Journal of Personality and Social Psychology, 57*, 212–228.

Fulmer, C. A., Gelfand, M. J., Kruglanski, A. W., Kim-Prieto, C., Diener, E., Pierro, A., & Higgins, E. T. (2010). On 'feeling right' in cultural contexts: How person-culture match affects self-esteem and subjective well-being. *Psychological Science, 21*(11), 1563–1569.

Fung, H. (1999). Becoming a moral child: The socialization of shame among young Chinese children. *Ethos, 27*(2), 180–209. http://doi.org/10.1525/eth.1999.27.2.180

Garner, P. W., & Estep, K. M. (2001). Emotional competence, emotion socialization, and young children's peer-related social competence. *Early Education and Development, 12*, 29–48.

Geangu, E., Benga, O., Stahl, D., & Striano, T. (2010). Contagious crying beyond the first days of life. *Infant Behavior and Development, 33*, 279–288.

Gelfand, M. J., Raver, J. L., Nishii, L., Leslie, L. M., Lun, J., Lim, B. C., ... Yamaguchi, S. (2011). Differences between tight and loose cultures: A 33-nation study. *Science, 332*(6033), 1100–1104.

Greenfield, P. M., Keller, H., Fuligni, A., & Maynard, A. (2003). Cultural pathways through universal development. *Annual Review of Psychology, 54*(1), 461–490.

Gross, J. J., & Thompson, R. A. (2007). Emotion regulation: Conceptual foundations. In J. J. Gross (Ed.), *Handbook of emotion regulation.* New York, NY: Guilford Press.

Grossmann, I., Ellsworth, P. C., & Hong, Y. Y. (2012). Culture, attention, and emotion. *Journal of Experimental Psychology: General, 141*(1), 31–36.

Güngör, D., Karasawa, M., Boiger, M., Dinçer, D., & Mesquita, B. (2014). Fitting in or sticking together: The prevalence and adaptivity of conformity, relatedness, and autonomy in Japan and Turkey. *Journal of Cross-Cultural Psychology, 45*(9), 1374–1389.

Gyurak, A., Gross, J. J., & Etkin, A. (2011). Explicit and implicit emotion regulation: A dual-process framework. *Cognition and Emotion, 25*(3), 400–412.

Halberstadt, A. G., Fox, N. A., & Jones, N. A. (1993). Do expressive mothers have expressive children? The role of socialization in children's affect expression. *Social Development, 2,* 48–65.

Halberstadt, A. G., & Lozada, F. T. (2011). Emotion development in infancy through the lens of culture. *Emotion Review, 3*(2), 158–168.

Hardin, C. D., & Higgins, E. T. (1996). Shared reality: How social verification makes the subjective objective. In E. T. Higgins & R. M. Sorrentino (Eds.), *Handbook of motivation and cognition: Vol. 3. The interpersonal context* (pp. 28–84). New York, NY: Guilford Press.

Hatfield, E., Cacioppo, J. T., & Rapson, R. L. (1994). *Emotional contagion.* Cambridge, MA: Cambridge University Press.

Heine, S. J. (2003). An exploration of cultural variation in self-enhancing and self-improving motivations. In V. Murphy-Berman & J. J. Berman (Eds.), *Nebraska symposium on motivation: Cross-cultural difference sin perspectives on the self* (Vol. 49, pp. 118–145). Lincoln, NE: University of Nebraska Press.

Henrich, J., Heine, S., & Norenzayan, A. (2010). The weirdest people in the world. *Behavioral and Brain Sciences, 33,* 61–135.

Higgins, E. T. (2016). Shared-reality development in childhood. *Perspectives on Psychological Science, 11,* 466–495.

Hochschild, J. L. (1995). What is the American dream? In J. L. Hochschild (Ed.), *Facing up to the American dream: Race, class and the soul of the nation* (pp. 15–38). Princeton, NJ: Princeton University Press.

Hong, Y. Y., Morris, M. W., Chiu, C. Y., & Benet-Martínez, V. (2000). Multicultural minds: A dynamic constructivist approach to culture and cognition. *American Psychologist, 55*(7), 709–720.

Isley, S. L., O'Neil, R., Clatfelter, D., & Parke, R. D. (1999). Parent and child expressed affect and children's social competence: Modeling direct and indirect pathways. *Developmental Psychology, 35,* 547–560.

Jasini, A., De Leersnyder, J., Kende, J., Gagliolo, M., Phalet, K., & Mesquita, B. (2018). Tell me your friends and I'll show you your emotions: A social network study on emotional acculturation, Manuscript under review.

Jasini, A., De Leersnyder, J., Phalet, K., & Mesquita, B. (2018). Tuning in emotionally: Associations of cultural exposure with distal and proximal emotional fit in acculturating youth. *European Journal of Social Psychology, 49*(2), 352–365.

Kashima, Y. (2008). A social psychology of cultural dynamics: Examining how cultures are formed, maintained, and transformed. *Social and Personality Psychology Compass, 2*(1), 107–120.

(2016). Cultural dynamics. *Current Opinion in Psychology, 8,* 93–97.

Kashima, Y., Klein, O., & Clark, A. E. (2010). Grounding: Sharing information in social interaction. In K. Fiedler (Ed.), *Social communication* (pp. 27–77). New York, NY: Psychology Press.

Keller, H., Yovsi, R. D., & Voelker, S. (2002). The role of motor stimulation in parental ethnotheories. The case of Cameroonian Nso and German women. *Journal of Cross-Cultural Psychology, 33,* 398–414.

Keltner, D., & Buswell, B. N. (1997). Embarrassment: Its distinct form and appeasement functions. *Psychological Bulletin*, *122*(3), 250–270.

Kim, H., & Markus, H. R. (1999). Deviance or uniqueness, harmony or conformity? A cultural analysis. *Journal of Personality and Social Psychology*, *77*(4), 785–800.

Kitayama, S., Markus, H. R., Matsumoto, H., & Norasakkunkit, V. (1997). Individual and collective processes in the construction of the self: Self-enhancement in the United States and self-criticism in Japan. *Journal of Personality and Social Psychology*, *72*(6), 1245–1267.

Kitayama, S., Mesquita, B., & Karasawa, M. (2006). Cultural affordances and emotional experience: Socially engaging and disengaging emotions in Japan and the United States. *Journal of Personality and Social Psychology*, *91*(5), 890–903.

Koopmann-Holm, B., & Tsai, J. L. (2014). Focusing on the negative: Cultural differences in expressions of sympathy. *Journal of Personality and Social Psychology*, *107*(6), 1092–1115.

Kuppens, P., van Mechelen, I., Smits, D. J. M., de Boeck, P., & Ceulemans, E. (2007). Individual differences in patterns of appraisal and anger experience. *Cognition and Emotion*, *21*(4), 689–713.

Lebra, T. S. (1992). Self in Japanese culture. In N. E. Rosenberger (Ed.), *Japanese sense of self*. New York, NY: Oxford University Press.

LeVine, R. A. (2004). Challenging the expert: Findings from an African study on infant care and development. In J. P. Gielen & J. L. Roopnarine (Eds.), *Advances in applied developmental psychology. Childhood and adolescence: Cross-cultural perspectives and applications* (pp. 149–165). Westport, CT: Praeger.

Lewis, C. (1995). *Educating hearts and minds*. New York, NY: Cambridge Press.

Markus, H. R., & Hamedani, M. G. (2007). Sociocultural psychology. In S. Kitayama & D. Cohen (Eds.), *Handbook of cultural psychology* (pp. 3–39). New York, NY: Springer.

Markus, H. R., & Kitayama, S. (1991). Culture and the self: Implications for cognition, emotion, and motivation. *Psychological Review*, *98*(2), 224–253.

(1994). The cultural construction of self and emotion: Implications for social behavior. In S. Kitayama & H. R. Markus (Eds.), *Emotion and culture: Empirical studies of mutual influence* (pp. 89–130). Washington, DC: American Psychological Association.

McIntyre, A., Lyons, A., Clark, A., & Kashima, Y. (2003). The microgenesis of culture: Serial reproduction as an experimental simulation of cultural dynamics. In M. Schaller & C. Crandall (Eds.), *The psychological foundations of culture* (pp. 227–258). New York, NY: Psychology Press.

Mesquita, B. (2003). Emotions as dynamic cultural phenomena. In R. J. Davidson, K. R. Scherer, & H. H. Goldsmith (Eds.), *Handbook of affective sciences* (pp. 871–890). Oxford, UK: Oxford University Press.

(2010). Emoting a contextualized process. In B. Mesquita, L. F. Barrett, & E. R. Smith (Eds.), *The mind in context* (pp. 83–104). New York, NY: Guilford Press.

Mesquita, B., De Leersnyder, J., & Albert, D. (2014). The cultural regulation of emotions. In J. J. Gross (Ed.), *Handbook of emotion regulation* (2nd ed., pp. 284–301). New York, NY: Guilford Press.

Mesquita, B., De Leersnyder, J., & Jasini, A. (2018). The cultural psychology of acculturation. In S. Kitayama & D. Cohen (Eds.), *Handbook of cultural psychology* (2nd ed., pp. 502–535). New York, NY: Guilford Press.

Mesquita, B., Karasawa, M., Haire, A., Satoko, I., Hayashi, A., Idzelis, M., … Kashiwagi, K. (2006). What do I feel? The role of cultural models in emotion representations, 1–54. Unpublished manuscript.

Mesquita, B., Vissers, N., & De Leersnyder, J. (2015). Culture and emotion. In J. Wright & J. W. Berry (Eds.), *International encyclopedia of social and behavioral sciences* (2nd ed.). Oxford, UK: Elsevier.

Miller, P. J., Wiley, A. R., Fung, H., & Liang, C.-H. (1997). Personal storytelling as a medium of socialization in Chinese and American families. *Child Development, 68*(3), 557–568.

Morelli, G. A., & Rothbaum, F. M. (2007). Situating the child in context: Attachment relationships and self-regulation in different cultures. In S. Kitayama & D. Cohen (Eds.), *Handbook of cultural psychology* (pp. 500–527). New York, NY: Guilford Press.

Morling, B., & Lamoreaux, M. (2008). Measuring culture outside the head: A meta-analysis of individualism-collectivism in cultural products. *Personality and Social Psychology Review, 12*(3), 199–221.

Moscovici, E. L., & Naffrechoux, M. (1969). Influence of a consistent minority on the responses of a majority in a color perception task. *Sociometry, 32*(4), 365–380.

Newland, R. P., & Crnic, K. A. (2011). Mother–child affect and emotion socialization processes across the late preschool period: Predictions of emerging behaviour problems. *Infant and Child Development, 20*, 371–388.

Perunovic, W. Q. E., Heller, D., & Rafaeli, E. (2007). Within-person changes in the structure of emotion: The role of cultural identification and language. *Psychological Science, 18*(7), 607–613.

Ramírez-Esparza, N., Gosling, S. D., Benet-Martínez, V., Potter, J. P., & Pennebaker, J. W. (2006). Do bilinguals have two personalities? A special case of cultural frame switching. *Journal of Research in Personality, 40*(2), 99–120.

Ross, M., & Wang, Q. (2010). Why we remember and what we remember: Culture and autobiographical memory. *Perspectives on Psychological Science, 5*(4), 401–409.

Rothbaum, F. M., Pott, M., Azuma, H., Miyake, K., & Weisz, J. R. (2000). The development of close relationships in Japan and the United States: Paths of symbiotic harmony and generative tension. *Child Development, 71*(5), 1121–1142.

Röttger-Rössler, B., Scheidecker, G., Funk, L., & Holodynski, M. (2015). Learning (by) feeling: A cross-cultural comparison of the socialization and development of emotions. *Ethos, 43*(2), 187–220.

Ruffman, T., Lorimer, B., & Scarf, D. (2017). Do infants really experience emotional contagion? *Child Development Perspectives, 11*(4), 270–274.

Ryder, A. G., Alden, L. E., & Paulhaus, D. L. (2000). Is acculturation unidimensional or bidimensional? A head-to-head comparison in the prediction. *Interpersonal Relations and Group Processes, 79*(1), 49–65.

Sam, D. L., & Berry, J. W. (2010). Acculturation: When individuals and groups of different cultural backgrounds meet. *Perspectives on Psychological Science, 5*(4), 472–481.

Savani, K., Morris, M. W., Naidu, N. V. R., Kumar, S., & Berlia, N. V. (2011). Cultural conditioning: Understanding interpersonal accommodation in India and the United States in terms of the modal characteristics of interpersonal influence situations. *Journal of Personality and Social Psychology, 100*(1), 84–102.

Schwartz, S. H., & Ros, M. (1995). Values in the West: A theoretical and empirical challenge to the individualism-collectivism cultural dimension. *World Psychology, 1*, 99–122.

Smith, M., & Walden, T. (1999). Understanding feelings and coping with emotional situations: A comparison of maltreated and nonmaltreated pre-schoolers. *Social Development, 8*, 93–116.

Solomon, R. C. (1984). Getting angry: The Jamesian theory of emotion in anthropology. In R. A. Shweder & R. A. LeVine (Eds.), *Culture theory: Essays on mind, self and emotion* (pp. 238–254). Cambridge, UK: Cambridge University Press.

(2004). *Thinking about feeling: Contemporary philosophers on emotions.* Oxford, UK: Oxford University Press.

Stein, N. L., Trabasso, T., & Liwag, M. D. (1993). The representation and organization of emotional experience: Unfolding the emotion episode. In M. Lewis & J. M. Haviland (Eds.), *Handbook of emotion* (pp. 279–300). New York, NY: Guilford Press.

Stephens, N., Markus, H. R., & Phillips, L. T. (2014). Social class culture cycles: How three gateway contexts shape selves and fuel inequality. *Annual Review of Psychology, 65*, 611–634.

Szczurek, L., Monin, B., & Gross, J. J. (2012). The stranger effect: The rejection of affective deviants. *Psychological Science, 23*(10), 1105–1111.

Townsend, S. S. M., Kim, H. S., & Mesquita, B. (2013). Are you feeling what I'm feeling? *Social Psychology and Personality Science, 37*, 451–463.

Triandis, H. C. (1995). *Individualism and collectivism.* Boulder, CO: Westview Press.

Trommsdorff, G. (2006). Development of emotions as organized by culture. *ISSBD Newsletter, 49*, 1–4.

Trommsdorff, G., & Friedlmeier, W. (1993). Control and responsiveness in Japanese and German mother-child interactions. *Early Development and Parenting, 2*, 65–78.

(2010). Preschool girls' distress and mothers' sensitivity in Japan and Germany. *European Journal of Developmental Psychology, 7*, 350–370.

Trommsdorff, G., & Heikamp, T. (2013). Socialization of emotions and emotion regulation in cultural context. In S. Barnow & N. Balkir (Eds.), *Cultural variations in psychopathology: from research to practice* (pp. 67–92). Cambridge, MA: Hogrefe Publishing.

Trommsdorff, G., & Rothbaum, F. (2008). Development of emotion regulation in cultural context. In M. Vanderkerchkhove, C. van Scheve, S. Ismer, S. Jung, & S. Kronast (Eds.), *Regulating emotions: Culture, social necessity and biological inheritance* (pp. 85–120). Malden, MA: Blackwell.

Tsai, J. L., Knutson, B., & Fung, H. H. (2006). Cultural variation in affect valuation. *Journal of Personality and Social Psychology, 90*(2), 288–307.

Tsai, J. L., Louie, J. Y., Chen, E. E., & Uchida, Y. (2007). Learning what feelings to desire: Socialization of ideal affect through children's storybooks. *Personality and Social Psychology Bulletin, 33*(1), 17–30.

Tsai, J. L., Miao, F. F., & Seppala, E. (2007). Good feelings in Christianity and Buddhism: Religious differences in ideal affect. *Personality and Social Psychology Bulletin, 33*(3), 409–421.

Tsai, J. L., Miao, F. F., Seppala, E., Fung, H. H., & Yeung, D. Y. (2007). Influence and adjustment goals: Sources of cultural differences in ideal affect. *Journal of Personality and Social Psychology, 92*(6), 1102–1117.

Valiente, C., Eisenberg, N., Shepard, S. A., Fabes, R. A., Cumberland, A. J., Losoya, S. H., & Spinrad, T. L. (2004). The relations of mothers' negative expressivity to children's experience and expression of negative emotion. *Journal of Applied Developmental Psychology, 25*, 215–235.

van Kleef, G. A. (2016). *The interpersonal dynamics of emotion: Toward an integrative theory of emotions as social information.* Cambridge, UK: Cambridge University Press.

Vander Wege, B., González, M. L. S., Friedlmeier, W., Mihalca, L. M., Goodrich, E., & Corapci, F. (2014). Emotion displays in media: A comparison between American, Romanian, and Turkish children's storybooks. *Frontiers in Psychology, 5*, 1–12.

Verkuyten, M., & Pouliasi, K. (2006). Biculturalism and group identification: The mediating role of identification in cultural frame switching. *Journal of Cross-Cultural Psychology, 37*(3), 312.

Vignoles, V. L., Owe, E., Becker, M., Smith, P. B., Easterbrook, M. J., Brown, R., … Villamar, J. A. (2016). Beyond 'West versus East': Global variation in cultural models of selfhood. *Journal of Experimental Psychology, 145*(8), 966–1000.

Wang, Q. (2007). 'Remember when you got the big, big bulldozer?' Mother–child reminiscing over time and across cultures. *Social Cognition, 25*(4), 455–471.

Conclusion

Laying the foundations of affective social learning

Fabrice Clément and Daniel Dukes

C.1   The affective social learning triangle

When we came up with the idea of combining three of the key notions in social sciences – *affect, social and learning* – we could not have anticipated that our neologism – affective social learning – would trigger so many fascinating thoughts and associations of so many researchers coming from so many different perspectives. Indeed, the views expressed and the analyses completed within these chapters are so rich and so varied that it would be presumptuous to try and summarize each contribution. However, needless to say, each author has forced us to rethink at least one of the main aspects of affective social learning (ASL). Our principal goal for this concluding chapter then, is not to provide a summary of each of the chapters, explicitly addressing each point as we write, but rather, it is to use the various thoughts and reflections contained within to rethink and improve on the design of ASL. Having sketched out the plans for ASL in earlier works (Clément & Dukes, 2013, 2017; Dukes & Clément, 2017), the first few pages of this book constitute, perhaps, a first true draft. Equipped with the intellectual tools provided by the chapter authors, it seems time, as we approach the book's end, to properly lay the final foundations of ASL.

However, before we begin, we would like to highlight what we feel is novel and original in this conceptualization of the transmission of – in comparison to similar concepts, and to other ideas that are similarly named.

There is of course always some arbitrariness in the choice of a concept, but it seems that the nature of the processes we have in mind necessitates a new concept. Another potential candidate name might have been something like *affective acculturation*. However, this name would have suffered from two disadvantages. First, acculturation is often understood in the literature as the 'cultural modification of an individual, group, or people by adapting to or borrowing traits from another culture' (Merriam-Webster

This chapter is co-authored and the authors share responsibility equally for its contents.

Dictionary). In this sense, it could be seen to be a behavioural and emotional 'corrective'. Given that our primary aim is to detail the processes
by which individuals become to incorporate a cultural form of life, this
sense is too specific for ASL, as in all the examples we used above, chiefly
refers to our *primary socialization*. The second conceptual error would
be to attach to the phenomenon the term *culture* itself – instead of *social*
learning. This could be problematic from a phylogenetic perspective, as
we wanted to favour a continuity with non-humans. From a naturalistic
perspective, it seemed easier to focus on cases of social learning, without
ruling on the case of culture itself. ASL is anchored in the belief that some
of these values exist outside of language and that they can exist in non-
human primates and in other species, but it is not always clear to what
extent we can describe these species as having cultures, although it is
easier to describe the individuals that collectively make up the species,
as social beings.

Clearly, ASL is not to be confused with socio-emotional learning (SEL)
either. While the titles are strikingly similar, SEL deals more with the
mechanics of emotion recognition and expression themselves, such as
relationship skills, social awareness, empathy, conflict resolution and
decision-making. In short, it deals with how to manage one's emotions to
have a positive, fulfilling life. Many of these programmes appear to either
be implicitly or explicitly inspired by serious academic research (e.g.
Camras & Halberstadt, 2017; Halberstadt, Denham & Dunsmore, 2001),
and there is now a great deal of evidence demonstrating how successful
these programmes are, not only in addressing socio-emotional problems,
but also in improving academic performance (Durlack, Dymnicki, Taylor,
Weissberg & Schellinger, 2011).

There are, however, other concepts that deal with themes that are
much closer to aspects of what we mean by ASL. For example, Gerben
van Kleef's emotions as social information (EASI) theory (van Kleef,
2009, 2016; van Kleef, de Dreu & Manstead, 2010) deals with how our
emotions, or, more specifically, our affective expressions, influence the
individual concerned. Van Kleef pinpoints two types of mechanism that
underlie the interpersonal emotional affects, inferences and 'affective
reactions' that help the observer, 'better understand the feelings, desires,
motives, and intentions of the person expressing the emotion, and to act
accordingly' (van Kleef, 2016, p. 38). In another profoundly social account
of emotion, Sally Planalp's book entitled *Communicating Emotion* (1999)
tackles questions of how emotions can be conditioned by those around
us in interpersonal exchanges and particularly focuses on the meaning of
emotion. While both of these books are concerned with socio-emotional
processes and about how we extract meaning from emotion (and thus,
by implication, affecting how we feel and how we act downstream), neither of them deals specifically with learning about a particular object – in

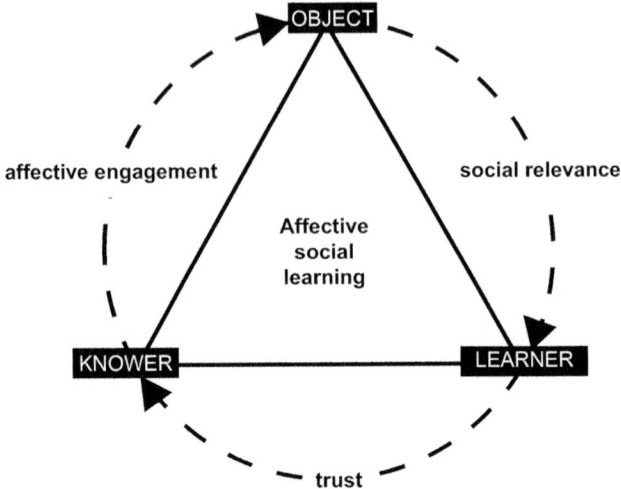

Figure C.1 ASL depicted as a relational triangle of object, source and learner.

fact, they are comparatively 'object free', at least in terms of our account here of ASL. Indeed, it is within this relational triangle, between knower, object and learner that ASL finds itself, and it is with such a triangle that we continue here (Figure C.1), as we remind the reader of how we characterized ASL in the introductory chapter.

The three points of this triangle are what we called the object, the knower and the learner. Thanks to the different contributions to this book, we will now be able to better specify what ASL is really about, to what extent the knower's identity is important, and what kind of mechanisms are necessary to learn in ASL. Moreover, we will be able to improve our descriptions of the sides of the triangle, each of them representing a specific relation (illustrated by the arrows): the (pre-existing) affective relation between the knower and the object, the affective relationship between the knower and the learner and the novel or modified affective link between the learner and the object.

C.2   The points of the ASL triangle

C.2.1   *The object of ASL*

Before describing the different components of ASL more carefully, it is important to remind ourselves of exactly what we set out to achieve in developing the concept itself. From an ontogenetic point of view, our idea is very much in tune with a line of research that insists on the fact that children are not isolated scientists, individually (re-)discovering what the world is made of, but rather, that most of what we know, believe or cherish is transmitted to us from others, via their *testimony* (Clément, 2010; Harris, 2002, 2012). However, even if emotions could be considered as a form of communicated information, as *affective testimony* perhaps (Clément & Dukes, 2017; Harris, Chapter 3, this volume), we thought that this explanation triggered the temptation to depict all learning processes as being intentional. After all, the notion of testimony usually involves the intentional transmission of some piece of information from one person (the knower/source) to another (the learner). However, various methods involved in certain anthropological traditions led us away from that particular temptation for two reasons.

First, anthropologists have produced numerous monographs that highlight the unbelievable variety of cultural forms of life. It is indeed fascinating from a scientific observer's point of view, for example, to consider how humans are shaped by the many different cultural demands made upon us, by each other – how many diverse ways there are for us to feel that we become the individuals that we are today, both fully realized and unique, simply by fulfilling the implicit and explicit cultural objectives that are considered as essential by our given community. But the differences in these forms of life, even within the same neighbourhood, can nevertheless still be quite radical: what can seem arbitrary and futile from an external point of view can be seen as essential and vital for those inhabited by the values they have inherited: the cultural practices of the Asian butcher in one part of the city can remain completely opaque to the African baker next door and again to those of the Jewish teacher across the street, the Catholic priest and the transgender actor, for example. And of course, each of us is likely to embody mixed cultural heritages, from the family we are born into, to the nation we belong to, to the job we have, the people we socialize with, the god(s) we believe in, etc. And yet, each of us can believe, to various degrees, that our culture has the monopoly on 'the truth' or on 'what is right'. One stark example of how ingrained these cultural values can go, how internalized they might become, is to argue that we are so accustomed in the West to living within our culture 'that it is easier to imagine the end of the world than to imagine the end of capitalism'[1] (e.g. Jameson, 2003, p. 76). Contemporary media seems filled with tales of the zombie apocalypse and impending environmental Armageddon, but relatively few people appear to be imagining how life could be in the West in a non-capitalistic future, for example. The deep (and largely unquestioned) conviction that what is at stake in a given

---

[1] This phrase is of disputed origin. The interested reader should consult Fischer (2009, esp. chap. 1).

culture (irrespective of which culture) is worth living for, and indeed, worth dying for, has been aptly named *illusio* by the sociologist Pierre Bourdieu (Bourdieu, 1998, p. 115).

Given the importance of these cultural incentives in the daily life of every human being, it seems crucial to better understand how the processes of adherence to such social values unfold. In an earlier study, we (Clément and Dukes, 2013), connected this line of questioning to the theory of cognitive appraisal by showing that these, sometimes seemingly arbitrary evaluations of what matters in any given culture can be considered an issue of *social relevance*: while our own private investigations may guide us in determining what is relevant to meet our own biological needs, other people serve as guides – as *proxy relevance detectors* – about what is socially relevant in order to fulfil our cultural aspirations. This theoretical twist enabled us to root the question of adherence in the burgeoning field of affective science and to make extensive use of other concepts: emotion contagion, social referencing, social appraisal and natural pedagogy. Our bet is that insisting on the importance of others' appraisals in the socialization process could offer many important insights about how to improve our understanding of how individuals progressively integrate and become an active part of a social group.

The second aspect of the anthropological tradition that encouraged us to develop a specific concept is the ethnological descriptions of the way cultural transmission tends to unfold in traditional societies. As summarized notably by Barbara Rogoff, explicit transmissions of cultural information are actually quite rare and, in any case, quite different from how it happens at school (Paradise & Rogoff, 2009): children essentially learn through observation, with a more or less active participation in the different activities of their community (Rogoff, 2003). In spite of this, children (as well as cultural newcomers) have many opportunities to learn about what is relevant in a (new) culture, simply by observing others' reactions, and, in particular, their affective reactions. In Clément and Dukes (2013), we insisted on the role of *interest*: observing someone being interested by an object, a person or an event is a very good proxy for appraising it as being worthy of attention, as being potentially socially relevant in a given context. But it can, of course, be extended to other emotions, like contempt, disgust or regret (Manstead, Rychlowksa, & van der Schalk, Chapter 8, this volume). Given the prevalence of such appraisal episodes, where the learner is observing a knower who is not really involved in a process of testimony, we included the novel concept of affective observation to add to the different ways by which we learn the affective saliences of our culture.

The *object* of ASL is therefore any input whose value can be appreciated by a learner thanks to some affective appraisals manifested, intentionally or not, by some member of a given cultural community. This can literally be anything – tangible or non-tangible, physically present or held in imagination, animal, vegetable or mineral, etc. In accordance with the appraisal school (and as outlined in the introductory chapter of this volume), it is not some intrinsic value of the object per se that is reflected in and subsequently recognized in the attitude (facial, bodily, vocal, verbal, etc.), but the value to the person(s) who is/are attending to it. The idea here is that while there are some objects that may have some universal value – a hungry, wild, murderous tiger, might be universally dangerous if it is on the loose, for example – the value of most objects, most of the time, is context dependent and in some cases culturally dependent. This cultural dependence can be captured in an expression, understood by someone else and, as such, transmitted. It is here where we find the beginnings of the concept of ASL.

C.2.2   *The knower in ASL*

We called the second point of our ASL triangle the 'knower' to highlight the fact that she is the one that already possesses and masters the knowledge of how to value a certain object – she is in some ways an authority on the subject of how to feel and of what matters to her. While traditionally in social appraisal theory this person has been seen as an influencer – from person to person, in ASL, importance is placed on the fact that her evaluations are implicitly the result of her personal history, of her culture, and that, as a consequence, it is possible to gain access to how her particular group feels or perhaps even, *should* feel, about the object in question – from culture to person. Thus, while naming this person *source* would probably be more in line with the psychological tradition (see Parkinson, Chapter 5, this volume; Fischer, Chapter 7, this volume), and may have been a good candidate here to update the title of *knower* in ASL as we lay the final foundations, we think a better candidate still is *model*. As described above, this *model* incorporates her culture(s) and is the result of her cultural moulds. In this naturalistic framing of the transmission of values, one that does not attribute ontological properties to *cultural representations* (Sperber, 1996), it is essential to figure out the 'material' supports of cultural forms. One of the vectors is the actual people who transmit, through their behaviours, emotions, speech acts, etc. the different elements of their culture(s). Whether intentionally or not, they model how they feel towards an object, perhaps through their behaviour, and, as a result, the observer *learns how to feel and behaves accordingly*. By their emotional reaction, the models provide, voluntarily or accidentally, precious information about the nature of the appraised object, its importance, saliency, desirability and perhaps more pertinently, its disgustingness, its scariness, its interestingness, etc. for her cultural group. Again, the recent line of research on testimony is particularly relevant when specifying the different properties of the model of ASL.

One danger of learning through social appraisal would indeed be the possibility of being misled by learning from some idiosyncratic relation that someone else entertains with a particular (kind of) object (Fischer, Chapter 7, this volume; De Leersnyder, Chapter 9, this volume). For instance, a child trauma suffered by Alfred could trigger a reaction of uncontrollable fear whenever he sees a red Ferrari. A little girl observing this model's (Alfred's) reaction could end up very negatively appraising these prestigious cars, an evaluation that would presumably be at odds with most of the other members of her group. It seems, therefore, very important that the social appraisal process includes some way of filtering the incoming information. The presence of such filters is presupposed by the epistemic vigilance hypothesis that highlights the fact that communication would not have emerged without some cognitive means to avoid manipulation (Sperber et al., 2010). Notably, communicated information seems to be automatically evaluated in relation to other representations that the learner already considers to be true (Clément, Koenig, & Harris, 2004; Koenig, Clément, & Harris, 2004). Of course, the epistemic vigilance hypothesis was designed to target explicit verbal communication, but there is no reason to imagine that information about social relevance is not subject to similar filtering processes. For instance, avoiding idiosyncratic preferences may be obtained by checking that the model's evaluation is not an exception but rather that it would be shared by the others of the model's group. And it has been shown that children automatically use consensus as a means to detect the reliability of a testimony (Bernard, Proust, & Clément, 2015; Corriveau & Harris, 2010; Morgan, Laland, & Harris, 2015). We can then expect individuals to adopt the emotional cues proposed by others with a certain degree of caution when they are learning what is socially relevant in their community – even if this does not prevent them from making mistakes entirely.

Another interesting question that has emerged in this book concerns the necessity of an *actual* presence of the model in order for ASL to take place (see Fischer, Chapter 7, this volume; De Leersnyder, Chapter 9, this volume). In other words, does the model need to be physically present with the learner in order to transmit a given value? This physical proximity seems inevitable in many cases. How can we imagine emotional contagion without real people to trigger mimicry, for example? However, it is not obvious that this presence is necessary in all cases – and even perhaps in some cases of emotional contagion. It might even be possible to imagine that some *virtual others* could play a more important role than real, present people. This is notably the case for fictional characters; in a sense, reading a novel could perhaps be seen either as an example of emotional contagion (the language used and the description could implicitly drive the reader to be affected by a certain affective atmosphere), affective observation (we incidentally observe certain affective reactions of some of the characters), social referencing (a book is chosen precisely because we expect that the heroes can inform us about how to value certain events or situations) or even naive pedagogy (a story can be intended to be a *bildungsroman*, with an explicit lesson about how to behave and feel in real life in tandem with an effort on the part of the author (the model) to anticipate and react to the virtual *learner*). In each of these cases, ASL might be possible without the model being literally present. Moreover, depending on the talent of the writer, the narrative and the stature of the characters could trigger a strong affective identification for the reader that could even reinforce the impact of the ASL. Studies of religion, too, can teach us about the importance of how gods or ancestors are reported to feel or behave, for example, as a way of defining how we should feel and behave towards the objects in our environment. While these can come second- or even third-hand, people can also be convinced that they have a direct line with a particular deity or even a guru who is guiding them, while praying, for example.

C.2.3   *The learner in ASL*

The final corner of our triangle is occupied by the *learner*. Even if intuitively ASL essentially concerns young humans, it is by no means restricted to them (Dukes and Clément, 2017). First, primatologists in this book (Schuppli and van Schaik in Chapter 1, and Gruber and Sievers in Chapter 2, this volume) show that it is very likely that non-human primates (notably chimpanzees, but also orang-utan) use others' emotional behaviour to make sense of their environment. Second, ASL not only concerns human children, but adults too. This is especially relevant when people are moving from one cultural group to another, when they are confronted with novelty, for instance, in the technological realm or when they have to evaluate a situation that is relatively complex and/or new to them, for instance when an important political decision has to be made. In such conditions, the uncertainty about the ongoing evaluation will trigger the individual's 'radar' to detect others' reactions.

On this learner side, one of the key questions, notably raised and detailed by Gruber and Sievers (Chapter 2, this volume) and Fisher (Chapter 7, this volume), concerns the competences and processes necessary to take advantage of the teacher's affective evaluations.

The case of emotional contagion is interesting because it could cover different kinds of situation. When the learner is directly involved in a relationship with the model, one would expect some direct mimicry. For instance, when a mother and her child are closely interacting face to face, the emotions of the adult will most likely influence those of the child, as in Trevarthen's observations (1979). In such cases, even if the triangulation with an external 'object' is not yet present, one would expect that the context where this emotional exchange happens would inherit at least part of the affective ambiance linked to it. For instance, let's imagine that positive affective exchanges are particularly intense at the weekend, when the parents retire from their busy city careers to their idyllic countryside home. It would be surprising if such contexts didn't influence these exchanges and that as a result, countryside, for this particular child, would subsequently be associated with a positive, perhaps even nostalgic feeling. What we have in mind here is actually very close to the *somatic markers* described by Antonio Damasio (1994). Alternatively, and more controversially perhaps, it could also be that the object in this direct interpersonal context is something like *being together*. It would follow then that, *being together* would be coloured by warm, positive affect and that the child would look to engage again and perhaps, more often.

The other kind of emotional contagion situation we had in mind is probably at the very edge of ASL since there is no direct contact between the learner and the model. It is possible to imagine contexts, such as the sports event example described in the Introduction to this volume, that systemically trigger some affective reactions (like excitation and joy) each time they occur. In such circumstances, it is most likely that a given context can be associated, *via* some form of conditioning, to positive or negative feelings, thus enabling a first evaluation of a given object. For instance, if each occurrence of a particular national flag is surrounded by a sense of respect and devotion, a positive association between these feelings and the flag's design will be established, even if the meaning of this symbol is not clear for the child. One could call these associations, lacking in precise intentional content, *affective connotations*. Their role in socialization processes may well be important, and this topic clearly needs further research.

To investigate the cognitive means necessary for *affective observation*, we have to remember that, in these particular cases, the learner has to identify the model's object of attention as well as the emotion that the object evokes. Therefore, even if it is not necessary for the two protagonists to interact directly, it is essential for the learner to detect the object of interest. In the developmental literature, these cases are related to 'joint attention', which emerges at the end of the first year of life (Tomasello & Rakoczy, 2003). In our case, this notion could be misleading because both protagonists are attentive to the same object but not in a 'joint' way. From a cognitive perspective, it is also important to note the passive–active role of the learner. It is *active* in the sense that she is engaged in an active exploration of her environment, using others' behaviour in order to seize what is relevant in their common environment. At the same time, it is *passive* because she is not voluntarily asking help or trying to get another person' attention; she is learning by observation – *eavesdropping* (as in Repacholi &

Meltzoff, 2007). While we insisted on the fact in the Introduction that the learner in affective observation was actively seeking information, we did not intend to suggest that they had been looking at the model to see what they could learn, as has been privately suggested to us. Rather, what we meant was that child is scouring the environment, looking for anything that might capture their attention and only then, incidentally, might start focusing on the other because that person appears to be behaving in an interesting, relevant way. This exploratory motivation to explore could be derived from a very basic seeking mechanism, like the one proposed by Panksepp (for instance, Alcaro & Panksepp, 2011). What could be specific to humans (and possibly other highly social species) is that this inquiry automatically takes advantage of others' experience when deciphering the different affordances of the environment.

Social referencing is, by definition, more active from a cognitive perspective than the two earlier processes. The learner is inhibiting her ongoing action in order to explicitly turn her attention to a more experienced person in order to get some help. This competence seems more complex, in the sense that it involves metacognitive abilities enabling the learner (1) to assess her own uncertainty about how to evaluate a given action/object, (2) to identify that another person has access to better information than herself, in order to (3) eventually modify her ongoing behaviour once informed by the model (see Gruber & Sievers, Chapter 2, this volume, for a breakdown of what is cognitively required for each part of ASL). We are therefore plainly in the realms of explicit inquiry, even if the depth of the investigation may remain rather superficial and relate either to a disambiguation of an ongoing action, or to the appropriateness of a certain reaction. Whether social referencing is developmentally prior to affective observation needs to be investigated (Clément & Dukes, 2013). It could be, for example, that the scaffolding involved in how the affective information is directly communicated and tailored to the individual in social referencing helps the younger infant to follow, but it could equally be the case that the young infant makes unguided associations between other people and objects before then. Given that both experiences are likely from a very young age, it may turn out to be difficult to identify a developmental hierarchy.

From that perspective, the cognitive abilities engaged in *natural pedagogy* seem even more complex to us. Indeed, the learner has a certain objective and, by collaborating with the model, she can, step by step, approach her goal. From a cognitive perspective, this type of acquisition matches closely to what is traditionally involved in learning. But it is interesting to note that most of the cognitive load is borne by the model who notably has to monitor the level of understanding of the learner, to scaffold the information in order to reach the learner's zone of proximal development and, emotionally, to keep the learner motivated to learn by constantly arousing her interest.

C.3   The different relations in ASL

Having explored and updated the three points of our triangle – learner–model–object – we will now turn to describe what this book has taught us about its three sides or, in other words, about the *relational* aspects of ASL.

C.3.1   *Learner to model*

It is important to note that, as Brian Parkinson reminds us (2017; Chapter 5, this volume), the relationship between learner and model is not static: although the paradigmatic case of ignorant child and knowledgeable adult may lead us to believe otherwise, within one interpersonal interaction, the identity of the knower and the model can change several times.

Furthermore, and as many of the chapters in this volume insisted, every learner will learn from several models throughout their lifespan. This was even the case for non-human primates like orang-utans, where young learners tend to track their mothers, while older ones observe their peers (Schuppli & van Schaik, Chapter 1, this volume). From an evolutionary perspective, this is not so surprising. After all, learning from an under- or mis-informed source is potentially harmful because it could potentially trigger some non-adaptive behaviours. Given that ASL can be seen as a kind of testimony (Harris, Chapter 3, this volume), and what we have said on epistemic vigilance earlier, we can expect a certain cautiousness on the part of the learner concerning the model(s). In relation to the ASL framework, we hypothesized two kinds of filtering. First, when the model is intentionally expressing an emotion, he has to be *benevolent*, with a desire to provide affective information, the belief of which would benefit the recipient. Indeed, this particular characteristic of the model seems to be evaluated early in development (Bernard et al., 2015; Mascaro & Sperber, 2009). In the case of ASL then, one would expect the kind of emotional attachment the learner has to the model to play a major role; if the learner endures a toxic relationship with the model, this could lead her to use his appraisal in a non-deferential way. Indeed, it could even have the reverse effect and push the learner to value the object differently. On the other hand, one would expect that people engaged in a harmonious relationship will converge in their appraisal. However, when the model is unknown to the learner, this goodwill can also be inferred by some cues. For instance, people who are smiling tend to be more trusted than people expressing anger (Clément, Bernard, Grandjean, & Sander, 2013; Todorov, 2008).

Another important factor for this type of trust is group belonging. A long tradition in social psychology, and more recent research in developmental psychology, has shown how models that are detected as in-group members are much more likely to trigger confidence in the learner. In other words, we are more likely to trust someone we feel we have a lot in common with, than someone with whom we don't (Bryne, 1997). In the case of ASL, one can even suppose that the affective appraisal of an out-group triggers an inverse appraisal by the learner (as mentioned earlier). For instance, an out-group member's expression of contempt could trigger interest for the object. Inversely, an expression of interest by an out-group member could lead the learner to consider that an object does not deserve any interest (see Manstead et al., Chapter 8, this volume, for an illustration of these kinds of processes and a review of the relevant literature).

Second, the model has to be *competent*, or at least more competent than the learner. Indeed, the learner has to believe that the person is a comparative authority on the subject. A rather new but growing field in developmental psychology has shown that even young children are able to assess their respective level of competence (or incompetence) compared to a communicator (see, for instance, Harris, 2012). In the case of ASL, this detection can also be linked with group membership; indeed, it would not make sense for anyone considered to be an out-group member to be viewed as competent in evaluating the different objects in a given cultural environment.

We have previously characterized the relationship between learner and model as one of trust. Certainly, trust plays a part, but, perhaps *deference* would be a better word. Trust suggests a two-way relationship whereas we really want to focus on how the learner perceives the level of competence about the model. In a sense, it is possible to feel that a person is not very trustworthy but, in certain contexts, to defer to her anyway because her authority in a domain is acknowledged. In that context, to defer means to give up on a personal experience and to rely on somebody's knowledge.

Of course, the relationship between the learner and the model is only relevant here if we are to argue that the *decision* to learn is at the least, quasi-automatic, rather than entirely automatic as argued by Mumenthaler and Sander (2012, 2015, Chapter 6, this volume). Clearly, only in cases where the identity of the other person is taken into account in some way can the relationship between the learner and model have any significance on the social transmission of value. Further research is needed to uncover more about the socio-affective inferential mechanisms involved in social appraisal, perhaps by running the study with members of in-groups and out-groups.

C.3.2   *Model with the object*

Another side of our triangle links the *model* with the *object* where different levels of engagement can be observed by the learner. One aspect is the intensity of the expressed emotion. An intense fear towards an object will most likely result in a different evaluation (and expression, consequent action, etc.) by the learner than a mild anxiety. An interesting aspect of ASL, picked up by Agneta Fisher in Chapter 7, is that emotional reactions can be compared. For instance, a learner could discover from someone else's affective reaction that her own emotion is not appropriate to a particular object in their cultural environment. Making this social comparison can result in modifying the evaluation of different objects: the learner may gather from her new friends' reactions that a certain kind of music may not be worthy of such intense enthusiasm, contrary to what she supposed. This is also the field of many cultural 'markers', different ways of making ones' emotions public (see De Leersnyder, Chapter 9, this volume). The level of engagement of the model is also mentioned in Chapter 1 by Schuppli and van Schaik and we think that it is an important and hardly addressed issue. In a way, it is not only the intensity of the emotional signal but also its sincerity that counts. This is notably the case in natural pedagogy. It is not rare to observe parents or teachers insisting on the intrinsic values of a given cultural object without really 'believing' it. In other words, the communicated emotion is perhaps not really experienced by the model and this discrepancy can often be detected by the learner. On the contrary, a silence and/or a rapid gaze toward a valued object could profoundly affect a learner if they evaluate his behaviour as, for example, a discreet sign of respect and, as such, as an important object for the model.

C.3.3   *Learner to the object*

To complete our triangle, attention turns to the relation that connects the *learner* to the *object*. We called this *social relevance* because, by the end of the cycle of ASL, the object will have become loaded with a certain socially acquired value for the learner. It is important to note, however, while most of the examples we have provided throughout the Introduction and in this Conclusion have been *cultural* in nature (a rugby team to support, a certain music style to admire, a way of behaving in public, etc.), there are of course examples when the object is simply social, and has nothing to do with culture. Let's imagine a novice skier on a glacier, for example. Not very confident on the slopes yet, he hears a sudden cry from one of the skiers ahead of him. Even though our intrepid hero cannot see the danger himself (a crevasse, for instance), he will change course to avoid any risk. This is a case of ASL, although, as stated above, this is not a cultural example.

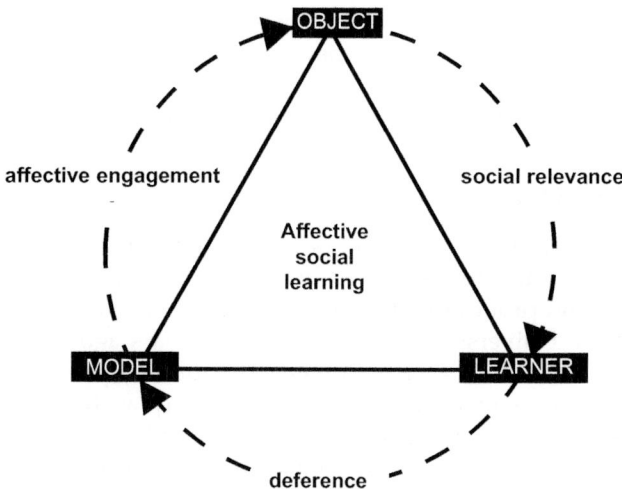

Figure C.2 The (socially modified) ASL model.

Of course, not all objects are dependent on an external appraisal as an individual can evaluate objects, perhaps for some idiosyncratic or physiological reason. One interesting question perhaps concerns the extent to which such personal appraisals can be modified or *overridden* by ASL. In the case of emotion contagion, it is difficult to predict the consequences of a negative social appraisal by the model in a context that has previously been evaluated as positive by the learner. Is it possible, for instance, for the soothing effect of a warm bath for an infant to become completely unpleasant because of the dull anguish a parent might have of water? Affective observation is mainly related to saliency detection but, here too, it is possible that some objects would attract the learner's attention independently of the model's emotions. For social referencing, it is interesting to highlight that the paradigmatic experiment involved a toy that the child was already eager to reach, on the other side of the apparent cliff. And teachers are well aware that learners' attention is not always available and that the preoccupations of one person are not always those of another. In other words, there are many cases where learners are not blank affective slates but rather encounter objects that are already partially evaluated. Part of this appraisal may lie in their personal predispositions (being sensitive to certain sounds, for instance, or having perfect pitch), some being genetic, others socially inherited. In any case, these dispositions will involve a familiarity, a 'natural' ease with certain objects that could counteract, or considerably favour, ASL.

Given these reflections and modifications, each one either motivated by the authors of these chapters, or in articles and books we have read subsequently or in discussions with people at various conferences, we have learned from others how they feel about ASL, what they think is important to highlight or change and we have begun to lay the foundations of this novel concept (see Figure C.2).

C.4   The future of ASL

This concluding chapter does not pay enough tribute to the fascinating and worthy contributions offered by all the authors of this book. We are happy (and proud) that this concept, invented on a table in a small corner of the University of Neuchâtel a few years ago, has triggered so much interest from so many diverse disciplinary perspectives. The idea that others play an essential role in the way we build our knowledge has definitely gained some impetus recently. Our proposal was simply to extend the idea of testimony from the learning of skills or propositional knowledge to the way that different elements of our environment are enlightened by others' attention, interest and affective evaluations. In other words, how we are all influenced by others in the way we evaluate what is worth living, fighting and, sometimes, even dying for.

Many questions remain, and we have highlighted areas that we think need particular attention throughout this Conclusion. Additionally, we have not made much distinction thus far between different *kinds* of values. While it seems *natural* to give importance to others when explaining how people develop feelings towards modern painting, rugby or béchamel sauce, it is perhaps less obvious in the case of moral values, for instance. Could there be such a thing as *a moral cliff*, where we look to others to help us with the many moral questions we each face every day? On one hand, one could begin to wonder about the extent to which what we consider as valuable is *entirely* the result of our given cultural upbringing. Our intuitive resistance to this idea has to be thought through. On the other hand, one could also wonder about the extent to which some very positive human values, such as universalism or humanism, for example, are also dismissed, particularly when they are being applied to people belonging to one unfavoured out-group or another.

Finally, in these cosmopolitan times of ours, in an age when it has become acceptable to present *alternative facts* and accuse others of distributing *fake news*, the sharing of a common knowledge base is apparently becoming more and more complicated and, as a direct result, cultural values are seemingly becoming more and more entrenched. With some optimism, we can hope that ASL could help us better understand how the transmission of values can make life full and accomplished without encroaching other forms of life characterized by values that are different, but perhaps not *so* different, after all.

References

Alcaro, A., & Panksepp, J. (2011). The seeking mind: Primal neuro-affective substrates for appetitive incentive states and their pathological dynamics in addictions and depression. *Neuroscience and Biobehavioral Reviews*, 35(9), 1805–1820.

Bernard, S., Proust, J., & Clément, F. (2015) Four- to 6-year-old children's sensitivity to reliability versus consensus in the endorsement of object labels. *Child Development*, 86, 1112–1124.

Bourdieu, P. (1998) *Practical reason, on the theory of action*. Stanford, CA: Stanford University Press.

Byrne, D. (1997). An overview (and underview) of research and theory within the attraction paradigm. *Journal of Social and Personal Relationships*, 14(3), 417–431.

Camras, L. A., & Halberstadt, A. G. (2017). Emotional development through the lens of affective social competence. *Current Opinion in Psychology*, 17, 113–117.

Clément, F. (2010). To trust or not to trust? Children's social epistemology. *Review of Philosophy and Psychology*, 1, 531–549.

Clément, F., Bernard, S., Grandjean, D., & Sander, D. (2013). Emotional expression and vocabulary learning in adults and children. *Cognition and Emotion*, 27, 539–548.

Clément, F., & Dukes, D. (2013). The role of interest in the transmission of social values. *Frontiers in Psychology*, 4, 349.

(2017). Social appraisal and social referencing: Two components of affective social learning. *Emotion Review*, 9(3), 253–261.

Clément, F., Koenig, M., & Harris, P. (2004). The ontogenesis of trust. *Mind & Language*, 19(4), 360–379.

Corriveau, K. H., & Harris, P. L. (2010). Preschoolers (sometimes) defer to the majority in making simple perceptual judgments. *Developmental Psychology*, 46, 437.

Damasio, A. R. (1994). *Descartes' error: Emotion, rationality and the human brain*. New York, NY: Putnam.

Durlak, J. A., Weissberg, R. P., Dymnicki, A. B., Taylor, R. D., & Schellinger, K. B. (2011). The impact of enhancing students' social and emotional learning: A meta-analysis of school-based universal interventions. *Child Development*, 82(1), 405–432.

Dukes, D., & Clément, F. (2017). Author reply: Clarifying the importance of ostensive communication in life-long, affective social learning. *Emotion Review*, 9(3), 267–269.

Fischer, M. (2009). *Capitalist realism: Is there no alternative*. Ropley, UK: Zero Books, John Hunt Publishing.

Halberstadt, A. G., Denham, S. A., & Dunsmore, J. C. (2001). Affective social competence. *Social Development*, 10, 79–119.

Harris, P. L. (2002). Checking our sources: The origins of trust in testimony. *Studies in History and Philosophy of Science*, 33, 315–333.

(2012). *Trusting what you're told: How children learn from others*. Cambridge, MA: Harvard University Press.

Jameson, F. (2003). Future city. *New Left Review, 21*, 76.

Koenig, M. A., Clément, F., & Harris, P. L. (2004). Trust in testimony: Children's use of true and false statements. *Psychological Science, 15*, 694–698.

Mascaro, O., & Sperber, D. (2009). The moral, epistemic, and mindreading components of children's vigilance towards deception. *Cognition, 112,* 367–80.

Morgan T. J. H., Laland, K. N., & Harris P. L. (2015). The development of adaptive conformity in young children: Effects of uncertainty and consensus. *Developmental Science, 18*, 511–524.

Mumenthaler, C., & Sander, D. (2012). Social appraisal influences recognition of emotions. *Journal of Personality and Social Psychology, 102*(6), 1118–1135.

(2015). Automatic integration of social information in emotion recognition. *Journal of Experimental Psychology: General, 144*(2), 392–399.

Paradise, R., & Rogoff, B. (2009). Side by side: Learning by observing and pitching in. *Ethos, 37*, 102–113.

Parkinson, B. (2017). Comment: Respecifying emotional influence. *Emotion Review, 9*(3), 263–265.

Planalp, S. (1999). *Communicating emotion: Social, moral, and cultural processes.* Cambridge, UK: Cambridge University Press.

Repacholi, B. M., & Meltzoff, A. N. (2007). Emotional eavesdropping: Infants selectively respond to indirect emotional signals. *Child Development, 78,* 503–521.

Rogoff, B. (2003). *The cultural nature of human development.* Oxford, UK: Oxford University Press.

Sperber, D. (1996). *Explaining culture: A naturalistic approach.* Oxford, UK: Blackwell.

Sperber, D., Clément, F., Heintz, C., Mascaro, O., Mercier, H., Origgi, G., & Wilson, D. (2010) Epistemic vigilance. *Mind & Language, 25*(4), 359–393.

Todorov, A. (2008). Evaluating faces on trustworthiness: An extension of systems for recognition of emotions signaling approach/avoidance behaviors. *Annals of the New York Academy of Sciences, 1124*, 208–224.

Tomasello, M., & Rakoczy, H. (2003). What makes human cognition unique? From individual to shared to collective intentionality. *Mind and Language, 18*, 121–147.

Trevarthen, C. (1979). Communication and cooperation in early infancy. A description of primary intersubjectivity. In M. Bullowa (Ed.), *Before speech: The beginning of human communication* (pp. 321–347). Cambridge, UK: Cambridge University Press.

van Kleef, G. A. (2009). How emotions regulate social life: The emotions as social information (EASI) model. *Current Directions in Psychological Science, 18*, 184–188.

(2016). *The interpersonal dynamics of emotion: Toward an integrative theory of emotions as social information.* Cambridge, UK: Cambridge University Press.

van Kleef, G. A., de Dreu, C. K. W., & Manstead, A. S. R. (2010). An interpersonal approach to emotion in social decision making: The emotions as social information model. *Advances in Experimental Social Psychology, 42*, 45–96

Index

Page numbers in **bold** refer to figures.